HEALTH, WEALTH & HAPPINESS

Sept. 30/05
To. Leo

Live with Passion

HEALTH, WEALTH & HAPPINESS

YOU **CAN** CONTROL YOUR DESTINY!

DAVID SINGH
with Albert E. D'Souza

ECW PRESS

Published by ECW PRESS
2120 Queen Street East, Suite 200, Toronto, Ontario, Canada M4E 1E2

NATIONAL LIBRARY OF CANADA CATALOGUING IN PUBLICATION DATA

Singh, David, 1953–
Health, wealth & happiness: you can control your destiny / David Singh
ISBN 1-55022-597-9

1. Success — Psychological aspects. I. Title
BF637.S8S586 2003   158.1   C2003-901899-7

Printing: Marc Veilleux Imprimeur Inc.

This book is set in Minion and Trajan

The publication of *Health, Wealth, and Happiness* has been generously supported by the Canada Council,
the Ontario Arts Council, and the Government of Canada through the
Book Publishing Industry Development Program.   Canadä

DISTRIBUTION
CANADA: Jaguar Book Group, 100 Armstrong Avenue, Georgetown, ON, L7G 5S4

UNITED STATES: Independent Publishers Group, 814 North Franklin Street,
Chicago, Illinois 60610

PRINTED AND BOUND IN CANADA

ECW PRESS
ecwpress.com

CONTENTS

SECTION ONE

ONE MAN'S JOURNEY
From a Poor, Third World Country to a Rich Canadian Life

SECTION TWO

WEALTH
Practical, Realistic Money-Management Strategies

SECTION THREE

HEALTH
Secrets for a Long and Healthy Life

SECTION FOUR

THE JOURNEY CONTINUES
The Creation of Destiny Health Solutions

SECTION FIVE

HAPPINESS
Your Pathway to Success

*This book is dedicated to my mother, Latchmin Singh.
Her strength, dedication to family and capacity for forgiveness
have been important lessons for me, in my journey.*

SECTION
ONE

ONE MAN'S JOURNEY

FROM A POOR THIRD WORLD
COUNTRY TO A RICH CANADIAN LIFE

PREFACE

When I first thought of writing this, my latest book, I immediately wanted to call it *HEALTH, WEALTH AND HAPPINESS*. The reasons were clear to me from page one: I wanted to describe the quite extraordinary ups and downs of my life and career, the story of harsh poverty in a Third World country, dreams driven by education and action in a new land, dreams fulfilled with the creation of Fortune Financial and Infinity Mutual Funds — and dreams crushed with the sale of both. I wanted to show how it was possible to land on Canadian soil with $22 in my pocket, and to become a millionaire many times over, just over two decades later. And most importantly, I wanted to share with readers how to achieve not only wealth, but health and happiness, too. This desire to create my fourth book came out of more than mere vanity. I wanted to inspire other men and women by what I had accomplished despite my humble beginnings, and share my faith that my newest company, Destiny Health Solutions, will achieve even greater success than Fortune and Infinity. I expect to take many thousands along with me on a journey to wealth, health, and ultimately, happiness. If a young immigrant of colour can make it in this tough, often heartless world of cutthroat capitalism, why not every one of us — if we work together with love, trust, and hope?

On December 6, 1988, I created a financial planning company with a handful of others, with whom I made my first phone calls from a pay phone in a donut shop near our tiny, suburban office in Toronto, Canada. In less than a decade, Fortune Financial had made dozens of men and women into millionaires — both its own employees and many of its tens of thousands of clients — and had hired some 500 employees and over 750 financial planners, each of the latter averaging well over $150,000 a year in income. More than 100,000 Canadians had entrusted over $10 billion to our hands, in the (justifiable!) hope that we would help make *them* wealthy, too — and we did.

Our neighbours to the south often talk of "The American Dream," but dreams are not limited to below the 49th Parallel.

There is a "Canadian Dream" as well, and I am not alone in having lived it. Indeed, I am *still* living it — thanks to so many hard-working fellow Canadians who also dreamed of making a good, honest living, while assisting others along the way.

I made it. I built the Canadian Dream — and then lost it — well, most of it. But I am now filled with the same determination, passion and carefully developed plans to make it again, with Destiny Health Solutions.

The launch of my new company was planned for Spring, 2003 — a symbolic gesture — a time of rebirth, resurrection, hope, and faith. After I share with you my life story, I'll also lay out my views on *wealth, health,* and *happiness.* In the latter case, not only some philosophies of life, but also how I have gone about creating a new "happiness" for myself, and I pray, for countless others, with my new health products company. Why was I forced to sell my beloved wealth management and mutual fund companies? How did I eventually come to focus on health? How and why did I create Destiny Health Solutions?

Of course, you'll have to read the book. But its title gives you at least a suggestion of what will follow: the story of one man's successes, failures, and determination to make millions not only wealthier, but healthier, too. And as we all know, with both wealth and health, one cannot help but gain happiness!

— *David Singh*

CHAPTER ONE

VERY MODEST BEGINNINGS

The Canadian national anthem has a rather problematic first line — one that's rather self-conscious, for a nation of immigrants: "O Canada, our home and native land."

"Home," definitely; "native," rarely. Statistics show that two-thirds of the nearly four million people in the metropolitan Toronto area, for example, were born and raised somewhere else, and that "somewhere else" is often very far away.

This 49-year-old began his life singing a vastly different national anthem, which would probably sound quite alien to the most Canadians (except for the 150,000 plus fellow immigrants from my homeland who have chosen this wonderful country as their new "home and native land.") My real native land was on the major continent to the south of the Caribbean — Guyana. There, black and South Asian citizens made up nearly 95% of its tiny population of just under 700,000.

A GLIMPSE OF GUYANA — WHERE I CAME FROM

Guyana is both a country and a state of mind. Indeed, just as most North Americans would think "Antarctica" when they hear the word "penguin," most of them would think "Guyana" only if they heard the phrase "poisoned Kool-Aid." For until the horrific mass suicide in 1978 of the followers of the American cult leader Jim Jones, Guyana was as unknown to the global consciousness as Herzogovina and Chechnya were, until their own, recent tragedies in the last years of the twentieth century.

But Jim Jones and his pathetic disciples were not native to Guyana any more than snowstorms. Guyana is situated on the northeastern coast of South America, bounded on the north by the Atlantic Ocean, on the east by Suriname, on the south and southwest by Brazil, and on the northwest by Venezuela. If you don't have a map at hand, just imagine the southeast Caribbean as a giant question mark, with the Virgin Islands and Antigua near the top curve, Martinique and St. Lucia as the bottom of the curve, and Trinidad and Tobago as a dual dot at the bottom. Due south of that giant question mark is the only English-speaking country on the continent of South America, and my true "native land," if no longer my home — Guyana.

Like Canada, Guyana is an independent country within the British Commonwealth of Nations and went through periods of violent struggle until Great Britain recognized its independence in 1966. Unlike Canada, Guyana is relatively small; its 214,970 square kilometres making it slightly smaller than the United Kingdom, excluding Northern Ireland.

Natives called the Arawaks once lived in Guyana's humid, swampy territories before being displaced by the Caribs, powerful warriors who would dominate much of the region before moving on to the islands to the north. It is estimated that there were half a million inhabitants of what the indigenous population called "Land of Much Water," before the Europeans arrived on Guyana's shores. Today, there are less than 45,000 Amerindians left, divided among nine ethnic groups. Clearly, South America was no kinder to its aboriginals than Canada, Australia, and other colonized countries.

It was as far back as the 15th century that the Spaniards "discovered" the coast of Guyana — to the surprise of the natives who had lived there for centuries — which they labeled "Costa Brava," or "Wild Coast." These early explorers expressed no interest in settling there, nor did Christopher Columbus himself, who sailed near its coast in 1498, but made no attempt at a landing. The British navigator, Sir Walter Raleigh, visited the area in 1595, this voyage followed by several failed attempts to establish permanent settlements in the country.

Finally, the Dutch showed an interest — inspired by the legend of El Dorado, the dream city of gold. They built the first fort in the country in 1616, followed by a second settlement eight years later.

As with so many countries that were colonized by European powers during the last millennium, Guyana changed hands several times over the years. The British began a massive introduction of slaves in the late eighteenth century to grow and harvest sugarcane. They finally seized the land from the Dutch in 1781 — losing it to the French just six months later. The French held on for only two years themselves, before restoring it to the Dutch, in 1783.

Notwithstanding the agonies of slavery and the grandeur of slave revolts, the shuffleboard of European domination continued; the British seized the colony again in 1796, then handed it back to the Dutch in 1802. But just one year later, the British recaptured it, ruling it until May 26, 1966, when the much-abused country achieved its independence, and British Guiana gave way to a new name — Guyana.

Colonization not only brings with it great turmoil, it also creates strange bedfellows. The countless slaves who managed to escape from their plantations very often ended up in the jungle with the Amerindians. This led to a racial and cultural interaction that resulted in the group referred to today as "bush blacks."

With the emancipation of all slaves within the British Empire in 1834 — it took nearly another three decades and a civil war for the United States to achieve the same act of humanity — the United Kingdom found it necessary to bring over more slave labour for its many planters. (Two-thirds of the ex-slaves had withdrawn their muscle from the plantations.)

And so, unlike the African slaves, all of whom had been spirited from West Africa, immigrants began to pour into Guyana from all over the world — Europe, Africa, the West Indies — and, in my own family's case — from East Asia.

Between 1835 and 1882, over 30,000 Portuguese labourers arrived in Guyana, most of whom died in the brutal conditions of the still-primitive colony. Then, another 42,500 African immigrants arrived between 1835 and

1930, the majority caught by Brazilian and Cuban ships which had continued to smuggle slaves long after abolition.

Eventually, the demand for a massive labour force moved the planters to bring over labour from India, between 1838 and the end of World War One. This group included my own ancestors. The numbers were overwhelming; nearly 240,000 East Indian "contractual immigrants" were recruited to work on the sugarcane plantations of British Guiana. This helps explain why East Asians make up over 50% of Guyana's population, and how they managed to re-elect Cheddi Jagan as prime minister several times since independence. (Indentured immigrants from China also came to the country between 1853 and 1909, but their numbers were only around 14,000, accounting for just two percent of Guyana's current population.)

This so-called indentured system was eventually abolished, due to British resistance to such policies of near-forced immigration — but not before it brought my grandparents to Guyana, and led to a profound impact on the tiny country's culture, heritage, and politics. In fact, a perusal of Guyana's countryside will uncover such originally East Asian place names as Delhi, Lucknow, Madras, Cundalore, Calcutta, Lahore, Gujurat, Malabar — even Bombay!

And that, briefly, is the history of the country where I was born and raised; the place which is my *real* "home and native land," in spite of the Canadian anthem I sing so proudly today. True, the country's average temperature is 26 degrees Celsius — just under 80 degrees Fahrenheit — but the legal system is based on English common law, and its educational system is strongly British — factors which undoubtedly made my eventual migration to my new "home and frozen land" a far easier leap than what many of you readers, your parents, or grandparents went through, when they immigrated to Canada.

However, last year, Guyana had an annual per capita income in the low hundreds of dollars (which is in the bottom ten percent in world ranking), ferocious inflation rates, a dollar worth only about *one-half a U.S. penny*, widespread underemployment, and violent racial politics between blacks and East Asians, all of which had influenced me to seek out the grander opportunities of the "True North" of Canada. And as this book will show, my move paid off very well indeed, despite wild swings between success and failure along the way.

AND SO, I AM BORN

Sometimes, simply the name of a birthplace can inspire confidence, if not visions of glory and romance; Paris! New York! Moscow! Well, not in my case. I was born on October 3, 1953, in a tiny village in Guyana named — believe it or not — Canal #1. (You may be impressed to hear that there is a Canal #2, as well.)

It was called Canal because there was a small river, like a canal, which flowed through the diminutive community, with a bridge connecting it to the other side. Canal #1 had only one street, with people living on both sides, not unlike some of the minuscule towns of the Canadian prairies. I'm not sure how many people lived in my community, perhaps a few hundred. It's even smaller today, since so many have left. (I've already noted that approximately 150,000 Guyanese make their homes in Canada, and when you consider that there are barely 700,000 left in that country — down strikingly from over one million in the 1980s — that's a remarkable number. Imagine if seven million people up and left Canada, or over fifty million migrated from the U.S., in only two decades. It's sad that Guyana's agonizing politics have caused so many to leave their homeland.

Both my mother and father were born in Guyana, in 1924 and 1930 respectively — and both lived in suburban Toronto until my father's death in 1999. My mother and four of my siblings continue to live there. My great-grandparents came over from India, during that unpleasant labour situation which I described earlier. My father's parents were both born in Guyana, but his grandparents were born in the old country. My mother's father was also born in India, making that connection all the closer.

To give you an idea of how little we got around in the old days, my mother, Latchmin Persaud, was born in the same tiny village in which I took my first breath — Canal #1. My father, Sew Singh, was born in Kitty, another little community not far from Georgetown, the capital city of what was then British Guiana. Their families were subsistence farmers, and the two went to the same school in Canal, where they met. They were married in the thriving metropolis of Canal #1 in 1945, in the sacred Hindu ceremony. My father was 20, my mother was 14.

Back then, not only did East Asian Guyanese tend to marry young —

they had children like it was about to be outlawed. My mother had eight brothers and five sisters. She first worked on her father's farm of ten acres, where they raised oranges, pineapples, cassavas, and more. When she married my father, they purchased land, also approximately ten acres, in Canal #1. There, along with the several hundred residents of Canal, they lived in a tiny house with their acreage out back, where they grew bananas, sugarcane, and various other tropical fruits. This was perhaps a dozen miles from the capital city of Guyana, and about ten miles from the Atlantic Ocean.

My parents worked together on their modest farm, slowly building it up until it had some six head of cattle, thirty chickens, thirty ducks, and a half-dozen lambs. Twice a week, they would make the long, arduous journey to Georgetown to sell whatever their rapidly growing family had not devoured. While their only source of income was the farm, and my parents both had only a few years of schooling, my family was still considered "lower middle class" by Guyanese standards, because they had a decent-sized farm and a liveable income.

My mother and father eventually had thirteen children, eight of whom are alive today. Two of my siblings died at birth, one at age 17, and two others at the ages of 50 and 34. The latter brother left two pre-teen sons, and I was able to fly home, and build a place for them to live — a six-bedroom home, with two indoor bathrooms (still a luxury in Guyana) — on the lot of the house I grew up in. How lovely to be able to help my family, thanks to my good fortune in Canada.

All of my siblings attended school, and as the fifth child, I was no different — at least not in that respect. But my father realized early on that I had an uncommon thirst for academics: "David was like all the others, and looked like them all, but he was the only one who 'took' to education. He didn't like working on the farm."

How does such a large family cope? It was a lot easier to manage such a family in Guyana than its counterpart would be in Canada, I assure you. We lived in a two-bedroom house, so we never managed to have meals together, because there was simply no room to do so. We slept five in each bedroom, although there were only two beds. My parents slept in the kitchen.

Guyanese homes would look exotic to Canadians. Most are built on stilts because of floods and snakes. (I guess every country in the world has its own drawbacks; Canada could certainly be warmer in the winter.)

To give you an idea of how my family ended up, my oldest sister is a homemaker who lives in South America; the second oldest, a brother, had his own farm in Guyana before recently passing away; the third, a girl, died at birth; the fourth, my immediate older brother, died in his teens of a brain tumour. After me is another brother, also a farmer in Guyana; a sister, who's a homemaker in Guyana; then a sister/homemaker who also moved to Toronto; next was a brother who also recently died — he had been a farmer in Guyana. My two youngest sisters are both homemakers in Toronto. The baby of the family is a brother who recently completed school in Canada, and is working in a factory here.

CHAPTER TWO

A GUYANESE EDUCATION

I started school at age five, but then, everyone in Guyana goes to school, at least for a short time. Indeed, whatever one's attitude toward colonization, it cannot be denied that the British had a positive impact on our educational system; today, Guyana's literacy rate is an impressive 98.6% for men and 97.5% for women. Yet, while more than 90% attend primary schools, only a little over 50% reach the secondary level. And with only around 250 students per 100,000 Guyanese in university, one can easily see why such large numbers have to leave the country for higher learning.

My village was principally East Indian and split between the two major faiths of our ancestral home of India — Islam and Hinduism — so when I finally went to school, there were only two or three blacks in class with me. There have often been considerable tensions between blacks and Indians in Guyana; one need not be white to be racist. Unlike in the old country of my ancestors, there has never been bloodshed between Guyanese Muslims and Hindus — although there has been conflict. Here, too, the diversity of Guyana would serve me well; I had many Muslim friends, growing up. What a fine preparation for a promising future in the multicultural Canada of the last three decades!

In Guyana, none of us were staunch Muslims or Hindus, and although I could well have been a Sikh in India (considering my surname), that heritage was lost over the generations. Indeed, I never saw a man wearing a turban until I came to Canada! The blacks in Guyana were primarily Christian, and the dominant religion — because of our teachers and the British influence — was Anglican. That faith would prove to be important to me over the first two decades of my life.

My memories of growing up go back far earlier than that scary first day in school, of course. Our home was fairly comfortable, although crowded. My four brothers and I slept in a little corner of the bedroom floor, with bedding made of burlap, and sheets made from old dresses. As I recall, going to bed was more a looking forward to getting up.

As anyone who has been raised on a farm knows, it's not an easy life. We would start the day at 5:00 a.m., help around the farm, and only then, go off to school. (The majority of Guyanese farm kids, perhaps understandably, don't continue their education past the age of ten or eleven.)

As I recall, I actually began to do the milking of cows and goats by the age of six. I was fortunate in that my parents tolerated my immediate distaste for farm work; I was the only one of the children who truly despised working there. I got along pretty well with my many brothers and sisters, but we weren't terribly close. We were not the types to sit around and talk much.

Of course, there are advantages to subsistence farming, such as simple, healthy eating! We lived on yams, breadfruit, vegetables, and an endless variety of tropical foods. So we ate extraordinarily wisely, without knowing it; no junk food from North America ever entered our tiny house. We couldn't have afforded it, anyway.

Physical discipline was rigorous in our home, and we were called up short for just about anything you could imagine — cows not tied up properly; chickens not fed the correct amount. There were several other punishments, as well; going to bed without dinner, or having to sleep outside the house. Some believe this is culturally acceptable in many Caribbean, South American, and East Asian communities; I fear that they may be right. Corporal punishment remains acceptable in Guyanese schools; canings are still common. It's simply the way things are done there.

Beatings were a fact of life in our village, and probably throughout the entire country, as well. It was caused by many factors: poverty, cultural tensions, and, to some extent, alcoholism. There wasn't a specific age at which one was beaten, unlike voting or the age at which one can legally purchase cigarettes; toddlers as young as one or two were often slapped around.

THE LIFESAVER — SCHOOL

And so, after feeding the cows and enduring whatever punishment I was in for, I headed off to the local school. Perhaps comically — when one considers the student body — it was called McGillvery Government School, a name which had something to do with the British army or earlier landmasters — two of my least concerns. (There are many such place names, right across Guyana, attached to most towns in which the British set foot.) McGillvery Government School served all of Canal #1, and it held approximately 300 students.

The school seemed quite huge then. It was a half-mile walk from our house, which might seem far to today's youth, but it was nothing to us. The school had two floors, and one giant, open hall, so groups of students would sit in their classes in various areas, with some 30 to 40 kids in a class. (Recent studies claim that there is one primary teacher for every 46 students in Guyana, which is probably close to double the student/teacher ratio in Canada today, and obviously not very conducive to learning.)

Our teachers were Hindu, Muslim, Catholic, and Anglican, both East Asian and black. And in spite of the "One land of six peoples, united and free," which we sang daily in our national anthem, it was immediately clear where the power lay; every single one of us — regardless of religious or cultural backgrounds — *had* to study Christianity. To be honest, that was just fine with me, and it made it easier for me later, when I taught in an Anglican school in the jungle.

We had to recite the Lord's Prayer four times a day — and this was taken very seriously. We also sang "God Save the Queen," and we meant it, too. As children, we saw no irony in this, any more than Jewish children growing up in the Canadian prairies during the same period would have found the Christian prayers insulting; it was simply something you were expected to do. After all, we had absolutely zero outside influence in our lives — no movies, no television, no newspapers. The closest ones were in Georgetown, which was more than an hour away by ferry. (In the 1990s, a floating bridge was erected, so that the journey from Canal #1 is shorter today.)

Since the country became independent of England in 1966 — eight years before I left for Canada — there has been a growing awareness of Guyana's past. There have been dozens of books published about the country's history, and its heroes; altogether, far more information is now available. (What Guyana needed was its own Pierre Berton, Canada's most prominent popular historian.) By the time I left in 1974, a new cultural sensitivity was beginning to emerge in my homeland.

But growing up in the 1950s and 1960s, there *were* no Guyanese heroes. England was still viewed as the "New Jerusalem" when I was a child, but when Guyana finally gained its independence, England rapidly lost its hold on our collective imaginations and lives, and Canada and the United States quickly replaced the United Kingdom as the promised land. Every one of my childhood friends eventually went north — and I would, too.

In school, it was typical for children to be caned, on a daily basis, for actions as slight as talking out of turn. One had to read aloud to the teacher, and if the student didn't recognize a word, or couldn't spell it properly, that unfortunate soul was caned. Girls were caned only on the hands, but boys were punished on the buttocks, as well. These canings were given out far more liberally than our education. You could get one or two canings for not spelling properly, or perhaps six or seven for fighting with other kids.

I am embarrassed to admit that when I started teaching, in my mid-teens, I would inflict the same corporal punishment on my students. In retrospect, I can't believe that I did such things. Indeed, when I taught school in the jungles of Guyana, the female teachers often admitted that they lacked the energy to do the dirty deed, and they would send their students to *me* to be punished! Sadly, I would agree to administer the punishments, as requested.

Sitting in my home in suburban Toronto in the first years of the 21st century, I shudder every time I think about what Guyana's educational system allowed, but I cannot deny it; that was the way it was. I was not a "nerd," as my beautiful and intelligent daughters might have taunted a fellow student in their high school days; I was simply the "good kid." And, I'm pleased to report, I was not mocked or punished for being so keen at my studies.

I was also involved in track and field, and was intensely athletic. Not surprisingly, in our racially conscious society, it was "expected" that the blacks in each school would be active in track and field, so I always found myself the only East Asian in that sport. True, cricket was the number one sport in Guyana, closely followed by soccer, but track and field was my true love.

There were areas in which the school system was sensitive to religious and cultural diversity. For instance, the school was closed on certain holidays. There were calendars published with holidays documented for practically everyone. Hindu holidays, which occurred in March and November, were respected, and the school was closed for them. Still, there was no question which religion was dominant in the Guyanese school system. I found myself reading the Bible a great deal, and I soon knew a lot about Christianity. Indeed, I probably received more education in that faith than my own daughters, who attended Catholic schools in Canada. (The latest arrival, lovely Julia, is still too young for kindergarten.)

Religion was only one of many subjects in Guyanese schools. Others included mathematics, history, and literature, which were all studied in depth. I was moved by my studies of religion, and I've tried to incorporate its values in my personal life, as well as in my business, even though I don't belong to a church today. I see religious belief as a medium — a source of education that provides rules to live by. I always viewed my daily Bible readings as a guide to how to act in one's everyday life.

I used to pray every night, and I came to see myself as a spiritual person. As the great Canadian humourist Stephen Leacock writes in his hilarious "Gertrude the Governess" literary parody, the heroine's aunt taught Gertrude all the tenets of Christianity — "and also Mohammedanism, to be sure." Well, I certainly covered two major religious bases like the fictional Gertrude; I studied, lived, and loved both Hinduism and Christianity.

There was a Hindu temple approximately a mile and a half away from our home, and I walked there every Sunday morning, and sometimes during the week. That religion touched me deeply, as well — to be honest, a lot more deeply than my studies.

My parents would occasionally take us to religious functions, but like so many children, we did not understand what was going on. I did go to sunday school to study my faith, but we did not have any leaders who were truly knowledgeable in the subject. People got caught up in what they had to do, but they were rarely truly involved in it. They didn't always know what they were doing, or why. I know very little about Hinduism as a faith because I was never really taught much about it. My parents were similarly ignorant; they did not speak Hindi. As my father told me shortly before his death, "We had prayers in our home and respected religion very much. But we didn't learn from our own parents much, only the prayers we wanted to pray in Hindi. But our kids learned in English, so they pray in English. Still, we kept the Hindu religion." I can't disagree with him about that; we did as best as we could.

From my earliest years, I always knew that I would escape Guyana. Maybe I would go to university in Georgetown; I wasn't sure. But I knew that somehow, somewhere, I would make something of my life. I wanted to do better. I hated working on the farm, and I wanted to be smart. I wanted to be an academic of some kind. I didn't consider myself brilliant, and I still don't. But even as a child, I longed to be like smart people, and I looked up to them. I never looked up to people with money, but those with brains? Always.

It was my little secret, and I wouldn't share it with anyone; someday, I promised myself, I'd get off the farm and into a more dynamic, interesting life. It wasn't shame that kept me from telling others my secret plan; it was the lingering doubt as to whether or not it would ever really happen.

I may not have been happy with my home life, but I cannot deny that my father was a very hard-working man. He always wanted to do the best he could for his rapidly growing family. His intentions were good, but he made many mistakes in farming. (I would later make quite a few mistakes as a young entrepreneur in Canada, as you'll soon read.)

When I was only about ten years old, my father did a daring thing; he left our village and our family, and leased land far from our home, in another part of the country, in a place called Berbice.

On a map of Guyana, Berbice is less than an inch to the southeast of Canal #1, but the distance was far to travel, as there were no highways, like in Canada or the U.S. This was very far from our home, and he actually had to live there. In the first few months, he traveled back and forth, between his two farms — first, alone, and then with my mother.

So as early as age ten, I was left alone in our house, without parents to return home to after school each day. Of course, it wasn't as traumatic as it may sound: my sisters took over the cooking, and we all continued with the much hated farm work together.

The land that my father worked in Berbice was leased from the government, so we had to clear it ourselves, and it was not easy. I recall going to visit my father and mother at the second farm when I was about 11, and I immediately disliked it. The journey was long and arduous. We had to travel by bus along a dirt road, and it took at least six hours to get there. Often, there were huge holes and deep ditches in the road, and more than once, everyone had to get out and push the bus back onto the road. Then, once we neared the farm, we had to walk through thick jungle to finally reach it! By the time I eventually visited, I saw that he had cleared only a little patch, and built a small hut on stilts.

Indeed, the Berbice farm was far from idyllic. It was not like farming at the "more civilized" Canal #1, which had been worked for decades. It wasn't even fertilized. There was lots of land to work on, but one couldn't farm very much of it because everything had to be done manually; there was no machinery, of course. My father grew bananas and pineapple there, but he couldn't plant sugarcane, because the land was so "new," and machinery was needed to work the new land. Fortunately, pineapple was always a successful crop because it could be harvested annually. My father eventually planted sugarcane once the logs, which had been cut down to clear the land, were finally moved.

As the years went on, my family's financial situation continued to deteriorate. While my father was farming in Berbice, the Canal #1 farm was neglected, the efforts of myself and my siblings notwithstanding. My father never managed to generate enough revenue because pineapple and bananas require a full eighteen months to make a profit. My father could not successfully farm both plots, and he had no money coming in for nearly two years. When the Berbice crops finally did come in, my father found that it was impossible to transport the produce to market. To top it off, the water supply was poor. As my father reminded me, years later in Canada, "It was a very hard time for us, David." Indeed, it was.

And so, quite unlike the average teenager in North America in the 1960s, I found myself working long hours for several months to help support my family. My siblings and I continued to help out on our Canal #1 farm, but we were forced to work as labourers in the village, where we were lucky to earn about 50 cents a day.

THE FAMILY SCHOLAR CONTINUES HIS EDUCATION

Despite my family's precarious financial situation, I was still intact; I continued to get straight As, and was the top student in primary school. Finally, after grade nine, I went to high school — the only one of the eleven surviving Singh children to do so. It was sublimely gratifying to me that I had done it. The realization of my dream seemed ever closer.

There are two kinds of high schools in Guyana: private schools, for which the student has to pay; and government-run schools, for which the student has to pass an extremely difficult exam. The first time I took the test, I didn't pass.

And so I went to the government secondary school, called the West Demerara. It took about 90 minutes to get there. The bus came at 7:30 a.m., and I was on my way to my secret goal: a real education.

There were some 300 students at West Demerara, with an average of two dozen in each class. As before, our teachers were Muslim, Hindu, and Christian. I made many friends, some of whom are still close. Yet as I worked my way through high school, I was no longer the straight-A student I had once been, and nowhere near the academic level that I desired.

In grades 11, 12, and 13, I was consistently among the top quarter of my class. This was hard for me after years of being the number one student throughout primary school, but I had to learn to accept it.

Perhaps more important in terms of my spiritual growth and future leadership in the business world was my involvement in community work, and a religious youth organization. My family respected me for getting involved in these activities. To be frank, there wasn't much to do in a village the size of ours, and boys of all sorts of backgrounds used to steal or throw stones at buildings, and get into all kinds of trouble. I was more attracted to helping with community affairs, eventually becoming one of the leaders of the Canal #1 Hindu Youth Organization.

In retrospect, I believe I became a leader of that youth group as a way of separating myself from my despised situation at home. A friend started the little organization, and was its first president; I was its first secretary. My job was to take minutes of our meetings, which took place on Sundays. The mandate of the organization was not particularly profound — simply to get together. We did things like go to one another's houses and sing Hindu songs. The important thing was, it kept us from getting involved in less savoury activities.

We also offered help to people in mourning, and visited their homes. When we sang in Hindi, we didn't know what the words meant, but I found the experience spiritual, nonetheless. We also did fundraising, and helped out around the temple, which was a single, small building in the heart of Canal #1.

We had approximately 40 members, equally split between the sexes. But there was no dating and no drinking — a powerful argument for life in small, Third World villages! These young people went to the church and held on for dear life; aside from the youth group, there was little else to do. (No, there wasn't any dancing, either.) Our little youth group lasted three years, until its leaders moved off into new directions.

One often wonders just how deeply religion and a sense of decency sinks into a person, no matter how involved the individual is with such things. A depressing example of my own failings during this period of my life occured when my older brother first fell ill in December 1968, when I was barely 15 years old, and heavily involved in the Hindu youth group. One day, he came in from working on the farm, complaining of a painful headache. We had no idea that it was the beginning of the end.

I'm ashamed to say that my response to that first, horrifying moment by my dying brother's side was shockingly immature and unsympathetic, even for a 15-year-old. I still recall, with great mortification, what I said to him: "I'm sick and tired of your games! Saying that you can't see!" How on earth could I have reacted so cruelly to a brother whom I loved? I simply can't explain this, nor can I fathom how easily I slid into the pattern of cruelty which I had experienced at home and at school, when I eagerly caned the children I taught, just a few years later.

My brother, Dyal, continued to worsen, and by April, he was dreadfully sick. The medicine which the doctors had prescribed did not help at all; nothing seemed to work. Various ancient Hindu remedies were recommended, but, in spite of my sincere involvement with the youth group, I was very skeptical of such religious and mystical suggestions.

Slowly, I watched him fade away. Nearing the end, Dyal was unable to eat, and weighed no more than 80 pounds.

In the days before he passed on, we would carry him out to sit by the orange trees each morning. I did not resent the attention we paid to him, but I was hardly aware that he was actually dying. None of us had any idea that he had a fatal brain tumour.

On May 16, 1969, my father left home about 7:00 a.m., as he did on most days, to start his long day working on the farm. As I was getting ready to go off to school, I looked at my brother, lying in a hammock, and I noticed that his face was changing colour — turning blue. He had been singing for several minutes, and suddenly stopped. I knew that something was seriously wrong, so I yelled for my mother, who was in the kitchen. She came running, looked at him, and began to scream horribly. She knew that the worst had happened: my older brother had died.

She sent me into the fields to tell my father; it took me about 15 minutes, running, until I reached him. Weeping, I broke the news to him, and he reached out and put one hand on my shoulder and said, "Everything will be okay." I recall that moment as the very first time that my dad had ever shown emotion — if I can call it that — towards me. His lack of emotional support would take a heavy toll on my life over the years. Today, I hug my daughters Elesha, Shayna, Kendal, and Julia endlessly, and tell them, often, how much I love them, and how special they are. I also frequently hugged both of my parents — especially my dad — whenever I saw them, and I do the same with my brothers and sisters. Is it possible that I'm trying to get the emotional support that I had longed for so much, all those years? I'm not sure, but I know that it feels wonderful whenever I am hugged, or when I hug someone.

Unlike my parents, I didn't break down in tears when Dyal died, but his passing reinforced my skepticism about life and human existence. This was not a rejection of my Hinduism, however, which continued to be a source of strength and camaraderie in my life — as would Christianity.

My brother's body lay in our house for the next several days, after the funeral home had prepared it. My youth group came over and sang songs to comfort my family. As I think back on this sad event, I realize something of which I was unaware at the time; almost the entire village, and half of the students from my high school, came to our home — but only vaguely did I notice how people recognized me — who I was.

Hindus usually cremate their dead, but we chose not to cremate Dyal. It was easier and more frugal to bury his body. He lies in a cemetery near our home in Canal #1, but with no marker on his grave. After my brother's burial came the traditional mourning period of 11 days.

Back in high school, I realized that I was hardly the goody-goody that I had been in primary school. On one occasion, while taking the bus home, the old vehicle finally broke down. The authorities proceeded to take all the girls home first, and left the boys to wait by the bus. We got together, found some shovels in nearby houses, and vandalized the bus, breaking down the seats. For this, I was forbidden use of the bus, and had to go to school by taxi from then on. I don't recall the cost of that, but it was an expense which hardly endeared me to my already alienated father.

When exam time rolled around, we all wanted to stay inside at lunch to study. Yet for some reason or other, the school created a new rule: all classrooms were to be closed over lunchtime. The following morning we lined up, as usual, girls in one line, boys in another. But several of us refused to enter the school, in protest of the new lunchtime rules. Most of my friends backed down from our mini rebellion, but I insisted on going through with it. (These leadership skills would stand me in good stead three decades later when I would found a major financial planning company in the New World.) For this bold act, I was expelled for three days, and beaten six times. Naturally, the punishment and beatings continued when I got home in the evenings.

As so often happens in the lives of serious students, there was one teacher whom I greatly admired. His name was Latiff Ayoub. He was Muslim, and he taught math and physics up to grades 11 and 12.

He was exceedingly brilliant, and probably only in his early 20s when he taught me. I called him Mr. Ayoub — and I still do. He dressed immaculately, and he was quite smart; I soon promised myself that I wanted to be precisely like him: an impressive, trustworthy, solid teacher.

Until I was about 16, there was no electricity in our home. We simply used a bottle of kerosene with a wick inside it, and I would study next to it. Only after I had earned some money teaching school in the jungle, was I able to help install electricity for my family. Fortunately, there was no mocking from my family, who could see that I never used homework as an excuse to get out of chores — and I had a lot of homework, too.

I was about to begin a new adventure, at an early age which will be surprising to most readers of my story; I wanted to teach — and I would end up in the heart of the jungle. The concrete jungles of Canada were still beyond my wildest dreams, even if they were to surround me, less than a half-dozen years in the future.

CHAPTER THREE

THE TEENAGE
TEACHER

I left high school after grade 12 because I wanted to go away and become a teacher. True, I could have gone to teacher's college, which was a requirement for employment in some schools, including those in my village. But many did not. If I had wanted to teach in my village, for example, I would definitely have had to attend teacher's college. But to teach in the jungle, as I did for several memorable years, one did not need to go to college, and for an obvious reason: no one wanted to work there — except for me.

I actually began my brief teaching career in January, 1970. *I was barely over 16!* At the age when most Canadian teenagers are checking their faces for pimples — and possibly flipping burgers at the local fast-food outlet — I was instructing young people who were often within weeks of my own age! I wonder what kind of chaos would have ensued, had North American teenagers been allowed to teach their peers during the rebellious years of the early 1970s.

So why did such a young fellow make such a momentous decision? Well, farming was simply out of the question because I hated it so profoundly. The only other choices open to a young man of my age and education were to go off to the big city (Georgetown, Guyana — population of 100,000, only

19

about half the size of Regina, Saskatchewan) and work in a bank, or maybe go into what we called public services.

At that tender age, the only two things that really interested me were teaching and public service, probably because most of my older friends were pursuing professions in those fields. (I was hardly the trendsetter back then, as I have tried to be in the world of Canadian business, finance and now health care — but I was only 16, please remember.) I sent applications to people in both fields in Guyana, but no one responded.

Then came a small ephiphany, in the form of an ad in the country's only daily newspaper — *The Guyana Chronicle*. It was nothing special —just a regular ad, not unlike the ones for teaching in Japan or Hong Kong which appear regularly in Canada's two national newspapers, and probably those in large American cities as well. I wish I still had the ad, but if memory serves me correctly, it went something like this (see if you would have applied for the job):

TEACHER WANTED
*A teacher is needed for a jungle school near the
Rutinini River, run by Anglican missionaries.
Write to Father Cole, Bartica.*

I suddenly found that I had to go deep into the jungles of Guyana to try to land a job and earn some money, or my family just might lose their farms. Though I would someday have dozens of offices in every province across Canada, I had rarely been more than a few miles away from my small native village, Canal #1!

North American newspapers often describe thousands of people who line up for hours for what are only *potential* jobs at a major industrial plant. I didn't have to worry about any lineups, but I had to travel a great distance simply to reach the interview stage.

The first thing I had to do was get to a small town called Parika. It was nearly a two-hour drive from Canal #1, and that was only because the roads were fairly good (by Guyanese standards), thanks to the relatively populous nature of the area. But Parika was only the start; I then had to take an eight-hour ferry ride, almost due south, to the frontier-like town of Bartica, which one might call the Dawson City of Guyana, but without the ice and snow of Canada's northern gold-mining towns.

If you have never heard of Bartica, here's a description from a Guyanese tourist guide:

Bartica is situated at the junction of the Essequibo and Mazaruni Rivers. This is the hub for the mining community in the North West of Guyana. The town is a hive of activity, as the miners pass through on the way to their claims further in the interior. The river stelling (wharf) and market are colourful and exciting; the pioneer atmosphere is still strong in the town.

Now, if Bartica had been my final destination, that would have been fine. But that was only where my *interview* would take place! An eight-hour ferry ride through the jungle, just to be interviewed! I was terrified, but I knew that I had to go to work, that I had to make some money for my family.

It's not by chance that Guyana means "Land of Many Waters," but I had never seen so much water in my life. My passageway is often called "the mighty Essequibo River," and with good reason. At its mouth — the Atlantic Ocean — it is 21 miles wide, and boasts 365 islands, one for every day of the year. In fact, it is so wide, it contains one island that is actually bigger than the country of Barbados.

There were no roads to take me to Bartica, and so, like Marlow in Joseph Conrad's *Heart of Darkness*, I found myself ferrying deeper and deeper into the interior of my yet-unexplored native land. I would discover no evil, like Conrad's Kurtz, but rather, kindly fellow teachers and loving Amerindian students. But first, I had to land the job.

I had always vaguely understood that only the northernmost portion of Guyana was inhabited, and the rest jungle; but like the average Canadian's limited knowledge of the Northwest Territories and the Yukon, my own understanding of my home country was quite limited until those first few months after I turned 16. Once I got just a few miles away from the relatively populated cities and towns, I was in the thick of it — literally. I was surrounded by jungle undergrowth and mountains. (Guyana is extremely mountainous, and has one of the steepest, most impressive waterfalls on the planet, the Kaieteur Falls.)

Unlike Conrad's ill-fated Marlow, I actually had a priest waiting to greet me in Bartica. He knew I was coming, and it was a great relief to see him waving to me from the dock. Father Cole was an English priest — caucasian — and from the United Kingdom. He was a most pleasant man, and he took me to his house, which stood next to the Anglican church in Bartica. After a brief interview — I sensed that I was not up against many others for the position — he asked me a question I would never dream of asking prospective employees at the major companies I would run years later, up in Canada: "Are you *really* interested in this job?"

I replied in the affirmative. After a few days at Father Cole's little home in Bartica, we went off to see the school. You can imagine how thrilling the "huge" town was, to an impressionable lad of barely 16 years of age! Probably not much different from the gold rush days of the Klondike in Canada or California in the U.S., Bartica was always buzzing — 24 hours a day. It was filled with all the vices of a boomtown, which must have kept Father Cole very busy, when not watching over his jungle school and the local church. The population was less than 10,000 back then, but since the town was situated on the edge of rocks and mines which contained untold riches, it was inevitable that Bartica would become the hub of Guyana.

From Bartica, two major rivers split off, to the northwest and southwest — the Cuyuni and the Mazaruni. Father Cole and I continued our descent into the Heart of Employment in a paddleboat. It took another two hours of floating through the deep, dark jungle to get to St. Edward's Anglican School, which would be the centre of my life and livelihood, for the next few years.

The tiny community — and I mean tiny — made Canal #1 seem like Tokyo by comparison, both in density and population. It wasn't much to see; there were three buildings, somehow cut out of the jungle — a church, a school, and a house attached to the school (in the latter, I would live). The community was populated mostly by the local natives, or Amerindians, who lived spread out, their domiciles scattered along the river like grains of sugar.

There were no signs of life except for another small boat or two. When our paddleboat docked, we stepped out onto some rocks, and there it was. To a teenager long used to hating farm life and beatings, it was as if I had died and gone to heaven! To me, there was so much potential for fun, I didn't think I'd ever want to leave.

Sure, this jungle community lacked the excitement of bad and busy Bartica, and it was much smaller than my hometown. I looked around and really *didn't* see anything happening: there wasn't a living soul, as far as my eyes could see. Just jungle, jungle, and more jungle. All I could see amongst the foliage were little wooden buildings on stilts.

(Sadly, when I returned to the minuscule community a few years ago, while visiting my siblings and their children who have remained in Guyana, every building was gone — destroyed, fallen down, flooded — who knows? Such is the life of the Amerindian in South America.)

The church school was a missionary school, set up to educate the Amerindians. There were maybe four dozen children who would be taught in the one-room schoolhouse by me and Mrs. Jordan, a married black woman in her late thirties, who lived in Bartica and commuted every day to and from the little school.

And so I was offered and accepted the job. The month was January, the year 1970, and I greeted the new decade — one which would end on the frozen streets of Toronto — with a strange new return address to scrawl on my postcards to Canal #1.

We were given a published curriculum, but as anyone might guess, our job was hardly to push academic excellence — these were students who would invariably remain in the jungle, and hunt deer, birds, and fish. For the Amerindians, this was a fact of life — and death. These children did not need physics, nor would they use English or Guyanese history, in the world in which they and their parents happily lived.

So many of the "courses" offered were really survival techniques. As I joked at the time, the most useful ones should have been called *How to Swim in the River 101*, and *How to Walk Safely Through the Jungle 409*. Not surprisingly, it was my students who would teach me to avoid the many poisonous snakes — even boa constrictors — which shared the jungle with us. This brings to mind the lovely ancient expression, "From my teachers I learned much, from my peers I learned a good deal, but from my students, I learned most of all." In the case of potentially fatal snakebites, I *gladly* welcomed the insights offered by my Amerindian students!

Upon my arrival, I had a week free before starting my job, so I headed back to Bartica that evening with the Anglican priest, and then took the long ferryboat and taxi ride home, to tell my family of my good fortune. I actually lacked the money to make the two-way trip to my home in Canal #1, and then back into the jungle for my new teaching job. This forced me to sell several of my schoolbooks to some of the children at the high school. Otherwise, I couldn't have afforded to return to my Amerindian students! To paraphrase a famous old commercial, I've come a long way, baby — at least since then.

I never did meet the teacher I replaced at the jungle school, and it's probably for the best; if that person had been killed by a poisonous snake before I had been hired, I certainly didn't want to know. Nor was I given a cornucopia of educational supplies; as I walked around the tiny school, I found only small stacks of paper, a few dozen pens, and lots of old books.

On my first day, Mrs. Jordan sat me down and described to me what I was expected to teach. I recall not being terribly intimidated by the fact that I was merely a teenager, about to teach other teenagers, as well as younger children. I knew that I needed this job, and that fact easily overcame any fears I might have entertained.

Of course I also knew that this job was temporary — an exotic means to get where I wanted to get, until I found something else which would assist me in my eventual escape from home, farm, and country.

From the very beginning I sent every penny of my paycheque home, because I knew how much my parents, brothers, and sisters needed the money — *all* the money. Indeed, I actually took credit at all the grocery stores in Bartica, where I would do my shopping — until it got to the point where I had to start holding back at least a little money from my weekly financial care package to Canal #1, so I could pay off my debts.

Oh, yes — the pay. I made an impressive sixty Guyanese dollars a month —about $30 U.S. Not much, you might think. But in Guyana in the 1970s, that kind of money went a long, long way — even longer, in fact, than a 12-hour taxi, ferry, and paddleboat trip from Canal #1 to my little Amerindian village.

I would stay and teach at St. Edward's Anglican school for nearly two years. What a superb preparation for a future life in North America, building a multi-million-dollar business from nothing (and with "snakes" everywhere, in the form of lawyers giving bad advice, public commissions which would threaten my very livelihood, and many other obstacles).

DAVID, KING OF THE JUNGLE

What was the first day of school like? Extremely interesting. The schools I had attended in Canal #1 were well-organized, with large, overflowing classes. In this jungle school, however, there were approximately three dozen children. I decided, as they poured into the classroom — really just a single, large room (Mrs. Jordan was teaching on the other side) — that I held for them great expectations.

As the children came in and sat down, I noticed they looked different from the East Asian, black, white, and mixed-race children I had grown up with; these were *native* people — Canadians would call them First Nations or aboriginals — with the square cheekbones and darker skin one often identifies with those ethnic groups.

I introduced myself to them, and found them extremely shy — and with good reason — they were so isolated from the rest of society; from the rest of the country. Indeed, the Amerindians even lived far from one another, in the thick jungle. They ranged in age from about five to sixteen, and when they spoke English, it was with a strong, thick Creole accent, like a Haitian speaking French.

The school day began at 9:00 a.m., and ended at 3:00 p.m. I would begin by teaching grade one, spend perhaps 20 minutes with those young pupils, and then move on to another "class" in another area of the room. So I had a few groups working, and a few doing nothing. Of course, not far away, I could hear the sweet voice of Mrs. Jordan, teaching her own classes.

Most of the studies were in English, science, and math, depending on the level of the students. There were only two students in grade ten whom I had to teach; soon after, both left the jungle school and went off to a school in Bartica, and did very well.

But it was clear from the start that most of our attention would be lavished on learning sheer survival skills.

I must admit, I was well-liked. When I returned to Guyana more than two decades later, the buildings may have been swallowed by the jungle, but not the fond memories. Several of my former students still recognized me, as I made my way to their primitive homes once more, this time as a Guyanese-Canadian who had "made it" in the First World.

There was some racial tension at the school, since there were only a few East Indian and black students amongst a vast majority of Amerindians. One would hear the occasional racial slur during the day, but not against me. They called me "sir," in the typically British fashion — and what teenager, whether teacher or student, wouldn't love to receive respect like that?

Outside of school, my students were kept busy fishing and hunting with their families. Unfortunately, they would also make their own alcohol at home, and would frequently drink away their weekends. But I never heard about drug use in the community.

Not unlike my Hindu background, the Amerindians had big families. And not unlike my experiences at the (comparatively) huge Canal #1 schools, there was a picture of Queen Elizabeth on one wall, and large crosses on all the others. Each day would begin with "God Save the Queen," and various Christian prayers. To the best of my knowledge, there was no strong native religion still existing in the jungle, and the Amerindians all considered them-selves Christian.

I received no mail except for brief cards from my parents once a month. After six months — I was still not yet 17 — my father actually came to visit me for a weekend. He saw the tiny house I lived in, and the kerosene lamp by which I would read every night until 9:00 or 10:00 p.m. But what really trou-bled him was the hammock in which I slept. I explained that there were huge snakes which would often fall from the roof, and occasionally into the ham-mock, as well.

As we were lying there in our hammocks, my father suddenly sat up. "We just have to get out of here!" he cried out. "We're going home tomorrow!"

This was shockingly unusual behavior for my father; I had never felt that he had paid any attention to me or my siblings. To hear such a protective, loving statement was memorable and meaningful to me. It has stuck in my mind ever since.

However, I couldn't help thinking how strange it was that my father — who had done so much in his life, even braved the jungles to build a second home on a second farm, so far away — could not stand what his son David was experiencing in the jungle! I think it was the total isolation there which he could not tolerate — and it was so very isolated. He begged me again to come home with him, but I flatly refused — this was only six months after I had begun my teaching career.

About a decade ago, I asked my parents how they felt now about my expe-rience in the jungle: "Bartica was so very far away, and we missed you a lot. You came home only rarely. But we were happy you were teaching, and continuing your education, my mother told me." (I *was* continuing to study, as you'll soon read.) "You were always sending money home from there, then more and more. We were very thankful for that. And you sent letters home, too."

After my father left — without me — I began to travel monthly to the "big city" of Bartica, two hours away by paddleboat — then, every two weeks to buy groceries. I also dated women there.

The days turned into weeks, then months, as I continued to teach my students, and continued to study, myself. During lunch breaks, I would go next door to my tiny (and usually snake-filled) hut and prepare my modest meals — usually rice and fruit. I also baked my own bread on weekends. And at the end of each school day, I would either take walks through the jungle (avoiding you-know-what), or study to further my education.

I returned to Canal #1 for the first time since beginning my teaching job in the jungle, in July or August, 1970, shortly before my 17th birthday. It was nice to come home, I must admit. It was the first time that I felt a sense of security — that I had money and that I could buy things.

Of course, I knew that I would not stay in that tiny jungle village forever, but I still had no plans to leave Guyana. Sure, I knew I wanted something bigger and better than what I had, and I had long considered going to the University of Guyana in Georgetown. Oh, I was determined that I would do well with my life — but that was the extent of my dream at the time. Building a large financial planning business, or a network marketing company selling quality health products, was nowhere in my sights during those difficult years.

That first summer home from the jungle, I went into the capital city of Georgetown every day, the way any North American teenager might wish to hang around the local mall. My friends and I used to hang around together, go to the movies, and other such activities. And, naturally, I continued to work on the farm that summer with my brothers, but not as much as I had before.

That September, just before my 17th birthday, I returned to Bartica and the jungle school, and continued to teach my Amerindian students through 1970 and 1971, and did not move on until September, 1972, making it two years at St. Edward's Anglican School. While there, I managed to complete the third and fourth years of the Guyanese educational system, all three forms of teacher's qualifications — I had to go all the way back to Georgetown to take the exams — and found myself receiving a "generous" increase in pay: ten or fifteen dollars more each month.

Over those years deep in the jungles of Guyana, I grew close to Father Cole, and I traveled with him a good deal. I would go to see him in Bartica every second weekend and assist him in his various obligations.

For instance, he used to minister to prisoners on an island situated about halfway between the town of Bartica and my little school. He went there once a month to conduct services, and I became fascinated by the experience. And so, the small-town Hindu lad found himself helping with the Anglican services, before a rather ethnically-mixed congregation (albeit a captive one). The island-prison was surrounded by four walls. Perhaps Alcatraz, the famous prison situated off the coast of San Francisco, might have the better view and the more romantic history, but this was pretty exotic for me. As you may well imagine, there were all kinds of inmates there, from petty criminals to murderers, and I was both entranced, yet somewhat fearful, to join in the singing of the Christian hymns. I never left my Hindu faith, but I cannot deny that I grew fond of the Anglican religion, and felt that it was an important part of my life.

By the time I finished my *Heart of Darkness* stint, I was about to turn 19. I had long since asked for a transfer to another school in Bartica, and for more than the obvious reason that I was tired of the loneliness and isolation of the tiny jungle village. I had been studying and passing all those teacher's examinations, please remember, and I soon found myself more qualified than over four-fifths of the teachers in the more attractive school in Bartica. In fact, now that I think about it, I was probably the most qualified teacher in that important frontier town, my age notwithstanding.

Yet after many months of requesting — nay, begging — for a transfer to the larger school, I was still stuck at St. Edward's. I eventually figured out why; Father Cole's assistant just did not like me. There are many times in one's life when it pays to get along with those in power, and this was certainly one of those occasions. After all, he was in charge of accepting all teachers for the Bartica Anglican School. I needed him on my side, but failed to accomplish that.

For two consecutive years, in fact, I would formally ask for a transfer, and the answer always came back in the negative. Finally, after considerable frustration on my part, the principal of the school in Bartica, John Palmer, asked for my services, and put great pressure on Father Cole's assistant, Father Lowe, to get me in there. (I had the good fortune of previous acquaintance with Mr. Palmer.) When I left my little jungle village, it was a quiet farewell, because everyone knew that I would continue to see many of them during their expeditions to the frontier town, just a two-hour paddleboat ride away.

And so, in the fall of 1972, as I was about to enter my 20th year, I began to teach at the Bartica Anglican School. As one of 30 teachers, I found my duties far more specialized: I had my own class — grade two — with approximately 20 children, mainly blacks and East Asians (but some Amerindians, as well). I happily said good bye to *Avoiding Snakes 101* and hello to reading, writing, and arithmetic!

I was now making $100 a month, which was clearly a big-time salary. I joined two friends in renting a little house — downstairs was a bookstore, but upstairs was a two-bedroom apartment. One of those friends now lives in Montreal and — these things happen — ended up marrying my girlfriend. The other friend, also of East Asian descent, taught in the local Catholic school. (The only tensions between the Anglicans and Catholics seemed to occur when their respective teams met on cricket and soccer playing fields.) It was only a ten-minute walk to school, with nary a snake to be seen along the way.

Civilization at last! I went home to Canal #1 far more often now, as frequently as once a month, although I soon had a girlfriend in Bartica, so I began to visit my family far less often. Indeed, I recall one period when I didn't visit my family for eight months. My parents were exceedingly upset — but such is the power of love. With my knowledge of the Bible, I could always paraphrase the Book of Genesis, and tell my family that the Lord ordered us to "leave our families and cling" unto a mate.

I also wasn't sending home as much money as before. By now, I had begun to move my sights quite a bit beyond the equatorial borders of Guyana, to north of the 49th parallel; I had begun to put money away for the first airplane journey of my young life. (One can get pretty tired of ferries and paddleboats, let me tell you.)

Fortunately, things had picked up a little back at Canal #1, so sending home only half of my salary seemed sufficient. At this point in my life, I was no longer assisting Father Cole. But then I was not involved with any specifically Hindu activities, either. Thinking back, I realize that I was never very religious; even when I taught and was so active in the Hindu youth group, my involvement had always been primarily to keep myself busy, and keep away from bad company. But then, I've always wanted to do things differently from other people, and I've always kept myself from becoming too preoccupied with any one thing, religious or otherwise.

By the time my first full year was up at the Bartica Anglican School, I was determined to come to Canada. Why such a distant, freezing goal? For the same reasons tens of millions have migrated to new nations over the past several centuries; a family member or warm acquaintance had chosen to move to Canada, and wrote back describing its attractiveness. One close friend had recently left for that unknown northern country, and before he left, I recall talking with him about what we would be doing in our respective futures. "I'd like to go there, too!" I told him. The feeling grew stronger and stronger inside me that Canada was where my future would lie. The nation of Canada would be both my fortune, and my "Fortune Financial," and eventually my newest dream — a series of quality, healing products manufactured by Destiny Health Solutions. But the first two of those dreams would not come true for another 14 years.

When I met my former beloved from Canal #1, not long ago, she told me, "You never told me that you were leaving Guyana until three weeks before you boarded that plane!" She had been greatly upset, and reflecting on my actions then, I couldn't believe that I had done that. But then, I didn't tell my parents until one short week before I left. I just got up one day before my family and blurted out, "I'm going to Canada!"

No one believed me. They bombarded me with questions: "How are you going? Where will you live? Where will you get the money for the flight?"

I simply told each of them, "I have it all planned out."

But really, I did not.

During this distracted and confused period of my life, I had been in touch with an old friend who had left Guyana for Toronto several years before, and had gone to George Brown College, an academic institution with several campuses around the city. With his kind assistance, I got in touch with the college, sent them all the information they requested, and stayed in close contact with them. (The thought that, just over a quarter-century later, I would actually sit on the Board of Governors of that same college, and found the first diploma-granting course in financial planning in all of Canada, would have been laughed off by me as quickly as if I had been told that I would walk on the moon in the next few decades.)

In fact, I had mentioned to my parents several months before that I was "thinking of going to Canada to study." The problem was, of course, that my family had no money, or even financial statements, to send to George Brown College or to immigration authorities, to verify that I would be supported, should I prove to be a burden to the country.

At first, my father was extremely helpful. He took me to someone in Canal #1 who was quite well off, whom he hoped would give us some kind of letter to prove that they would be responsible for me, and promise I would be financially supported, should I ever need such assistance in Canada. Alas, they refused to give us such a letter. We were back to square one.

So I returned to the principal of the school where I had taught in Bartica the previous year — the man who had so generously helped me escape the jungle school — and he gave me the letter I needed. If it hadn't been for that man, I would probably still be in Guyana.

The letter was simple; if I ever fell on hard times while studying and living in Canada, he promised to support me. He was a Christian black man, generously helping out an East Asian Hindu — the sort of relationship which my often-tragic country of Guyana sure could have used over the past half-century.

To this day, I have no idea why that kindly principal did such a wonderful thing for me. But I did see him again when I returned to Guyana four years after coming to Canada, and I thanked him profusely at that time.

Meanwhile, with the potentially life-changing flight north rapidly approaching, I continued to improve myself as a teacher. I took a series of difficult teacher's exams called "The Third Class," but in retrospect, they were more like the third degree: they were on twelve different subjects, ranging from arithmetic, geometry, and algebra to history and geography; from biology and hygiene to literature and art; I had to learn them all in order to pass.

Very few people actually passed this torture test. You sat and wrote it for three days straight. (Who needs slavery or colonialism to be mistreated? We ethnics can do it to ourselves!) I had to drag myself off to Georgetown to go through this hell.

In the entire country, only two people passed these ferociously difficult and diffuse tests that year — 1973. No one had ever passed them in the history of the town of Bartica.

I was one of those who achieved that goal.

There were reasons that Bartica's teachers had never "made it" before I managed to; first, as mentioned above, the tests were excruciatingly difficult. Second, Bartica was a remote location in our country, and it was rare that anyone would take all that trouble of time, travel and hard work to study for them.

Suddenly, I achieved instant celebrity status in Bartica — my own

15 minutes of fame. I even began to give evening classes to my fellow teachers, most of whom were far older than my 19 years. This gave me further recognition, and those courses were highlights of my several years of teaching. I received no extra money for this; it was simply one of the ways in which I wanted to "pay back" the school for being so good to me, by taking me out of the jungle.

And so, I edged closer and closer to the airport and a future in a country "cold and oceans" away, to quote Leonard Cohen. I was on a real high. I had become very qualified as a teacher in my country, and I had also become the coach of the track-and-field team at my school, which in turn was involved with a dozen other schools across Guyana.

Quite similar to what we have in Canada, teams were divided into regions, and I had set a goal for myself — not unlike the goal I had set to pass those near-impossible comprehensive teacher's exams: I wanted to become the head coach of the entire region, so I found myself coaching children and then taking them to meets all over Guyana. My experience as a "national" track-and-field coach was another highlight in the first two decades of my young existence in Guyana.

All these life-shaking events took place during the last year that I would live in my native land. All that year, Canada grew larger in my mind and in my thinking.

In retrospect, I'm not sure why I had focused so strongly on George Brown College in Toronto. I had no real career ambition at that time; I simply wanted to do well — in something. The subject of engineering just sounded interesting, so I applied and got accepted to the college in that field.

According to the stringent (but understandable) immigration rules for students coming to Canada, I had to buy a round-trip ticket. It cost $600, which was half a year's salary. But I had saved enough, and I did it. I also had to pay, in advance, the tuition for a full year, which was another $250. It may not sound like much now, but it was a towering sum to a teenager who had been earning around $100 a month, and sending half of that home to his family for the previous year.

It was late August, 1974, nearly 30 years before I began writing this book. I would soon turn 21. I packed whatever clothes I owned — they fit easily into one small suitcase. There is usually a huge farewell party for those who leave the country, but I didn't have one. I had broken the news at home only one week earlier, and I didn't want to make a big deal about it. I just wanted to go.

Still, everyone came to see me off at the tiny, wooden departure hall at Georgetown's modest little Timehri International Airport, painted in the traditional colours of the Guyanese flag: yellow, green, black, red, and white. The building seemed crowded by my huge family, alone; my parents, my brothers, my sisters, all seeing me off.

As I boarded the British Airways jet, I looked back at the family — and the country which had brought me so much pain, yet so many insights and a powerful ambition to succeed. I guess I should have been scared. I wasn't, though. I was more fascinated with the endless possibilities which lay ahead.

The plane swept up off the worn tarmac. As I looked down at the vanishing countryside and the rapidly receding South American continent, I found myself silently reciting the National Pledge of my country, which I had spoken in unison countless times over the previous 15 years:

> I pledge myself to honour always
> The flag of Guyana
> And to be loyal to my country
> To be obedient to the laws of Guyana
> To love my fellow citizens
> And to dedicate my energies
> Toward the happiness
> And prosperity of Guyana.

It was hardly disloyal to want to start again, was it? I had been obedient to its laws (by and large); I had loved my fellow citizens. But the time had come to work on my own personal prosperity, and in doing so, bring financial gain to both my native Guyana, and the new, as yet unknown country to which I was rapidly flying.

CHAPTER FOUR

INTO THE CONCRETE JUNGLE

It was August 24, 1974, when I landed in Toronto with $22 in my pocket. I was 20 years old, and seemed to have collected enough memories, both good and bad, to last a lifetime. But like any new immigrant to a new land, I was quite literally, and physically, beginning a whole new life.

Everyone has something which stands out in his or her life — falling in love, one's first job, and so on. What stands out for me — the tallest, free-standing memory, if you will, is the recollection of my first glimpse of the CN Tower as the jet came in for a landing at Toronto International Airport. The village from which I'd just arrived had fewer people living in it than in any of the towering apartment buildings I saw below me.

In the jungle, after that two-hour paddleboat ride from Bartica, I used to study by a little bottle lamp, and sometimes a firefly would come by and flicker a bit of light near my head. Through the thatched roof of my small hut amongst the Amerindians, I could see the stars flickering above — the same stars which can be seen above Canadian cities (when the air is clear enough) — but I never knew that back in Guyana. Beneath the rapidly descending plane, were what seemed like a million flickering lights. Primitive fireflies had become fluorescent, after only a few hours of flight! That was my first impression of Toronto. I had felt comfortable on the plane because there was someone else on it from Canal #1 who was coming to Canada for a brief vacation. At least I knew somebody!

Before I left Guyana, I sent a message to a distant relative who had been living in Canada for six years. He turned out to be more distant than I could have imagined in my worst dreams. He was supposed to pick me up — at least that's what I had thought. (He later claimed that he never received the message.)

I got off the plane in this very alien city, and there was no one to greet me, and no place to go. I tried to phone my relative, but no one was home, and for the first time I began to panic. I had no money! "What if this person really did not want me to stay at his place?" I asked myself. Maybe that's why he chose not to pick me up!

Luckily, Kenneth Singh (no relation), the person from my hometown whom I had recognized when boarding the plane, was still in the airport, waiting for his luggage. He promptly offered to take me to his place, which was at Queen Street and Lansdowne, in the southwest part of Toronto's downtown.

I stayed at my compatriot's home that night, with people whom I really didn't know; true, they had lived in the village of my childhood, but we were hardly good friends.

The next morning, I phoned my distant cousin once more. This time he was home, and he picked me up. But he soon made it clear that I would not be able to stay at his place for very long; he had only a one-bedroom apartment, and two of his brothers were already living with him. By my second week in Canada, I had to go and find myself another place to live. How lucky that it was still summer, and I had not yet encountered one of this nation's often-brutal winters.

For the first time in my life, I was in a city where the majority of people were white, and I was a member of a distinct, "visible" minority, as they love to put it in Canada. I immediately felt different, and didn't know how I should conduct myself with others. I was certainly very conscious of the fact that I was different. I also noticed, for the first time, how tall people seemed to grow here. Fortunately, at the beginning, no racial slurs were directed towards me.

I remained in the general area of Queen Street — just a few blocks north of Lake Ontario — for the next few weeks, and moved around quite often.

My first rent was a then-costly $20 a week, so I had to find a job as soon as possible. (I had come on a student visa.) My initial employment experience in my new, chosen land was at Harvey's.

My job could not have been more menial; I was to wash the toilets and the floors. I stuck with it for two weeks, but then, because of my first experience as a victim of racial discrimination, I left.

I had already begun classes at George Brown College, which would last until five o'clock each afternoon. I started in the industrial engineering program, but after a few months I realized that I just did not have what it took to become an engineer. I remember one day when we had to take apart a water valve and then put it back together. I was the only student in the class who ended up with extra parts at the end of the exercise! But what I like to call flexibility — a quality which would serve me well over the years — came in very useful, and in January 1975, I switched to the business administration program at the college, from which I would eventually graduate, with honours, in the summer of 1977.

Still, those years were overwhelmingly challenging. After finishing each day's class in the late afternoon, I would go off to my job at Harvey's, where I worked until two o'clock in the morning. I would grab only three hours of sleep each night, before returning to my classes the next day.

On shift, when I had just finished mopping, the assistant manager came down and screamed at me, "I don't like the way you're mopping!"

Before I even had a chance to reply, much less defend myself, the young man picked up the pailful of dirty water and splashed it across the floor I had just finished cleaning. "The mop is waiting over there for you," he snarled at me.

I told him that I was not going to do it again, at which point the assistant manager grabbed me, pushed me against the wall, and shouted, "You Pakis come here to this country, but you're not going to get out of this store until you mop this floor over!" This was hardly the time to explain to the fellow that my heritage was Indian, not Pakistani. I simply announced to him that "I'm not going to redo it!"

"You'd better!" he shouted back.

I marched upstairs and walked out, without saying anything further.

The next day, I informed the manager that I was not coming back. He told me that I was welcome back on the job anytime I wanted to return.

This unhappy event occurred on the day before my 21st birthday. I had truly come of age — in terms of human (and inhuman) relationships. The following day, October 3, I received the nicest birthday gift possible: I applied for work at the Hyatt Regency Hotel (today, the Four Seasons) on the edge of the famed Yorkville area of Toronto, and was offered a job as a dishwasher, which I accepted.

I had been in Canada for little over one month, and already I had learned an important life lesson: I knew that I would hear the derogatory term "Paki!" in reference to myself many more times. Unfortunately, I would not be proven wrong in my expectation.

In retrospect, when the manager at Harvey's used racist language against me, I didn't lash back because I was both afraid and enraged. Moreover, I wasn't sure how to respond; I was not used to slurs of any kind, and just wasn't familiar with these kinds of experiences. I had been in shock, more than anything else.

My hours at the Hyatt were from 5:00 p.m. until 2:00 a.m. And my wonderful new job? I was to wash pots and pans. (As so many women joke about housework: it's dirty work, but someone has to do it. So why not a recent immigrant to the country?)

It's difficult to compare the two jobs, because I had worked at Harvey's for only two weeks. But I liked it better at the attractive hotel almost at once, because no one stood over me, watching my every move.

Ultimately, I spent some 18 months at the Hyatt Regency, and I grew to enjoy the job very much, my dishpan hands notwithstanding. I think I was pleased with it because it did a similar thing for me that teaching in the jungle had done; it left me with a lot of time to think. Back in the jungle, on those long, dark, and lonely nights, there was no one to talk to. I found myself spending countless hours, days, and even weeks, thinking of the things I wanted to do with my life.

Now, barely over a year out of the darkest jungles of South America, I had long periods of time in which I could think of the things I'd done in my life — how I had taught Amerindian children in the jungle school; how I would come home each evening to my little hut and read and study, never speaking to anyone.

Here in Toronto, I had not yet landed a job which was conducive to communicating with people, and that's how my earliest relationships went:

not talking too much. This was one of the things that my now ex-wife would often complain about — that I didn't communicate sufficiently with her. Now, in mid-life, I talk a great deal more, but I still do a lot of internalizing, and do a lot of planning on my own, both in my private life, and in the world of business.

Occasionally, I had regrets about leaving Guyana, and I had frequent longings to return home. But they were never strong enough to act upon. When I once asked my father about that time in both of our lives, I was taken aback when he told me, "We didn't hear anything from you for two years, not even a single letter." Clearly, I was more focused on making it in my new home than I may have realized at the time.

That first winter — it was 1974/75 — was the hardest. I had rented a room with only a bed in it, nothing more. There were no extras, no sheets, blankets, not even cooking facilities. I was earning just enough money from my job at the Hyatt to pay the rent and buy some groceries. Today, I believe this sort of living would be described as "no frills."

Every night — the middle of the night, in fact, was when I got home, after work — I would collapse on my bed, and pull my coat over my freezing body. The room was bitterly cold. In fact, the day that I bought my first blanket still stands out in my memory as a very special day; it was such a big deal for me, at that time. I remember — with some embarrassment today — that I used to sneak food (let's call it what it was — it was stealing) from the fridge which was shared by the six tenants in our small building. I was never caught doing this, so I still must live with the guilt of those difficult days.

At the Hyatt, I was earning the minimum wage of the province of Ontario, which was $1.25 an hour back then. The fare on the TTC (the Toronto transit system) was a dime. I worked over 40 hours a week, on top of my business studies at George Brown, and each summer, I worked as much as 80 hours a week, in order to try to save some money for my tuition and living expenses for the coming year.

In fact, during my first four or five summers in Toronto, I was always studying or working, working or studying. This calls to mind that wonderfully insightful one-liner of the Canadian humourist Stephen Leacock: "I'm a great believer in luck; the harder I work, the luckier I get." I've ended up being very, very lucky in my life.

SUCCEEDING AT WORK, SUCCEEDING AT COLLEGE

For the first year and a half that I washed pots and pans at the Hyatt Regency Hotel, I made only one friend — a black man. Unlike me, he was always dressed beautifully. He was the only one of all the workers at the hotel who, when dropping off the pots at my station, would exclaim, "Hello!" and actually talk with me.

Then, after that initial 18 months, I was promoted to a better job. It was the first time that I wore a white shirt and actually looked clean — at which point, at least half a dozen other workers started to come over and sit with me at the same dinner table where I'd sat for the previous year and a half, when not a single person (with the exception of the man mentioned above) had ever spoken to me. The only thing I could change was the way that I would react to such situations, since my response appeared to be all that I had any control over.

I never encountered any racial prejudice from my fellow workers at the Hyatt, but on the buses to and from work, I met with a disturbing amount. I would be returning to my room late at night, and people would actually walk up to me and spit in my face. (Presumably for the crime of having dark skin, and maybe for taking all the good jobs away from real, native-born Canadians?) True, the men who would do this were never the high-class, well-dressed people; it was always the bums and the drunkards. But still, it bothered me greatly.

What kept me going was that I would tell myself again and again: "I'm not going to allow these ugly incidents to affect me." After studying self-help books and tapes, and attending numerous seminars, I have come to realize that you can learn things from every experience.

In my new, higher employ as a busboy, I began to encounter all kinds of discrimination, even from the well-dressed, purportedly cultured clientele. When I used to collect the used glasses and dirty ashtrays from a table, I would be asked, "How does it feel for a paki to work in such a nice hotel?" These sorts of nasty slurs angered me, but I refused to honour them with a response. It was always white people who would address me like that.

This kind of verbal abuse was surprisingly common, nearly three decades ago. Hotel guests would forever be calling me "paki" or "coloured boy." True, I was never called "nigger" while at the Hyatt Regency, but I would hear that vile term many times in other places around the city. As late as 1976, I was still working at the hotel, occasionally still washing pots, and still earning that very minimum wage.

When I arrived in Toronto and enrolled at George Brown, I quickly made it clear to my fellow classmates that I wanted to become president of the student council. Campaigning for the elected position was most informative, in terms of the racial tolerance of George Brown students at the time: I had my picture plastered all over the school on campaign posters, and when I came in each morning, every one of them was defaced with such epithets as "NIG-GER GO HOME!" and "PAKI! WE DON'T WANT YOU HERE!" I guess they just couldn't decide who they wanted as their fellow citizens — or what minority group I belonged to. I actually got a big kick out of this, and eventually, I was elected president. I am pleased to note that I was the first "coloured" person to ever be chosen by his peers for that position at George Brown College. I had run against two white students and one black, and the vote was very close. Similar slurs were used against the black candidate.

Recently, George Brown College was kind enough to dig up some copies of their school newspaper, *Full Moon*, from just prior to that election. It was fun to look at the tiny photo of myself, taken nearly two decades ago, which showed me with an Afro as large as the SkyDome, clutching a phone. Beneath the now-laughable picture was the enthusiastic electioneering of an eager new Canadian:

I am a third-semester marketing student and one of my major interests is organizational work. I have been involved in all kinds of organizational work for a long time and have gained a tremendous amount of experience. I enjoy taking the leadership role in organizational work [a bit repetitive there!] for I strongly believe that self-motivated people will cooperate to get things done if it is for the benefit of others.

This has been proved to me clearly through my involvement with Cultural Day. As coordinator for this occasion, I received all the cooperation I needed from all the groups involved, to make this day the success it was. As vice president of the Black Students' Union I also gained a lot of experience working with the students here.

I have a lot of plans for the St. James Students' Council to ensure that the good work the present executive is doing is continued and even surpassed. A lot has been done by the present executive, but there is still much more to be done for the benefit of all students here. [Note: I would end up being a continual praiser and constant supporter of my hundreds of sales reps at Fortune Financial, and later, Destiny Health Solutions.]

Forming an alumni association, encouraging all the clubs on campus to work together for a common goal, unity, setting up of staff and student-merit awards, getting administration to provide better facilities for students as soon as possible, getting the students' councils of all the other George Brown campuses to work together, and a bigger Cultural Day in 1977 are some of my plans for the coming year if I am elected PRESIDENT *of the St. James Students' Council.*

I PROMISE NOTHING BUT HARD WORK, DEDICATION, AND EFFICIENCY FOR A STUDENTS' COUNCIL DEVOTED TO WORKING FOR THE BENEFIT OF ALL STUDENTS ON THIS CAMPUS. *[Yes, all those caps were in the original; such was the enthusiasm of youth!]*

Thank you for your support and let us all work together to ensure unity and love, for together we will make progress.

As I leaf through these photocopies, I am struck by just how prescient it all was; the insistence on leadership; the willingness to praise others and avoid belittling their contributions; the sense of determination and the promise of "hard work" and "dedication" — even the list of all the things I was determined to do, if I was elected.

When Alexander Pope wrote that "as the twig is bent, the tree's inclin'd," he was referring to the way a child is raised, of course. When I considered these youthful words, I realized the twig of my life had been bent toward leadership. Under the self-penned headline *"Communication is David's 'Thing,'"* I wrote about my hopes for the campus, now that I was the new president of the student council:

> *The first thing the new executive will do is to improve the communication system on this campus. If we are truly going to promote unity among students here, then I see a dire need to first of all, improve communication among students. A weekly newsletter from the students' council will be our first endeavour to ensure that you know what is taking place at the students' council. You can be assured that everything possible will be done to ensure that all the*

sections — business and commerce, graphic arts, elec-
tronics, manpower, etc., are involved in the students'
council . . .

I was already showing signs of leadership which I never could have imagined, back in my tiny village of Canal #1, much less in the jungles beyond the frontier town of Bartica.

I studied at George Brown for three years, from the fall of 1974 to the summer of 1977. I took mainly business courses, and enjoyed most of them. One of my instructors was Jerry White, who, in one of those delicious acts of fate which sometimes occur in our lives, later became one of the top investment lecturers for the company I would soon create: Fortune Financial.

My classes comprised a mix of cultures, which is probably even greater today, considering worldwide immigration to Canada over the past few decades; there were Caucasians, Africans, Koreans, Chinese, Eastern Europeans, Caribbeans, Philippinos, and many other nationalities. At least three-quarters of my business classmates were male, and we tended to divide racially at lunch. With echoes of my youth in Guyana, blacks and East Indians hung around together.

I felt that I was getting an excellent education. Everything was new to me, of course, and I enjoyed it tremendously. When I graduated from the three-year course, I received an honours diploma in business administration. What I wanted back then in terms of a career was still vague in my mind; I knew I wanted some kind of position in business, whether sales or marketing. I was unable to put my finger on any particular job I would try to land. But somehow, I just knew I would succeed.

In my own recollection, I wrote home to my parents regularly — maybe once a month, but as time went on, I cannot deny it, I began to write less and less. I did not return to Guyana until March, 1978, after graduating from George Brown. As my father told me several years ago, still brimming with appreciation, "When you first returned home, you put in electricity for us!"

Before graduating from college, I left my job at the Hyatt Regency. This move paralleled my election as president of the student council. I was paid thirty dollars a week for handling that honour, which was enough to pay my rent. When I look back on those years, I'm also proud that I had insisted on our campus publishing a yearbook. I've been told that they have continued to put out a yearbook ever since that first one I inauguerated, back in 1976.

The next place of employment in my rapidly divergent career was as a sales clerk in a women's clothing store called Dalmy's. They hired me because of my educational experience at George Brown, and I quickly realized that I was the only male working there. I never encountered any kind of racist (or sexist) prejudice while working at that store, and I was employed there happily until May, 1977. It was a pleasure to be able to use some of the concepts which I had studied at college. After I graduated college, I left Dalmy's, and lived in a room I shared with a friend, until I got married in June, 1977.

My first job, after leaving George Brown, was in a fast food restaurant at the corner of Bloor and Yonge called Roy Rogers. Once again — except that the young newcomer was now clutching a diploma in business administration — I was doing exactly what I had done at Harvey's, three long and difficult years before.

There was simply no other job available at that time, so I took what I could get. (We immigrants tend to be that way.) I was newly married to a fellow student from college, and living in a one-bedroom apartment in the eastern suburb of Scarborough, which since has become part of the Greater Toronto Area.

My job at Roy Rogers was undoubtedly a step backward, in terms of both prestige and work experience, but I had already learned one of the seminal truths of my young life; if you treat every experience as a learning opportunity, then you'll never be afraid to go back and do something a second time — because if it's a learning experience, you know that it is only temporary.

In fact, one of the things I still hope to accomplish is to influence the Canadian school system to teach students to react positively to different, often difficult, situations. And let me tell you, the situation I found myself in at Roy Rogers took some work to react favourably to! Working there was downright embarrassing, after busing at a fine hotel, studying business administration, serving as a student-council president, and then as a clerk at a quality women's clothing store. Talk about three steps forward and nine steps back!

I was actually mortified that my wife might see me at what seemed to now be a demeaning job. I had told her that I was cooking at the restaurant, but in reality, I was cleaning floors and toilets. (Thank heavens for the wonderful work experience I had picked up during my tenure at Harvey's, shortly after I first arrived in Canada. Nothing is wasted in this world!)

I worked at this unpleasant, yet financially crucial job from July through September of 1977. One time, my wife came to see me on the job, and I actually hid from her, so she would not watch me in such a menial situation. But then, such are the ways of immigrants in a new land.

A SEMI-HAPPY LEAP INTO THE WORLD OF SALES AND ACCOUNTING

WITH FURTHER EDUCATION ALONG THE WAY

By the fall of 1977, I had been in my new "home and native land" for three years, had worked several thousand hours at minimum wage; survived three Canadian winters — no small feat, for a kid from tropical Guyana; earned a degree in business administration; continued to develop my leadership potential, first shown in Guyana with the Hindu youth group, and later by being elected president of the student council at George Brown College, fallen in love and gotten married; and learned how to become a World Class Cleaner of Toilets, Floors, Pots, Pans, and Ashtrays. I discovered that nothing in one's life is ever wasted; nothing.

I was about to begin a new phase in my life and career, and one — unlike the toilets of Harvey's and Roy Rogers — which would lead irrevocably to the creation of Canada's largest financial planning company just over a decade later, and, ultimately, the making of my own personal fortune.

It began in the same inauspicious way as my tenure in the jungles of Guyana; I looked for another job. I applied for a position at Sun Life Assurance because it was business-related (unlike Roy Rogers' toilets), and, to be frank, simply because it was *a job*. I landed the position shortly after the interview, and I became an insurance agent later that same month. (The insurance licence took only a few weeks to study for and receive.) This was the company that had made Canada-wide headlines when it pulled its head office out of Montreal, and moved it to Toronto. But for this still-youthful immigrant to the country, it was a glorious opportunity to spread my wings and learn about the world of sales.

I happily made the long journey on public transit from our little apartment in the eastern suburbs down to 200 University Avenue, because I was sure that it would be a very good learning experience. And it was. But I quickly realized that I wouldn't remain there long. To be blunt, I didn't like the pressure, and I hated the way that life insurance was sold to the public. (See my recommendations for Money Management Strategies in the Wealth Section of this book, below.)

As a child, I always liked to analyze things, and as an adult, I just refused to accept what my managers kept telling me — that "whole life" insurance was the best for our clients. Best for the insurance salesperson, undoubtedly, in terms of commissions and best for the insurance company, of course — but *what about the public?*

The sales records quickly showed my attitude; I was always selling more "term" insurance than any other kind, and more than anyone else in the office. So I sensed that I would not be long on the sales staff at Sun Life.

No, I wasn't fired, and, to be honest, I made a fair living working there. But I vowed that I would not stay at Sun Life longer than necessary.

How does one become a successful salesperson? You usually go to work on relatives and friends, and try to interest them in purchasing a policy. (True, friends can become irritated with you, but relatives are pretty well stuck with you, aren't they?) After you go through those people — not an inexhaustible list — you soon realize that you haven't learned the basic skills. I sure had not. What I did learn at Sun Life was how I would want to train my own employees, to assist them in becoming the best marketers possible, and working in the best interest of their clientele.

I stayed at Sun Life for less than a year. In August, 1978, my wife and I had our first child — a beautiful, healthy daughter whom we named Elesha, from the biblical word for Elizabeth. I was to start new studies at York University in September of that year. I wanted to continue in business, and York would allow me to take evening classes. I simply couldn't afford *not* to work.

And so, in August, 1978, I quit my position at Sun Life, and began a new job at Confederation Life. It was a nine-to-five job, unlike sales. My duties were to analyze budgets, working very closely with the company's marketing department, and reviewing sales projections for its branches.

In many ways, my work at Confederation Life, which went belly-up some years later, was my first real job in this country, and I saw myself staying with the company for some time. I had decided that I wanted to become an actuary, and eventually remained at Confederation Life for three years, as a financial analyst. I had begun there making $18,000 a year — a nice improvement from the minimum wages of Harvey's, the Hyatt, and Roy Rogers, and when I left, my salary was up to $22,000 annually.

It was a good time in my life, although I continued the arduous pace of the previous few years: I would take the subway to work — we had no car, of course; I would be at the office until five o'clock each day, and then I took buses up to the York University campus in the northwest part of Metropolitan Toronto, where I took more business courses, from 7:00 to 10:00 p.m., four nights a week. I earned an equivalent of five credits a year.

Understandably, my wife and I had no time for a social life. At the time, I had no thoughts of starting my own business — that idea would take another decade to come to fruition — but I did very much want to move up to being a manager.

The decade of the 1980s dawned far more promising than the previous one, which began with a ten-hour river ride into the jungle from my Guyanese village. I graduated from York University with a B.A. in Administrative Studies in May, 1981, and then left Confederation Life in October of the same year.

The reason I moved on was fairly prosaic; I saw a job advertised at Allstate which would pay a few thousand dollars more than I was earning at Confed — some $25,000 a year. Moreover, I felt that I had to try something new. My work had begun to be quite frustrating, and not only because I had completed three years of university education at York in the evenings. Although my confidence had grown considerably and I was not yet 28 years old, my manager at Confederation Life, who had been there for many, many years, refused to do any work on the computer. He was dreadfully old-fashioned, and I simply had to change jobs if I was going to grow professionally.

The sideways leap to Allstate was an unpleasant experience (even though the offices were in Scarborough, the first time I had ever worked so close to my home). I stayed barely over one year and left in August, 1982.

I simply didn't like my manager, and he didn't like me. Personal pressures were also building; my wife and I had our second daughter, Shayna, in August, 1981, and we purchased our first house in Scarborough that same year. My wife remained at home, taking care of our young children.

I must confess here to a rather strange attitude towards money; I just always assumed that it would come. I'm not suggesting that everyone should act this way, because it can get a little scary, doing things first, and then worrying about how to finance one's plans, later. But this has been a pattern throughout my life. I lacked the money to even reach the place where I had hoped to teach, in the jungles of Guyana; and I left for Canada without really knowing how I would survive; and I had no money whatsoever when I bought our first home. I had simply picked up the *Toronto Star* on a Saturday, while studying at York, noted that the housing market was going crazy, drove out to Scarborough, and declared, "I like this house! I'll take it!" I then went back to our tiny apartment and told my wife, "We just bought a house!" We argued for a week about that — at which point I had to figure out how I was going to pay for it.

Like so many young Canadians, my wife and I found it very hard to cope financially. We had a high mortgage, and two children, and my income simply wasn't high enough to care for everything and everyone. Then, in one of those twists of fate which can be so important in our lives, I ran into a friend and former countryman, Dax Sukhraj. He had joined the major financial planning company, Investors Group, three years earlier. He was doing very well, and he told me that I could do a lot better financially in *his* field. How interesting and ironic that years later, he became president of Financial Concept, the largest competitor of the firm I would later create myself — Fortune Financial.

CHAPTER FIVE

DEEPER INTO THE JUNGLES OF SALESMANSHIP

I joined Investors Group in August, 1982. I had made the decision that I had to get out of a salaried position. I needed to be in total control of how much I would earn, and had long since realized that I and my growing family simply *could not live* on $25,000 a year. I was running up a lot of debts, and I just wasn't making enough to make ends meet.

I knew absolutely nothing about mutual funds at that time. Absolutely zero. Interestingly, my move to Investors was my second choice; my first choice was to stay at Allstate, but as an insurance salesperson once more; I had even gone through the entire process of applying for that position there. True, I had not been pleased with my earlier experience as an insurance agent, but I was determined to take charge of my earning potential, and being in sales allows one to do that, for better or worse. (The "worse," I had already accomplished.)

After I had spoken to some of the insurance agents at Allstate, and found out how much they were making, and then spoke with my friend Dax and discovered what *he* was making selling mutual funds at Investors, the decision became very clear.

One must earn a mutual-fund licence; but that's very easy. It takes only a couple of days of study, and is hardly a difficult task. The biggest decision I had to make, really, was, "would I get into sales?" I decided to burn all my bridges, another of my risky approaches to success. At Fortune Financial, I used to explain it to my new agents like this: "You will do a hell of a lot better if you come to this business with the mind-set that you've burned your bridges behind you, and that you are going to make this thing work!" If you have no fall-back position, I always believed, then you *must* succeed.

And that's what I did. What's interesting about that philosophy is, that's not the way I live my life. I always have a back-up plan! And one of the main reasons that I have been so successful (even with some devastating setbacks along the way), is that *I've always had that back-up plan.*

So why such an inconsistency between the message I would often teach, and the way I've chosen to live my life?

Because I did not want to even think of the possibility that I could not make Investors work for me. I would have alternatives, within the framework of "making it work." If one strategy didn't succeed, I would have something to fall back on. But in my career path at Investors, I needed a single-minded focus.

Investors administered a kind of psychological evaluation to each potential representative — true or false, fill in the blanks, and so on. The first test, which lasted 15 minutes, was a timed test, and comprised a straight-forward list of 50 questions. A second test was a word survey, or temperament test. You then received the results, which were plotted on a graph. As an old acquaintance of mine, who was a rookie the same year as I was (and later became a regional manager at Investors), told me several years after: "Most sales companies give tests like this; they show that certain temperaments are more successful than others. We don't hire only people with that kind of temperament, but it may be easier for those who do well on it."

I failed! The ideal candidate, apparently, ended up with a graph which looked like a hockey stick. I guess mine ended up looking like a cricket bat; I'm not sure. (The tragic clashing of the Guyanese and Canadian athletic cultures!) But they decided that they would give me a chance, anyway.

I don't know why I didn't do well on the tests, and I'm not interested in knowing, to be frank. But I'll tell you what it did for me: it made me decide that there was no merit to it, and I would never, ever put anyone through such an evaluation. There were a number of things, in fact, that I experienced at Investors that I refused to use years later, with my own representatives, and one of those things was this kind of psychological testing.

A year and a half later, when I was a candidate to become a division manager — the company had two management positions in each office, division manager and manager — I had very good relationships with everyone. I was assisting at the branch and making a significant contribution, but I did not get the promotion. The person who landed the position had done nothing to support the branch, and his sales were nothing compared with mine. So why was he offered the job? Because his psychological test proved that he was an ideal candidate, and mine had not — apparently, I lacked the people skills and the patience. At least, that was what the test results showed! So, according to this little test, I wasn't supposed to make a good manager. Of course, it had also showed that I wasn't going to be a good salesperson, yet I had proven to be extremely successful in sales — and eventually became a very good manager as well, when I created my own financial planning company.

Still, this minor failure in my life didn't throw me, any more than those who spat in my face on Toronto buses, and the others who called me "paki" and "nigger." As the French say, "c'est la vie" — and my life in the world of financial sales was only beginning.

Today, when people come into the financial planning business, they come primarily to sell mutual funds. I'm not sure what it's like at Investors nowadays, but when I first joined that firm, mutual funds were not the predominant product, the way they would become years later. In fact, I don't recall selling a single mutual fund until several weeks after I joined. Back in the early 1980s, Investors had a product called The Money Accumulation Plan, which was more a guaranteed GIC-type product. (Guaranteed Investment Certificates are a low-interest, but extremely safe way of achieving both short and long-term savings goals.) Indeed, one of the things which made Investors strong over the years had been that the company never really promoted itself as a mutual fund company, in the way that Mackenzie and Trimark and others have in Canada. Investors began to do this more and more, to the point that mutual funds became the backbone of its business, although the company has always had other products.

When I started working for the company, I was selling a kind of savings plan in which the return was guaranteed to the investors. The mentality at

Investors — at least back then — was pretty much as in the insurance industry: they put you through some initial training for about two weeks; you learned some selling skills, some tax-planning ideas, studied the products which Investors offered, and so on. Training occurred over a ten-day period; two weeks of Monday through Friday studies.

Salary was awarded strictly based on commission, so one always had the grand potential of making absolutely nothing. A lot of commissioned positions are difficult to get going, and it was not easy for me. After eight months on the job, I found myself falling further and further behind in my financial obligations.

Call it bad luck, call it agony. But when I purchased our first house in 1981, it was during a type of hyper-inflation in Canada, and my initial mortgage was a towering 18.5%! The Bible has a word for this, and I think it's "usury." But interest rates began to fall soon after that, so I got fortunate: every six months, I would go back to my bank and renegotiate my mortgage. This is not necessarily a blessing, of course — every time I did this, I was increasing the mortgage, and there was a penalty. So my payments remained the same, even as the rates came down. (This is not the way I later taught financial planning at my company, I can assure you.)

After the training period, my work consisted of "getting out there" and trying to find people to talk to. As usual, I started off with friends and relatives. But I also went "door-knocking," also known as the dreaded "cold call," which is as loved by salespeople as much as "working on spec" in the freelance writing field. In the latter case, if the magazine doesn't print your article, you don't get paid for your work. Welcome to the world of cold calls; make a sale and make some commission on that sale; *don't* make any sales that day and come home with empty pockets and a wasted day and just as large a mortgage.

This was the way that most new people at Investors had to work. During the day, most reps sat around and did nothing. But I had made a decision that I was going to make this thing work, so I sought out every person at Investors whom I knew was doing well and peppered them with questions: "What's working for you? What makes you successful? How do you land sales?"

I was told by most: "You've got to talk to a lot of people." That was pretty much it. I didn't get much guidance from my colleagues at Investors. No one there was doing any business seminars back then, or sponsoring any other professional development activities. When I ran my own financial planning firm a few years later, I knew from this awful period what I had to do to help my own representatives avoid the anguish I experienced at Investors Group.

I quickly came to the potentially depressing decision that I was not about to learn from anyone at the firm, so I'd have to learn on my own. The question remained, however — how to get started? I had no money to promote myself; most of that was being poured into one of the tallest, freestanding house mortgages in the province of Ontario.

I started to figure out what I had to do to make a living at this. But, alas, figuring that out was one thing; getting started was something else. I went door-knocking, and I knocked on doors for the next year and a half. The routine was to sit in the office all day, doing little or nothing, and then at 5:00 p.m., I would pick up my briefcase and head off to apartment buildings and start knocking on doors, often with co-workers for company.

But getting into a building is almost as challenging as trying to sell financial plans to a prospective customer! As you know, one is not supposed to just walk into a building. Those signs that read *No Vendors Allowed, No Canvassers Allowed,* and *No Trespassing Will Be Tolerated* have been put up for a reason. You might have a suit and tie on; you might look eminently respectable on the streets of downtown Toronto, but you are not supposed to get into a building where you don't live — and to which you don't have a key. So I would wait until someone entered or left the place, and I would walk in after that person. If the landlord happened to see me entering this way, I was quickly ushered out.

Our manager had this all figured out. What we would do is, one of us would get dropped off in front of the apartment building, with no briefcase in hand; another would stay in the car. This way, lacking a briefcase, the first salesperson doesn't look suspicious. He or she might look like anyone else who is there to visit someone, and is waiting to enter. Once spy number one gets in, he goes to the side door of the apartment building, and spy number two, holding (very suspiciously) *two* briefcases, will be let in by his conspirator-in-sales. *Free-market capitalism in action!*

I cannot deny it; I felt very sleazy operating this way. I still recall the very first night I went out. I was so nervous, I went into the hallway and was sick everywhere. (I've heard since that this sort of action in the hallways of apartment buildings is frowned upon, even from legitimate tenants.)

Naturally, one learns tricks as one goes along. You knock and then slide one foot into the door, so they can't close it on you. (I never told you that this was state-of-the-art, high-tech salesmanship.)

These were some of the lines we used: "Good evening sir/ma'am. We are in this building, talking with people about government programs to save income taxes." (The buzzwords, of course, were "government," "save," and "taxes.") The chief product that we were promoting at that time was the Home Ownership Savings Plan. These were like RRSPS (or IRAS, in the U.S.), where the money is put toward one's retirement. These plans were specifically directed towards the purchase of a home — hence our working the apartment buildings of Toronto. What better place to discover future home-owners? If we made a sale, Investors would pay us a small commission.

Then we would say, "Do you have ten minutes to spare? May I come in?" One of two things would invariably happen: they would let you in, or they would send you on your way, and we'd move on. (I was not about to discuss anything while standing at the door.) If they said yes, I was at the kitchen table within nano-seconds. I would then give them my presentation. Either they would be receptive, at which point I would continue my spiel, or I would be quickly ushered out the door.

Most nights, I would not make any sales at all. And this was after knocking at several hundred doors. If I was lucky, I'd be allowed to give one, two, perhaps three presentations. Typically, we would do this until ten o'clock at night. Most evenings, the sales were zero; the most I ever made in one night — from more than a hundred door-knockings each evening — was three. (I can assure you, there were many nights during that first year when I would trudge home, reminiscing fondly about giant snakes falling into my hammock in the jungles of Guyana. Very, very fondly.)

The commission from these endless evenings of continual frustration, embarrassment, and near despair was often only $50. The most I ever made from the sale of one plan was $500. Come to think of it, I began to miss cleaning pots, pans, and toilets at Toronto hotels and fast food restaurants.

On those rare occasions when someone actually deigned to let this well-dressed young fellow into their lovely apartment, I would sit down and explain how these savings plans worked, the tax benefits of saving in this way for one's home, and so on. People might reject these well-explained plans because they didn't have the money, or they might be interested in hearing about the program in six months, but not that evening. We had several products to sell, but one thing Investors urged us to do was to "keep it as simple as possible." As time went on, each salesperson would hope to expand his or her product line, and, depending upon the sophistication of the client, one would offer other products as well.

The selling process was the easy part — it was getting in the door of the individual apartments, after so ingeniously sneaking in through the front door of the buildings — that was the toughest aspect of the sale. I had some very interesting experiences. Let's face it, when you get into a building, and then knock on a door, you don't know what is going on behind that closed door! (A little *Twilight Zone* music here.) I would walk up to one door, and discover a husband and wife beating each other up. I would knock on another door, and I'd hear a woman screaming, "No, he's going to kill me!" Other times I would knock on a door, it would open an inch, and I could smell marijuana fumes drifting into the hallway. On too many other occasions, I would get "You stinking fucking paki, get the hell out of here!" shouted into my face. "Thank you very much," I would say, like a true Canadian, and move on to the next apartment. Far more often, I would see a woman peek over a chain, or through the peephole, obviously filled with wariness and fear, and I would move on quickly further down the hall.

The toughest part of the job, of course, was when people insulted me. I didn't mind when they said they weren't interested. But it was the name-calling and the racial slurs which cut deep. Whoever wrote that famous childhood ditty, "Sticks and stones may break my bones, but names will never hurt me" was the greatest liar who ever lived.

Yet some people took it even further. They would invite me in — this happened on several occasions — and they wouldn't let me out — certainly not before I got my fill of racist insults. That was one more reason that we tended to travel in twos; that way, we could be reasonably sure we were not going to get beaten up. Can you imagine? I would just sit there at a man's kitchen table, watch him lock the door behind him, and listen to him berate me until he felt he was finished. "I'm sorry, sir, I'm sorry! I didn't mean to disturb you! Would you please let me go now?" What else could I say?

Once, my partner and I were invited in by a female voice behind the door. After we entered the apartment, we discovered two young women sitting on the couch, both in the nude, who cheerfully exclaimed, "Why not have a beer and take the rest of the evening off?"

"We'd love to have a drink with you, but we really have to work," was our mutual response. (In retrospect, such moments were rather more appreciated than the racial slurs.) As the months went on, I realized that I was making less at Investors than I had been making at my salaried job at Allstate. There were many, many times when I wanted to pack it in, and for countless reasons. For one thing, there was a tremendous amount of stress at home, since I was working most evenings long into the night, leaving my wife and two young daughters to fend for themselves. If I was invited into an apartment at 9:30 or 10:00 p.m., the presentation might take an hour, even 90 minutes, so I often would not get home until 11 p.m., even midnight.

The scenario: I'd arrive home well after dark, usually deeply depressed from not making any sales, and having earned no money. I'd be exhausted from the long day, and further upset over the fact that mortgage payments were due, and there were other bills to be paid. My wife would also be depressed — she'd been stuck at home with two little kids all day. But I had to work those long terrible hours, because it was the only way I could build up business, and even begin to make a living for my family.

I must confess, there was never a certain point when it "clicked," in the sense that I landed that one big sale. I had made the decision that I would stick with it, and in my first year at Investors, I ended up making $40,000 — even after all those months of nothing or close to nothing in commissions.

Things eventually began to fall into place; forty grand was reasonably good income for the early 1980s, especially considering that I had given up a job paying $25,000 to work at Investors. But it was still not enough to get me out of the financial straits that I found myself in, because I had incurred so many debts, and borrowed from so many people.

Yet things continued to slowly improve. In my second year at Investors, I made about $65,000 in commissions. I was still making a lot of those dreaded "cold calls," but I also started getting referrals, which often proved successful. At Investors, if you survive the first year in the business — no easy task, as you've just learned — then you get some help from the company. You see, many people who joined would not stay very long, and they would either leave the business entirely, or would move on to a competitor. But their accounts would stay at Investors.

There's no question that Investors could have given me — and many others — far more guidance. It's important to let people use their own initiative, and even struggle in this business — any business. But they need some direction, some guidance. They should be told what works, and what doesn't work.

In the mid-1990s, when I was running one of the largest financial planning companies in Canada, I was speaking with a young woman from Investors, who had phoned our office and told us that she was considering joining my firm, Fortune Financial. (We never, ever sought out prospective reps — that is something I insisted upon at our company.) One of the things that I told the woman, when she came in to see me, was that she should take some time before she decided to join us, and should set up several appointments with the most successful salespeople at Fortune. I gave her the names of these people.

"Don't take more than ten minutes of their time," I requested of her. "These are very busy people, and their time is very important to them." I even told her to take her watch, put it on the table, and keep track of the time which she would spend with these busy reps.

But still, I formally invited her to talk to these top reps, and find out what was working for them. After all, I said to her, "They were like you at one stage in their careers. And you can probably earn substantial amounts, just like them."

"This is unheard of!" the woman said to me. "At Investors, even my manager — who spends most of his time selling — doesn't want to talk to me. His door is always closed." She went on, with some anger, "You can never find an office door open around there, especially the doors of the most successful salespeople."

I asked her why.

"Because we're competing with one another!"

I recall telling her: "Successful people — the truly successful people in this world — do not compete with one another. Successful people recognize that they got to where they are because someone helped them along the way. And they are grateful."

That was one thing I always said to my fellow workers at Fortune Financial: "If we are successful, then we should be what I call 'truly successful' — and truly successful people never stop being grateful, and never stop helping others along their way to success." I was forced to sell my beloved company, but I'm proud that I insisted on this "sharing of success" with others.

So what led to my gradual success at Investors? I was determined to become one of the most knowledgeable people in the office, regarding the financial products we offered. I studied constantly, instead of sitting around talking and reading the newspapers, as many of my colleagues did. It was consistent with what I've always tried to do with my life; back in Bartica, I spent all my time studying, instead of going to the bars. At George Brown College, I had been determined not to be "just another student," and at Investors, I had sworn to myself that I would not be "just another financial planner."

I had no plans to take over Investors Group — not by a long shot. I merely wanted to be successful, to make enough money to live. I had no aspirations to make even hundreds of thousands of dollars. (That would come much later!) I just wanted to live a comfortable life, and to somehow stand out from the other people in the office.

The time I spent studying Investor's products would help me when I was talking with clients. They recognized that I knew the business, and that I was sincere, and that helped me make sales. True, I was never really strong at what's called "true selling skills," and that's why, as I am building up Destiny Health Solutions, I spend very little time with new hires on such things. My own definition of "true selling skills" differs radically from the "sell sell sell until you close" philosophy. I believe in showing the client the alternatives available; I expand the client's horizons and range of choices, and then I let him or her decide. That's my job, not "you need it, it's good for you — take it!" Like the Golden Rule of the Bible, what would be good for the prospective client was also good for me.

I was rarely in the office. Investors did not provide offices, just little cubicles that were the width of a bookcase, and all the reps were stacked next to one another, so there was really nowhere to bring a client to discuss our products.

In 1984 — the year that I left Investors — my annual income was about $75,000. My personal financial situation was starting to become more manageable by then, and when I made the decision to leave the company and join Tillcan Financial, I was far better off than I'd been in years. In the early 1980s, Investors had approximately 1500 reps across the country, and they had what they called their "sales leaders conferences." At these meetings, they gave out awards, some of them for "rookies." If you achieved a certain level, you were declared "Rookie of the Year." In my first year, I was one of five employees who enjoyed that honour, even with all the door slammings and racist attacks — and with only $40,000 in earnings. In my second year, I was probably in the top ten of the 60 or so agents in the Toronto office.

A FATEFUL DECISION

In the summer of 1983, I was at a trade show at the Canadian National Exhibition (CNE), in Toronto. Investors encouraged us to set up a little booth with an Investors sign, and the reps would buy space, in order to line up more prospects. Several of the agents took turns managing the booth, and as people walked by, the rep would approach them and ask, "Do you know anything about Investors? Do you have five minutes to chat?" The goal was to get their name and phone number, and call them later. (And you thought that the roller coaster was the most dangerous thing at "the county fair"? How wrong you were!)

While I was there, another booth nearby was being staffed by a man named Mike Lee-Chin, then president of AIC Investments. Mike approached me and introduced himself. He was with Regal Capital Planners at the time, and had always been phenomenally successful. He was their number one salesperson, so I had obviously heard of him. Everyone had. He drove a Rolls-Royce and owned a Ferrari and a Porsche. He had done very well for himself. I was always so impressed with him, I was almost afraid to answer his greeting. A West Indian like myself, who had done so brilliantly in this business! I was in awe of his skills.

Mike reminded me that he had begun his career at Investors, and then he asked, "What are you still doing there? You can do so much better on *this* side of the business!" (By "this side," he meant independent sales. Whereas Investors tended to sell only its own products, Regal had chosen to handle as many different mutual funds in which it had confidence, giving its clients far more choice in their investments.) Mike really was one of the few "good guys" whom I had met up to this point in my career as a financial planner. Until then, I had heard few words of encouragement or assistance from anyone.

"Look," he went on. "You're a good-looking guy. You dress well. I would love to help you if you decide to get out of Investors." He didn't say anything about joining him at Regal, interestingly enough.

"Mike," I told him fairly honestly, "I'm happy where I am, learning the business."

"How's this," Mike Lee-Chin concluded. "If you ever decide to leave Investors, just give me a call."

I don't know what triggered it, and I still don't, to this very day. But something happened that fateful summer; I started getting impatient at Investors. I found myself seeking out my old friend Dax again, who was at Versatile. Even Mike Louli — my old manager — had recently left the company to join Dax at his financial firm.

Then, some half-dozen others all chose to leave the Don Mills branch of Investors. I remember thinking, "Gee, there must be some reason that all these guys are leaving!" These were people whom I had looked up to, to some extent, including my own manager.

I approached these people, and asked each one privately, "Why have you chosen to leave Investors?" Their responses were invariably the same: "They have a limited range of products." "We want to offer more variety to our clients." "There are so many more things we can offer, as independents." To top it all off, Investors' funds were not thriving at that time in the market, and clients would often pull out the *Financial Times* survey and ask, "Look how your funds are performing, compared with Mackenzie! Compared with Trimark! Compared with. . . ."

I struggled over whether to leave Investors until December, and then, wondered *when* to leave. Finally, I began to tell the other sales reps that I was planning to leave.

As it happens, every top producer I spoke with gave me the same response: "If you're going to leave, *we're* going to leave, too."

Now, a new question arose — where to go? One of the first people I phoned was Mike Lee-Chin, at his Regal Capital office in Hamilton. We started to have discussions, but he was unable to get approval from Regal's president, Paul Rockel, to let me open my own office in the Toronto area, which was my immediate goal.

And so I made another fateful, and ultimately nearly fatal, decision; I approached a man who had been a vice president at Investors, but who had also left. I thought, "Here is a guy who was not only a manager, but even at the same firm as me. I should certainly speak with him about where my future might lie in the world of the independents."

He hired me as a manager of a branch in Scarborough, and several other reps left Investors and joined me at the new office — eight in all — each one of us eagerly working for a new company called Tillcan.

Many financial salespeople are still angry over that experience today, since Tillcan went under a few short years later. But that man did a lot of good things for me; he gave me the opportunity to start a branch for Tillcan at a time when I did not have any managerial experience. (I was barely 30 years old at the time.) Investors Group certainly did not want to give me that chance; they felt I didn't have the qualifications to be a manager — and I'd done so poorly on that stupid little exam, right?

So I was given that big chance to build a branch, and I've always been grateful for that — in spite of the horrors that eventually came to pass. I learned many valuable skills which allowed me to move on from Tillcan towards the end of 1988, and create Fortune Financial with several others.

What followed was an exceptional learning experience. I gained substantial knowledge, which inspired me to achieve far greater success. I became a manager at the new firm in December, 1984. The office was at Markham and Highway 401 on the northeastern edge of Scarborough, and it would be where I'd spend four wild and woolly years.

CHAPTER SIX

FORTUNE RISING

L eaving Investors Group was obviously a major move for a young man
barely into his 30s, with a towering mortgage and numerous debts, and
a wife and two young children at home. But such a risk was necessary; the
impact of so many friends leaving the company to move to the "other side"
of the business was enormous. I had tremendous respect for these people,
primarily because of the volume of business they had done; they had all been
reasonably successful in the amount of sales — and commissions — they
had been achieving.

As I noted in the previous chapter, I had no previous experience in management, nor many mentors, either. Within months, I built up a very
successful branch for the Scarborough office of Tillcan, taking it from the
original eight reps to as high as three dozen men and women, becoming the
number one branch in the country for the fledgling firm. With over two
dozen branches across the country by then, we were, by far, the branch gen-
erating the most business.

Between January, 1985, and September, 1988, I contributed a great deal to
Tillcan. It was an amazing learning experience for me. Becoming a manager
was an inspiration and a revelation. By Christmas, 1986, I was promoted to

vice president — one of three in the company at that time.

As a manager, I took on quite a few additional responsibilities; managing another branch in Canada's national capital of Ottawa, a third in Thunder Bay, Ontario, and a fourth in Saint John, New Brunswick — in addition to the Scarborough office. Yet the only compensation I ever received was what was called "override," or a percentage of commissions, which I was given for managing the home branch in Scarborough. I received zero compensation for working at the head office as a VP, nor at any of the other three, far-flung offices. I never asked for any, and I never received any!

Many readers may think that I was being foolish, if not naive, in this self-lessness. But that experience was very important to me, in that it was consistent with the way I have always done things in my life, from working in the Anglican church in Guyana to my desire to "get ahead" of everyone else, whether in school or in business. I have always felt that I should get out there and pay my dues often, and worry about getting paid only much later. I never asked how much I would be compensated for what I did — and to this day, I still don't. If I feel that my involvement in something will benefit me in some way, I will go ahead and do it, and not even think about remu-neration. In every case where I worked for someone else, I let them decide what the payment was going to be. I believe in this very strongly, and have maintained this attitude throughout my life.

But after the famous stock market crash in the fall of 1987, things did not go so well for Tillcan. In fact, many people around me started to feel that I was "too much of a company manager," in that they believed I had been withholding some possibly unpleasant truth about the firm's survival.

Yet it wasn't until April, 1988, that it dawned on me — the company was in severe financial difficulty. That fact had been hidden from me — and later on, that bothered me plenty. (Strangely, never to the extent that I felt hard feelings or animosity towards anyone. Whether this was naiveté or simply common sense, I'll let the reader decide.)

What I eventually learned, at the huge expense of both peace of mind and financial stability, was that it really was partly my fault. I believe that one should do things, and get involved. And if I am in something 100 percent, I'd better make damn sure that the people I work with are telling me everything. I simply trusted the president and owner of the company, and he did not keep me fully informed. It bothered me that no one told me to what extent our firm was in severe financial trouble. It made me look bad, and even dishonest.

Finally, we were informed that, in order to keep the company afloat, money was required from each of us. It was admitted — at last — that Tillcan was "encountering difficulties." This was certainly true. Perhaps foolishly, but out of a sincere desire to keep Tillcan afloat, I invested $60,000 of my own money into the floundering enterprise. I was the only one of all the managers present at that meeting who chose to do so.

Now, why on earth did a fairly intelligent, successful manager and vice president borrow money in order to do this? The reasons were clear then, and they still are now: I had a lot of faith in Tillcan's president, who had shown such faith in me less than four years earlier, when he had placed me in my first managerial position.

He had begun Tillcan from scratch, and had rapidly built up a promising company. Furthermore, I was deeply committed to the company, and I wanted to see it survive, and thrive. I felt profoundly responsible to the men and women around me, whom I had been telling, in complete honesty (based on what I knew at the time) that everything was okay. I was not eager to tell those same people that I had been wrong, that I had misled them.

I knew that I had done nothing wrong; I had merely been passing my employees information from my boss. And, frankly, I was not eager to admit my own failure in not asking the right questions about Tillcan's solvency.

I also chose to invest my own money based on verbal commitments made by other managers that they would invest, too. I later realized that not one of them had indeed invested; they all subsequently changed their minds. I had already gone ahead and taken out a second, and then a third mortgage on my family home to raise that $60,000, because I still did not have a single penny in savings at that time.

In fact, I never really made very much money in the business, when one considers the endless hours, and the four separate offices I had been managing. I had spent so much time and effort building Tillcan — dashing off to the Ottawa, Thunder Bay, and Saint John offices, as well as to the head office. It left me little time to spend with my own representatives in Scarborough, not to mention my wife and children.

I felt guilty for not being in the Scarborough office often enough, to offer guidance to my employees. To make it up to them (like the classic absentee husband or father), I gave frequent seminars on their behalf, to help drum up clients and business for them. I paid for all of these seminars, too.

But at the same time, I was growing; I was learning; I was improving steadily as a manager, seminar leader, and vice president of a major financial planning company; but I was not being rewarded financially, and the toll was growing.

The above might suggest substantial stupidity, gullibility, and lack of planning on my part, and I am not about to deny this. I still had a lot to learn, and I admit I made a lot of dreadful mistakes and wrong-headed choices. Naturally, I learned from my experiences at Tillcan. They forced me to be a more sensitive, generous boss when I started up Fortune Financial.

If anyone had recognized my contributions and treated me more fairly, I would have loved it. But it didn't happen. I was frustrated by this, but in retrospect, not terribly; the painful but valuable lessons gained from this experience ultimately outweighed the fact that I hadn't received money or recognition for all the things that I had been doing on behalf of the company.

And so, the fool and his money were quickly parted. I invested the $60,000, and then rapidly discovered that all the others who had promised to do so, had not. This was all acutely depressing, and I finally began to see the writing on the wall; the company I had worked so hard for was not going to survive. Added to this was another, immediate revelation, much like the writing on the wall which appeared to Daniel in the lions' den; I could kiss my $60,000 goodbye.

I had no savings, and three very large mortgages. My marriage was under dreadful strain. And if it had been available in those years, a few thousand Prozacs would have been very much welcome.

TRULY, THE FIRST ROBBINS OF SPRING

Fortunately, another life-changing moment had taken place just a few months earlier — I signed up for a two-week training course with Anthony Robbins, whom I had met at a conference in November of the previous year, and who had greatly impressed me.

Anthony Robbins is, as the millions who have purchased such popular self-help books as his *Unlimited Power* know, an extraordinarily dynamic, charismatic, inspiring lecturer. After reading that particular book, and discovering that he would be presenting a so-called "certification" course in

Austin, Texas, that June, I chose to sign up for it. By the time I had made that ultimately risky decision to put my money where my faith was, and to invest the sixty grand which I could not afford in Tillcan, I was already booked for my flight to the Lone Star state.

It could not have come at a better (or more bitter) time; the stress at home had reached a breaking point; I had stupidly not told my wife about the second and third mortgages on the house and my investment in Tillcan, and she subsequently found out, adding further layers of stress to the mountains already rising between us. She realized that she had not been part of such a key financial decision, and this added insult to injury. So the two weeks in Austin were really both good and bad; good, in that it took me away from everything which was driving me to distraction and despair; bad, in that my wife felt I was insulting her further, by escaping south of the border at such a horrible time in our lives.

I look back on that time with such mixed feelings, since I still don't know whether or not I did the right thing. True, the experience in Texas was ultimately life-changing and life-affirming, and it made me a better businessman and a better person. But it did not contribute anything to my marriage, and for that, I felt a tremendous amount of regret, and still do. But at that depressing time in my life, I just didn't know how else to juggle everything. Today, I feel that I would probably handle a similar situation with greater finesse and sensitivity.

In January 1995, the broadcaster Diane Sawyer dedicated a lengthy segment of her newsmagazine to the "phenomenon" of Anthony Robbins — and her program was often of the exposé variety. Indeed, when one watches the tall, lanky man in action — the exhorting of the troops; the whoops and hollers; the crazed dancing and exercising; the endless calls to success and rejections of negative thinking; even the fire-walking, in order to lessen fears and build self-esteem — one might think it a case of consciously provoked, near-religious hysteria. Yet, Ms. Sawyer's TV study of Robbins was surprisingly warm and even favourable, considering the surface glamour and glitter of his astounding personal wealth and success. (He earns countless millions every year, from books, seminars, and personal training; in the last case, several world-renowned figures have put him on individual, multimillion-dollar retainers, for support and guidance.) And I think that Sawyer was correct: even if the man were a fake or a fraud — which I could never believe — the impact on those who take his courses is often undeniably positive and even life-saving.

Such was Robbins' influence on my life. Those two weeks in Austin, Texas, undeniably changed my life forever. They were two weeks of the most incredible learning experiences I'd ever been through. If I were asked to identify the one person who has had the greatest single impact on my life (and there have been many), it would be Tony Robbins — in the ways that I should be looking at my life, how I could better put things in true perspective, how to come to grips with myself as a person, how to understand my emotions and better handle them — how I should deal with those, and countless other forces in my life, which I had clearly allowed to go completely out of control.

Classes began each morning at nine, and lasted until midnight every night. And this went on for 14 consecutive days at the hotel, with some 700 other people. I recall that there were only two Canadians, the rest mainly Americans and others from around the world; whether this paltry attendance by our countrymen can be blamed for Canada's negative balance of payments and huge federal deficits, I cannot prove. But I can think of many of our politicians who could have gained a great deal along with me.

There were lectures each morning, and break-out sessions, where you met in small groups and discussed subjects ranging from "the emotional aspects of your life" to "creating options and expanding your horizons." We spoke of setting the rules which we hoped to live by, regardless of what was happening around us; we discussed expanding our belief systems and defining our values in positive terms.

Why was I so impressed with the course, and these countless discussion groups? Because I'd been struggling with these issues for so many years, and here was the first opportunity in my life to bring them all together, and hear someone make sense of them. I realized I had been acting in ways that just seemed "the right thing to do," never really knowing whether or not these actions made sense, or were actually in my interest. Like a personal epiphany, I found myself thinking, *"This is what I've been doing! These are the psychological reasons behind what I've been feeling!"*

I started to feel better — that I had been on the right track. I found myself understanding why things had been going wrong in my life — such as my relationship with my wife — and felt some small consolation from the realization that there were reasons behind my actions. And if I didn't like the way things were going, I had control over them, and I could change them. I had control over the way I responded to my father's mistreatment of me as a child, and I could change how I felt about that, too! I was determined to make my life better from then on, because I felt much more in control of those actions and feelings.

Tony Robbins showed me ways in which I (and so many others there) could change my self-destructive actions, and in very practical terms. Let me give you a few clear examples: I have always believed in setting goals. But the way I had always set those goals was by thinking of the things I wanted to accomplish. Robbins, however, pointed out that one has to write those goals down, focus on them, believe in them strongly — and they would happen. That became an extremely powerful motivator for me. It's so simple and logical, really, but then, often the most inspired and inspiring things in the world are similarly simple and logical; think of the Ten Commandments and the Sermon on the Mount, from the Hebrew and Christian Testaments.

And so, I would write goals down. I would focus on them daily. *And they would come true.* If they did not come to fruition within six months, which may have been my deadline, then I was not to become frustrated; I was to focus on them again. The goals might take eight, ten, twelve months or more to become a reality.

That was crucial for me, because I realized that if things did not happen the way I wanted them to happen within the time frame I had set, that was no reason to become frustrated. True, I doubt if what I learned at the seminar would have necessarily saved me from my past confusions and dubious decisions, such as the $60,000 I threw away on Tillcan. I probably would have gone ahead and loaned that money to the firm, in spite of Robbins' teachings. But I do believe that I would have asked more questions about the stability of the company, and that had nothing to do with Tony Robbins, but rather with the substantial experience I've had in business since that fateful year of 1988.

During those life-changing weeks of profound learning experience in Texas, I walked, barefoot, over 42 feet of fire (which Robbins apparently no longer uses in his teaching — *now* he tells me!), and climbed a 60-foot pole, and stood proudly at the top. The objective behind those exercises is obvious, even to those unfamiliar with psychological techniques — to prove to oneself that there are no limits to the things you can do, if you set your mind to them strongly enough, if you focus on them sufficiently. And if you believe in yourself and your goals, then things will happen — even the most surprising and astonishing things.

Throughout my life, from the Guyanese classrooms of my youth, to the days of track and field, to my running for student council president at George Brown College, I have always told myself the same thing; *I am going to get the most out of this environment and situation that I possibly can.* These are things I've always practised, which is why I have little doubt that few others, among the 700 participants at that Tony Robbins seminar, benefited more than I did from those two weeks in Texas.

Lovers of American literature may recall that moving moment at the end of F. Scott Fitzgerald's classic American novel, *The Great Gatsby*, where the narrator is handed a list of "General Resolves," which the title character had written as a young boy in 1906: "No wasting time. . . . /No more smokeing [sic] or chewing./Bath every other day/Read one improving book or magazine per week/Save $5.00 [crossed out] $3.00 per week/Be better to parents."

The list is meant to be poignant and savagely ironic, since it is discovered shortly after the death of Fitzgerald's protagonist. But I felt no sense of poignancy or irony when I recently dug up my notes from that crucial period in my life. In fact, I have often looked back on them and reflected upon these words, over the half-dozen years since. Here are a few selections from that seminar:

- What is missing from my life?
- Set goal/design plan to help as many people as possible!
- Think of my "destiny" in terms of "consequences." (Note how I chose "destiny" for the name of my most recent entrepreneurial creation!)
- The quality of my life comes down to the quality of my evaluations.
- Superior evaluations create superior life.
- Everything we do in life is done to: 1) avoid pain; or 2) gain pleasure.
- To change something you don't like, change your associations to that thing.
- In spite of all the problems people are faced with in life,

somehow it seems that some people are always winning.
- Everything in life has four parts: 1) Cause; 2) Effect; 3) Direction; 4) Destiny.
- The quality of my life comes down to the quality of the questions I ask myself consistently.

And so on. Some of the exercises which Tony Robbins puts his followers through could well serve many high school students and college graduates today:

"Where was I five years ago?" we were asked. My answers — written in mid-1988 — clearly show my state of mind at that difficult time:

1.	Emotional	frustrated, confused
2.	Physical	same as today
3.	Spiritual	same as today
4.	Financial	not as well off as today
5.	Social	same as today
6.	Living environment	worse than today
7.	Love relationships	better off
8.	Children	less children
9.	Friendships	had more friends
10.	Career	worse than today
11.	Health	same
12.	Appearance	same
13.	Contribution	no change

This was followed by a most telling list of answers to the question, "Where am I today?"

1.	Emotional	stable, focused
2.	Physical	not as good shape as I'd like to be in
3.	Spiritual	okay
4.	Financial	would like to be better off
5.	Social	would like to socialize more
6.	Living environment	satisfied
7.	Love relationships	would like to improve
8.	Children	three

9.	Friendships	would like to have more friends
10.	Career	would like to improve
11.	Health	happy
12.	Appearance	not happy
13.	Contribution	would like to make significant improvements

Then, in answer to the question, "What's most important to me now?" I wrote down my "ends" and "means" values, the former referring to things, the latter to feelings:

My "means" values:
1. Money — enough to be able to do whatever I want to do.
2. Home — a large home on a large lot with beautiful landscaping, three-car garage, office, exercise room, etc.
3. Family — a loving and happy family.
4. Condominium in Florida — to be able to enjoy the warm weather during winter. (Guyana lives!)
5. Help my brothers and sisters financially.

My "ends" Values:
1. Love — to feel unconditional love for everyone and to feel loved.
2. Happiness — to feel happy and relaxed.
3. Power — to be able to influence people to be better individuals.
4. Confident — a feeling of being able to do whatever I want to do.

Eventually, we were all asked to write "mission statements." Mine was as follows:

"The purpose of my life is to be the very best person that I can be and to help as many people as possible to be the best they can be, striving each day to become a better person in whatever I do, and helping others to do the same. When I'm on a roll and working out perfectly, I feel confident, in charge, and happy. It motivates me to strive for even better results and continue the feeling of success that I had when things were on a roll. I want to share my success and feeling of delight with my family and for them to be as happy and proud of me as I am of myself. The purpose of my life's mission is to excel at what I do, help others to excel at what they do, to be happy, and help others to be happy."

A fairly tall order, perhaps, but here is where it gets even more interesting. Tony Robbins had us complete a further, stunningly insightful exercise; we were to make a list titled "everything I want." Like Fitzgerald's young Gatsby, I eagerly wrote down, in no particular order, 26 things, ranging from "A Mercedes 500 Series (black)" to "spend quality time with my children," to "be totally self-confident" and "a loving and caring person."

After making the list, Robbins had each participant put down when he or she wished to achieve that particular goal. So, for example, the Mercedes has "1" (as in "one year") next to it; the quality time with my children has "now" printed there, and so on.

(Might I mention, in rather amazed retrospect, that number 25 on my list was "write a book." And here I am, less than 15 years after I jotted down that seemingly unconscious thought.)

Then, the greatest shocker of all: Robbins had us search through our lists of "everything I want" and list the "top four goals" we longed to achieve, and describe them at some length.

When I came across this list of goals many years later, I was taken aback. Here they are, in all their prescient glory:

Top four goals

1. Be president of my own business
I am going to figure out a way to have my own business within the next six months. (There is a double underline beneath "six months.") This business will operate in major parts of Canada and possibly expand to other countries. The business will have something to do with financial planning plus personal development. (Health products would obviously take me a bit longer.)

2. Earn $200,0000 in the next six months.
I need $200,000 to set me on track to earn $1 million annually. Need a strategy.

3. Become top financial planner in Canada.
Will incorporate "Neuro Linguistic Program" (Tony Robbins' philosophy) skills.

4. Be a good parent.

Spend quality time with my kids. Be totally confident and be a loving, caring person.

I'll let my children (now numbering four lovely daughters) and colleagues decide whether I became "a loving, caring person." But the thought of starting my own business had not been a conscious one at that moment in my life; it was June, 1988, and I still had great hopes of saving Tillcan and working happily with the many reps in my four offices across Canada.

Naturally, one of the major rules of life is that we have to be realistic about things. For instance, to become the best major league pitcher in the world, a person requires some talent to throw the ball the right ways, at the right speeds, and so on. But that merely begs the question, "If one wishes to be a superb, world-class ballplayer, how does one get those talents in the first place"? One must go out and practice, and learn to develop those skills, over a length of time.

In other words, it's obviously not enough to merely believe that you want something to happen, so that it will happen. You also must put into place some of the practical things necessary to make it happen, and all those things have to come together to make it a whole; like pieces of a puzzle where each one is shaped differently, you must figure out how to place each piece to complete the picture. What Tony Robbins taught me was not merely "pie in the sky, wish and it will happen" nonsense — not by a long shot.

For instance, if there is a crash in the stock market that we have no control over — no different than the piece of a puzzle that has a weird shape — one must figure out how it all fits together. When that crash comes, one must make sure that things have been planned such that consideration has been made for things out of our control.

I know that when I drive to work, and the roads are wet from rain or snow, I have no control over this. I simply drive slower, and keep a careful eye out for those who will not be as careful. The fact that I have this firm belief that I will get to work safely today will not allow me to get idiotic about it, and drive at 200 kilometers an hour. I have to be careful, and balance the practical things in life and the things I have no control over, with the things which I do have control over, always keeping that balance, and not letting anything get too far out of hand. Balance is crucial, of course; I have set goals for my life, which I'll discuss below, ranging from family and health to career. But if I focus only on family, and focus so much on that one thing to the point that I ignore work or won't exercise, the entire edifice will crumble.

Looking back, I realize I didn't bond well with many people at that remarkable Anthony Robbins seminar, but that's mainly because of the strong, narrow focus that I had during those powerful two weeks: I had gone there for a reason, and that reason consumed my mind and thoughts totally.

I've always believed very strongly that people who attend forums, seminars, and self-help gatherings are really no different than people who go to church on Sunday, synagogue on Saturday, or mosque on Friday; one may be deeply moved and even spiritually uplifted by the experience, but it's what happens after you walk out that door that makes the difference. I have not stayed in touch with anyone with whom I shared those two weeks in Austin, so I can't say to what extent other particpants benefited from the experience. My goal was to leave the seminar with as much as possible, and I was determined to let that particular experience in Texas have a phenomenal impact on my life. So I bonded only when it was particularly relevant, such as in group discussions. Otherwise, I spent the majority of my free time in my room, going over my notes and vowing that I would change my ways.

SETTING ONE'S GOALS AND VALUES

If you have difficulty setting goals, and staying focused on those goals, I urge you to try a method I learned from that inspired man, Anthony Robbins. He suggests that we each set our goals in the following areas, and then analyze them, as follows:

(You may well wish to jot down your own notes here — see if you can gain as much as I did!)

1. HEALTH (and here I am, years later, creating products for better health!)
   a. What will happen if I am able to remain healthy at all times? (Here, one makes a list of all the things that would occur, if this were so.)
   b. How can I remain healthy at all times?
2. EMOTIONAL

a. What will happen if I always manage my emotions effectively?

b. How do I manage my emotions?

3. FAMILY

a. What will happen if I can always be a good father/ mother, husband/wife, son/daughter, brother/sister?

b. How can I be a good father/mother, husband/wife, son/daughter, brother/sister?

4. CAREER AND FINANCIAL

a. What will happen if I have a successful career and can earn X dollars each year?

b. What do I have to do to have a successful career and earn in excess of that amount?

In addition to identifying our goals, we must also clarify our values. Here are the values which I wrote down during my two weeks in Texas. You may well wish to fill in your own, on a separate piece of paper or two. (Surely the values which determine the meaning and purpose of our lives should be worth a few minutes of time!)

1. HEALTH — I must eat properly and exercise regularly.

2. LOVE — I want to love my family and to receive love from them.

3. SUCCESS — I want to make enough money so that I can do all the things I would like to do.

4. HAPPINESS — I want to be happy . . . and I want the people around me to be happy; I want to be contented and know that I am achieving my other values.

5. KNOWLEDGE — I must read good books every day, attend seminars, and feel that I am learning new things on a regular basis.

6. HONESTY — I must be honest with myself and with the people I have to deal with.

7. LEARNING AND GROWING — I must learn by reading every day and maturing in terms of the way I think and do things.

8 CONTRIBUTING — I must share my knowledge and experience with others, and help them to become all that they can be.

9. FLEXIBILITY — I must be flexible to make changes and not be afraid to make mistakes, and to learn from them.

10. INVESTING — I must ensure that my money is growing and that I am making financial progress. (Please see my essential chapters on wealth.)

11. BEING THE BEST — I must consistently strive to be the best in my field, and also the best at helping others to achieve their maximum potential.

12. SHARING — I must share my knowledge and experience with as many people as possible.

13. PERSONAL POWER — I want the confidence to do anything that I want to do, and the ability to access my "personal resources" whenever necessary. I also want the ability to affect changes in others.

14. CREATIVITY — I must come up with new ideas and methods of doing things. This will help me to become the best, so that I can, in turn, continue to find new ways to help others.

15. HAVING FUN — I must enjoy what I am doing; looking forward to each new day, and sharing my joy in life with people around me.

16. RESPECT FROM OTHERS — I want people to show care and appreciation for my genuine concern in wanting to help others.

17. CARING — I must care for other people's growth and development.

The million dollar question is, how does one realize these values in one's life? It is necessary for a person to establish what I call a "daily code of conduct" — a series of rules to live by — every day — if we expect to realize our values and goals. My own "daily code of conduct" is as follows:

Be happy. Be loving. Be passionate. Be honest. Be committed. Be caring. Be helpful. Be fun. Be healthy. Be confident.

Obviously, I have needed to follow the above code to ensure that I am enjoying this journey through life, and that every single day is a constant and never-ending improvement.

The final piece of life's puzzle, then, is for each of us to define a personal mission statement.

What's the secret? There really is no secret; to be successful in life, whether in the world of business or elsewhere, each person should put into writing their values, goals, code of conduct, and mission statement.

One should make a commitment to read these declarations every single day, and remain focused on making them a reality, always keeping in mind that life is a journey, and that, as in any journey, there will be ups, downs, challenges and setbacks along the way.

In the same vein, we should try not to dwell on the past, but learn from our failures, and then move on. According to Jim Rohn, whom I consider to be one of the most articulate and compelling speakers of our time, one way to learn to do something right is to do something wrong. We learn from failure, as well as from success. Failure must teach us, or surely, success will not reward us. Past failures and errors must prompt us to amend our conduct, or the present and the future will be little more than a duplicate of the past.

So, having a healthy and mature attitude about the past can make a major difference in everyone's life. One of the best ways to approach the past is to use it as a school — not as a weapon. We must not beat ourselves to death with past mistakes, faults, failures, and losses. The events of the past, both good and bad, are all part of life experience. For some of us, the past may have been a harsh teacher. (How many of you would include giant snakes falling into your hammock as a personal example?) But we must remember to let the past educate us and bring the value of its experience into our lives. Indeed, part of the miracle of our future lies in the past.

The past, in fact, gives us a wealth of experiences and knowledge. The goals we set for ourselves today can create an exciting future for us, but there is a price which must be paid, and people must decide whether they are prepared to pay that price today. At the risk of echoing what has become a cliché, there can be no gain without pain.

Within a few short years, I was the president of a major financial planning firm, so one could boldly state that the effect of that two-week seminar in Texas was entirely positive. But that would be incorrect. It had one hugely negative effect which was not unrelated to my dream of owning my own company; I focused so much on the growth and prosperity of Fortune Financial that I insisted on doing everything myself, and figuring out everything by myself, as well — without talking to my wife and making her a part of that exercise. That was one of the biggest frustrations for my very bright and able first wife, and I don't think she will ever forgive me for that. So I've paid a very heavy price for that aspect of my "top four goals," and so did my marriage. My vital relationship with my wife suffered greatly as a result of my determined focus upon career, business, and financial success. Clearly then, I did not focus sufficiently upon the personal aspects of my life.

I'll never forget the day I returned to my office at Tillcan, after attending Tony Robbins' seminar. I had just spent two life-changing weeks in Texas, focused on making myself a better person. (I recall that my roommate in Austin spoke only of "how much money I'll make as a result of this!" He was going to go back home, he vowed, and he would do exactly what Tony Robbins had urged him to do. When I called him a year later, he admitted that he had regressed, because he kept getting distracted from his goals. He just didn't have enough skills to put "this Tony Robbins thing" into place.)

My goals were much simpler, but nothing could have prepared me for the shock of learning, upon my return, that Tillcan was falling apart. Before I left Toronto, everything was fine, at least in my mind. I had invested the $60,000 in Tillcan, showing the boss and my fellow managers my faith in the company and my determination to keep it afloat, even to the point of mortgaging my house to the limit. What was going on?

I began to lose interest in my job and in the company. Then came the steady loss of my top producers, who kept leaving to join other financial institutions, as rumours spread that our firm was not going to survive much longer. Even the other managers started to leave. They quite legitimately had each come to the decision that they might as well back out of their promises.

Everything began to crumble around me. July and August went by, and I was making no money. My income had fallen precipitously, not long after I had taken those extra mortgages on my house. A deep depression began to grow within me — all this, so soon after those inspiring weeks with Tony Robbins down in the States! Absolutely nothing of that exciting experience was being put into action. My world was rapidly caving in.

Then, in September of that same momentous year, I met with several other surviving representatives from Tillcan at a hotel in downtown Toronto. The topic of discussion was inevitably what was happening at our company, and what would happen to us all.

Suddenly, one salesman turned to me and asked, "Have you ever thought of starting up your own company, David?"

"No," I lied. "It never crossed my mind." In fact, although I had written down that very goal during those two weeks in Texas — to become president of my own business — I really never focused on it, and hadn't looked at that sheet of paper more than once since those momentous days.

The salesman went on: "There are a lot of guys in the industry who have a lot of respect for you, David, and if you were to start your own firm, there's a good chance that most of them would join you."

I was both flattered and intrigued. It was the third week of September. Within one month — on October 13, 1988 — Fortune Financial was incorporated as a company in the province of Ontario and the country of Canada.

CHAPTER SEVEN

FORTUNE, IN MORE WAYS THAN ONE

M y recollections of the birth — really, the conception — of Fortune Financial, are as clear to me as if it were yesterday. I, and a handful of others, had agreed that we would create this new financial planning company, and that I would run it from Toronto. The only real strategic decision we made was a straightforward one: if we could build something, we were going to build it well. And so, we took the Re/Max model; we would not be responsible for any of the expenses in any of our prospective offices. But nothing else was discussed during that first, crucial day — the name of the company, commissions, payouts, the structure of the organization — nothing.

Upon recollection, maybe there was one more thing we talked about. Not unlike a man or woman coming out of a bad marriage, we agreed that, if we *did* start something, "Let's make sure we don't get ourselves into the same trouble that Tillcan got into." One way to avoid that pitfall, we agreed, was to make each manager completely responsible for the operations of his or her own office. It was only at that point that someone noted, "You know, that's similar to Re/Max," the wildly successful real estate firm. That was fine with us — we weren't out to create something completely innovative. It was a better mousetrap we wanted, not a high tech, nuclear-powered one.

To continue the marriage metaphor, we were all still married at the time that we were discussing a better kind of relationship in the future. Tillcan had not yet gone under; it was then October, 1988. The company would not declare bankruptcy until the middle of 1989, long after Fortune Financial had taken root, if not taken flight.

I was in the awkward position of not yet having spoken to my boss about our plans. And so, like a guilty husband who is having an affair, I continued to come to my Tillcan office daily, advising clients and selling product.

At other (still secretive) meetings, we realized that if we were determined to start a new company, we had to find a name for it. This proved to be a real challenge, because we just couldn't think of one; every name seemed to be taken! Then, fortuitously, one of my favourite reps at Tillcan — Tom Vandenberg — suggested "Fortune." He was, as his name makes clear, of Dutch heritage, and he wanted to call it "Fortuna," which means Fortune in that language. I had trouble with that, and said so.

"Okay, then," Tom said. "How about calling it Fortune 21, after Century 21?" Once again, I balked. *"Let's call it Fortune Financial,"* I said. Much to my surprise, when we did a search on that name, it had never been registered as the name of a financial planning company! So we filled out the papers to incorporate our new baby, and the tense waiting period began. And no, a certain well-known business magazine out of the U.S. never chose to sue!

It was now November, 1988. I still had not said anything to my superior at Tillcan, even though several of us had begun the process of moving off on our own. Then came that tense and cold day which I'll never forget — I simply walked into my boss' office, and calmly announced, "Look, I'm leaving, and I'm starting up my own company."

His response was immediate and not particularly surprising: "Leave my office right now!"

"But I'd really like to discuss my plans with you!"

"Get out this minute!"

"I didn't think you'd be so angry with me," I said, rather foolishly, in retrospect. Did I actually think that he would give me his blessings? "Okay, I'll leave."

As I walked out, I quickly thought to myself, "What have I begun here?" It was, in retrospect, a rhetorical question, since I knew the ugly tradition in this business; after I left Investors, they sued me, and even took me to court.

Investors Group, like so many other financial planning companies, believed that if a rep chooses to leave, and wants to take his clients along with him, the company should automatically take him to court. In my case, I was the only one who settled quickly, just a month later. The other fellows who got sued at the same time spent between $100,000 and $150,000 in legal fees because they had been determined to fight. Not me; I just settled quickly, even though it meant staying away from "their" clients. I felt at the time, if that is what it would cost me, then I would simply avoid their clients, and build my own clientele. So we settled — I think it was for two dollars — and it allowed me to get on with my life, and my career.

I had a real insight at that moment, and I vowed to put it into practice, just as soon as I had the power and situation to do so; after the hell that I went through when I left Investors, and after the way that I had been treated when I left Tillcan, I vowed to myself that I would never, ever make it difficult for employees to leave my company. For anyone who became part of Fortune Financial, I would make sure that individual enjoyed the process and the experience. Fortune reps would learn as much as possible, and I would present the information they needed to be quality salespeople as generously as I could. If they ever chose to leave, I would give them a hug, and a promise to remain friends: "Take your clients with you, and I'll support you as much as I can."

I had been deeply hurt by my experience at Tillcan — I had given so much of myself to the company — emotionally, physically, financially, and to see it all end so abruptly, so coldly — I felt that there was no justice in the world, but that I'd do my part to make sure that there would be in the future, for myself and for others as well. My $60,000 was clearly gone; I just had to let it go.

All of these things would shape the way I would conduct myself, and the way I would build my new organization which we had just christened Fortune Financial.

Meanwhile, several of us founders had begun the application process to get our company through the Ontario Securities Commission (OSC) as a mutual fund dealer. The first step had been to register our company, and that had us worried. Not that this is a complex problem — we simply got ourselves a lawyer and he submitted the application to the OSC under the

Fortune name. But we were told that it would take "probably a year" because the commission had become quite wary; a large number of mutual fund dealers in Canada had been dropping like flies, since the crash of 1987.

One major company out of British Columbia, National Financial Brokerage Corporation (NFBC), went bankrupt, along with its 600 representatives. Tillcan was about to sink, with its 350 reps; Stenner Financial, also out West, with some 300 employees, was having similar difficulties. So the securities commission was not eager to license any new company rising from such a huge pile of ashes, and understandably so.

The companies that were failing were mostly undercapitalized. Brokerage houses were selling themselves off to banks left and right, because they had been undercapitalized as well. It was a tough atmosphere to try another kick at the mutual fund sales can.

When we submitted our application, we had no idea where the financing would come from. I certainly had no money. And now we were told that it would take a full year to approve our application. Panic started setting in. True, more and more people wanted to join us, but I had nowhere to go. Oh yes, I could have gone to almost any company in Canada; I was receiving offers — life rafts, really — from all over the place. People came up to me and asked me to start branches for them. They knew that I had built Tillcan, and they saw my potential for helping them, too.

As I had done in the not-too-distant past, I began to canvass friends once more, to borrow money. I decided that I needed at least $100,000 in order to get Fortune off the ground. One of my sisters-in-law loaned me $15,000, and several other friends loaned me money, too. I soon raised the sum I felt that I needed. Another friend, Ernie Huckerby, raised the same amount, and it was a must that we both did so: we had to put up $35,000 with the securities commission as a security deposit. There were also legal fees, office space expenses, filing fees, and considerable operating costs. (This all sounds like a very powerful argument for millions of prospective entrepreneurs to consider "network marketing," which by its very nature, involves very little initial investment. This is only one reason why I recently began offering such opportunities within my latest company, Destiny Health Solutions.)

We knew we'd have no revenue coming in for several weeks — or likely, months — so we budgeted for $200,000, and we managed to raise it, almost overnight. And speaking of overnight — we had a fantastic bit of good luck; we obtained the licence from the osc on December 6, 1988 — *exactly four weeks* after we had applied for it! I had no idea why or how we got it so fast. I was not only ecstatic with joy — I was profoundly relieved. I had no desire to work briefly for another company for a short period of time, and then have to switch my licence all over again.

Ernie Huckerby was in London, Ontario; I was in Toronto. Getting a company started was very difficult. I worked hard — as I've tried to do all my life, but this time, I would be getting something in return for all the endless time, sweat, and effort. Then, a tense moment: I told Ernie, "We're 50-50 partners in this company, but I'll be doing most of the work. I think I should be given controlling interest in Fortune."

Initially, Ernie said no. "This is the way we started it," he told me, "and this is the way it is going to be." We yelled and screamed at each other, and we fought plenty for a long while, and then he finally agreed; he'd give me whatever I needed, in terms of percentages of ownership, to help Fortune grow and prosper. Ernie, the friend and gentleman he has always been, had actually given in to my request to let me have controlling interest in Fortune Financial. He could well have said (as he did at the beginning), "This is the way it is, and that's just too bad, David. Let's go and fight it out in court." And many new companies go that route, and end up dead, long before they ever have a chance to be born, and to grow. But Ernie Huckerby chose not to do that, and I'll forever be indebted to him — as would the many hundreds of employees and representatives of Fortune Financial and their tens of thousands of clients, over its decade-long existence as a thriving, respected company.

Thanks to Ernie's cooperation, our ownership of Fortune went from 50-50 to 75-25. By 1990, we were making commitments to several other representatives to whom we were going to give up portions of the ownership of Fortune Financial. We figured that this was as good a time to do it as any other. We had gone through the last few weeks of 1988 and all of 1989 sharing partnership equally, but by the middle of 1990, our new arrangement was settled.

And so we got our own licence to open as Fortune Financial on December 6, 1988. We set up a little office, having purchased as much used furniture as we could. It was 2,000 square feet, but big enough to make a go of it. Through the vibrant existence of Fortune Financial, I always had used furniture in my office, while most of the reps had brand-new, expensive pieces in theirs. I bought everything at garage sales; for instance, the chairs in my president's office were worth $2,000, but I paid $300 for them.

As soon as we were licensed, I had to rush around, from mutual fund company to mutual fund company, to complete putting the agreements in place. The few reps who had said that they would join me in the new firm had to get all their licences transferred over, so the first two weeks of Fortune's existence were very frantic.

It also turned out to be perfect timing, even though we hardly planned it that way; we started our business at year's end, when people in this business usually don't do very much — they're too busy with Christmas shopping. But this gave me and my assistants lots of opportunity for the last three months in 1988 to work non-stop getting everything in place, without very much business or sales to worry about. Why, we didn't even have order forms! Yet the timing could not have been better.

So, as of January, 1989, Fortune Financial was fully operational. Not that we were successful in those first two months — not by a long shot! Truly outstanding success would not come until 1992. In the first few weeks, we had only ten representatives — the same number with which Tillcan began — but with some key differences; a new, more symbolic name, and better working conditions for employees. The only difference between myself and the other nine was that I was running the business. I was responsible, and had a far larger picture to worry about. But I still had an office to worry about; just fewer reps than I'd had, back at Tillcan.

From the very first day of Fortune's existence, I was out there selling, and I continued working "in the trenches" until I had to sell the company, a decade later. I kept incredibly long hours — in the first few weeks, I believe I was putting in close to 24 hour days — but I had no money, so I still had to sell products to the public. I did not take a penny from the company for the first three years, because I was eager to see it survive. I managed to get by on my own commissions only, so every dime that came into the company would be directed to pay its bills.

The original ten employees soon expanded. I kept getting phone calls, and more and more people were asking what we were about, and whether they might be able to work for us.

At the time, I wasn't really sure why we were growing so much; we weren't doing anything that spectacular. Back at Tillcan, I was able to keep a three percent commission, whereas at Fortune, it was only slightly higher — 3.5 percent. So it wasn't because of some kind of huge payout that new people kept coming to us.

Certainly, the high commission payout was one of the features that attracted so many new reps to Fortune Financial. But most of the growth had accrued from people being referred to us. We never ran a single ad in any newspaper for employees or representatives. Indeed, right through the life of my new financial planning firm, not once did I ever phone anyone at another company — no matter how good they were — and try to recruit them for Fortune. This latter refusal to "cannibalize" other firms led to one of my favourite anecdotes from that frenetic time:

The best compliment I received in the first half-dozen years of our young company was in late 1994, when a very big product competitor joined us — Jack Gillis. I had known Jack for many years; we'd met at dozens of meetings and conferences, and I'd always found him a wonderful fellow. I also had tremendous respect for him because of the way he conducted himself and his business. So when he phoned me in the winter of 1994/95, and said that he had to talk with me, I was thrilled; he had been such a successful producer, with respect from the industry to match. After a few meetings, he told me that he wanted to join Fortune.

"What's the main reason you want to?" I asked, deeply flattered.

"Because you are the only person in all my years in the business who never approached me to join them! Also, I've heard so many good things about you in the industry — from fund companies, from your own people. But the main reason is, because you never tried to recruit me!"

That meant so much to me, because it had been a central approach of mine since day one. And since that same day one, the word was spreading; we were good people, we were a high-commission place, we were a company that they should talk to. I started getting phone calls from right across Canada! I would show up at a hotel or airport, and I'd always receive the same response: "You're not the sort of person I had envisioned."

I had to laugh. "What type of person did you have in mind?" I'd ask them.

"Well, we've heard so many good things about you and Fortune, that I expected you to be an older person. You look so young!"

It must have been all the fresh vegetables and fruit in Guyana. These exchanges took place some 15 years ago, when I was 35, and I must admit, I certainly looked younger then than I do today, at the half-century mark. Still, the response was typical; people usually expect someone trying to build a major company to be big, tall, probably white-haired (and, yes, probably white).

Most of the men and women who came to see us had been in the business and heard about "these new guys at Fortune." It was easy to check out the potential reps, and the screening process was not difficult. Many were referred to us through mutual fund companies; in fact, they quickly became our biggest source of referrals. After all, they are out there talking to people in our industry on a daily basis. So when they encountered someone who was not happy in their company, they'd be asked, "Do you know anyone good in this industry to talk to?" And the answer was very often: "Talk to David Singh at Fortune. He can be trusted."

I believe this was all payment for years of good, hard work. If I hadn't put my integrity and caring ahead of compensation and monetary rewards back at Tillcan, Fortune would never have started, much less flourished. If I hadn't continued to practise those attributes, Fortune would not have reached its extraordinary successes through the 1990s. Without that drive and decency, we never would have benefited so much from the countless referrals we kept getting. And we got them because I had focused so much on making sure that my integrity was in place; that when I said I was going to do something, it was quickly done. I was determined to put my employees' interests before mine, always. This attitude and determination continues with Destiny Health Solutions, in the new millennium.

What the Fortune reps got from me were things that they felt were important to them. They felt that they deserved those things that made them feel important and fulfilled, so they received things from me which made their lives better. I can break these benefits down into the personal side of their lives, and the business side. These two, I feel, are the most important parts in all of our lives; the side that pays the bills, and the side that keeps our emotional stability in place, and keeps us going.

On the business side, I delivered to my fellow workers at Fortune the things that I had always wanted in my life, but never had. I took the attitude of continually asking myself, in every situation: "Is this important to me? Would it make me a better person in business? If the answer was "yes," then perhaps other people would desire the same thing.

We made sure that we delivered the things that we said we were going to deliver. From a business perspective, if we told a representative that we would pay a specific commission, we made sure we delivered. Perhaps even more importantly, we decided that we were going to pay commission on a weekly basis. That was unheard of in the financial planning industry, but we chose to pay all reps promptly every Friday. We had those commission cheques ready, no matter what it took. We had only one office doing this, but we made sure that all commissions were paid, every single week, from day one.

This is probably why so many fund companies believed that Fortune wasn't going to survive for very long. We offered the highest commission in the business, and we were paying it to our reps every single week. This, of course, meant a lot of extra paperwork. We never missed a payday in the first 12 months. Fifty-two commission checks went out every Friday — or, at the very latest, Saturday or Sunday.

I also promised that I would support each and every representative with their business. Soon I began my "strategies for success" conferences, which proved hugely popular. From a business side, I delivered what I said I'd deliver, and I did the things the agents wanted, but rarely got, from their previous places of employment — good payout, weekly commissions, marketing support, and fair treatment. Not only that, I was in continual touch with them, and made each of them feel important. And they were important, too.

Soon my reps were speaking to mutual fund companies, telling them "how much David Singh is doing for me." And then those companies turned around and began to tell other people to talk to me. I trust that there will be a similar response to how I plan to treat my employees and fellow workers at my newest business, Destiny Health Solutions.

On the personal side, I made phone calls on a regular basis. And I picked up an approach from Anthony Robbins which is so very important, even though I had lacked this in my own life — at the seminar in Austin, we had to hug as many people as we could, every day, whether they were male or female. At first, I was extremely uncomfortable with this, but I got used to it. Back in Canada, I began to do the same thing — hug everyone. I kept doing this, and soon the guys felt happy to be a part of the organization.

At Fortune, then, through the majority of its existence, we were having a good time, enjoying ourselves, and doing very well in sales. These were the sorts of things which got to our competitors' ears, and to those who were working for other financial institutions; *maybe we should talk to the people at Fortune.*

Back at Tillcan, it had been constant war between the reps and the head office, because the former weren't getting their commissions on time, and we'd forever be yelling at the people in charge, "We're not getting paid!" The way of dealing with such complaints was always, "I don't know. I guess the girls at head office are not doing their job." As you can see, "passing the buck" is a tradition which is not limited merely to civil service or giant corporations!

From the very start of Fortune Financial, I took 100 percent responsibility for what went on, and never lost track of what was happening at my head office. I always met with my head office staff at 8:30 every morning, whether I was physically there or not. When I was in British Columbia in late 1994, for example, I would get up at 5:30 a.m., and handle the meeting by teleconferencing, even if it was only to bring me up to date.

Every manager had to keep me informed on what was happening: were there any complaints? What did you hear from the clients? Was there anything we should be aware of in the field? Here's what I'm hearing about you guys at the head office — and so on. So if someone came to the Scarborough branch, which was the head office of the firm, I was your manager. If you went to the London, Ontario, branch, Ernie Huckerby was the one in charge. And so it went, as offices popped up like apple blossoms across the country.

In retrospect, the reasons for our company's explosive growth were obvious. With all due humility (a very Canadian trait), here is a letter from a representative who worked briefly for Fortune Financial in the mid-1990s. I came across it while I was researching this book, and I was struck by its warmth and frankness, but most importantly, I think it would be good if you heard from somebody other than the author of this book, to get a sense of what we were doing right. This former employee worked for the Halifax office, had an Masters of Business Administration, and was a successful investment planning consultant, as his business stationery reads. His name is Layth Lorin Matthews, and his letter is dated October 21, 1996, a time when my firm was entering its most glorious — and soon to be most difficult — years:

Dear David,

I know a lot of changes have come down recently at head office, so I'm sure you don't have time for mushy letters, etc. But I have to do it.

As you know, I have sold my practice. . . Over the years it has been great to get to know you. I feel that you are my personal friend. It has been interesting to watch you over time and reflect back on myself. I have worked at five different investment firms in my retail career, both in the U.S. (in Seattle) and Canada. Of those, you are the first company president I have met with the discipline and fearlessness to expose his heart.

You have created a company here which offers substantially improved circumstances and challenges to brokers, who could be described as people too difficult to fit in anywhere. Really you just give them what they want and need, which is freedom and fairness and generosity. That's all very nice, but what makes you special is that you have had the discipline to keep on giving those things. That is truly amazing, to me anyway. Most firms squeeze the brokers into a corner with lower payouts and less security and then back off just before or just after a mass exodus. That is so stupid and it is obvious that the hands-off empowering approach that you take is the way of the future. People are becoming too smart for that other sh—. David, I feel that you are doing well by doing good. You're the best thing on the street, really.

Much love, and best wishes,
Layth Matthews

CHAPTER EIGHT

GROWING FORTUNE AND GROWING FORTUNES FOR EVERYONE

W e did not start off in December, 1988, with a plan to build Fortune Financial into the number one financial planning firm in Canada, a position we achieved by the mid-90s. No, our goal was merely to do things a little differently than our competitors; to love and care for our employees and associates; and to commit ourselves to always do what would be best for our clients.

The latter, especially, is still a serious problem at many mutual fund companies, insurance firms, and banks. Think of the billion-dollar fine leveled against one of America's top brokerage houses recently; the countless tales of insider trading, the scandals of untrustworthy analysts, corrupt accountants, and CEOs of giant firms who were spending more time purchasing hundred-million-dollar homes and ranches than they were running their companies honestly and properly. As I look back at the past few years, I am shocked by how tainted the entire process of money management has become in North America. (See my section on Wealth, below, to help you escape from this troublesome reality.)

And so, our company started to grow and prosper. From an extremely modest beginning of two branches, ten representatives, and three head office staff, we began to grow almost exponentially. Within one year, we were up to 60 reps, and $43 million in sales; the latter shot up nearly 200% to $125 million after our second full year, from 100 reps — a 67% change in that number. Two years later, we grew 117% in sales, up to $325 million, with 175 reps — a 25% increase from the year earlier. By 1994, we hit nearly $700 million in sales (a 44% increase from the previous year) and 250 reps — nearly a third more than the year before.

By the time Fortune Financial reached its peak in 1998 — barely a decade after its fragile birth in a difficult economic atmosphere, (after all, we set up shop only weeks after the stock market crash of 1987 shook world markets) we had some 750 reps in over seven dozen offices in all ten provinces of Canada, with annual sales in the hundreds of millions. In fact, we were managing over $8 billion in assets, so it wasn't just our planners who were doing well; clearly we were bringing a lot of satisfaction to many thousands of clients, also.

So what are some of the secrets behind this phenomenal success? (Beyond the kind words of that happy Halifax financial advisor in the letter quoted above?) And how do I plan to use similar wisdom to build up my new network marketing company, Destiny Health Solutions?

One of the first things Fortune Financial did was to invite mutual fund managers — the men and women who actually pick and choose the stocks which go into their products — to our managers' meetings. We recognized early on that the fund companies should know how we were building our company, and should be aware of what was important to our fledgling firm. We invited them all, but at first, only a handful of them came. Then, as the word got out that we were quality salespeople, and were running an impressive ship, more and more of them came — and at their own expense, too. Not only that, I encouraged them to pay to attend the meetings, which is how I managed to afford those gatherings. "It's an opportunity to meet my managers, and to impress them with your product," I'd say to each. I still had that *"I must know more! I must know everything"* attitude which pushed me towards more knowledge throughout my young life, whether in Guyana or at colleges and universities in Canada. And I knew that this longing for understanding would make my sales representatives better at their jobs, and help them to achieve better results for their clients.

Few successful companies or organizations, I would guess, had a sense of their direction and ultimate goal when they began. Did Henry Ford, as he tinkered with his first automobile on his Michigan farm, ever imagine gas stations around the world, and super-highways and suburbs across North America? I know that I did not! When we first received our mutual fund licence on December 6, 1988, I was completely satisfied with that. After all, that's all Tillcan had been — a mutual fund dealer. And earlier, at Investors Group, that's all I had done — sell mutuals. Indeed, most of the people in the industry were selling mainly mutual funds. Frankly, all I wanted to do was to build a good, reliable mutual fund organization, and that was that.

And that's what we were — at first. We just grew and grew — with a consistency and rapidity that suggested that this company would soon *not* be satisfied with selling mutual funds only.

In each and every case, the growth from British Columbia to the Atlantic provinces came through referrals, and referrals, alone. "What are they doing over in Fortune Financial?" One after another, men and women would call and see if I'd "be interested in opening an office" in this or that location. I would immediately book a flight and fly off to meet whomever expressed an interest in what we were doing; whoever was interested in becoming a potential associate of this rapidly growing financial planning company.

Initially, it was probably the high commission payout which attracted new people, or that's what I thought. But I quickly realized that was only part of the reason that agents wanted to be a part of this then-fledgling firm. No, the biggest reason that they all wanted to join Fortune was that they saw the opportunity offered by our company. At my firm, they could run their own show; they were largely in charge of their own destinies. I have vowed to give the same guidance, and the same freedom, to those who join my now-fledgling Destiny Health Solutions firm.

The explosive growth of the number of associates of Fortune Financial forced upon me a new realization: being a mutual fund dealer was not going to be enough to keep us alive and burgeoning. Not unlike a manufacturer who recognizes that the company must offer more than one line of gym shoes or more than one type of breakfast cereal, I realized that "man cannot live by mutual funds alone." I had to create an organization with a broader range of financial services than merely one which sold only mutual funds.

I've always benefitted from my ability to recognize and pick up on opportunities very quickly — and respond very quickly when I see something which can help myself, or others. To this day, if I read something interesting in a magazine on an airplane or in a doctor's office, I always sit and ponder it at great length, often running with the idea soon after.

And so, sometime during the first year of my tiny new company's life, I decided that Fortune Financial had to become a securities dealer if it was to continue to grow; we had to be able to sell stocks, as well. Which is how Fortune Financial Corporation was born, in 1989. Within one year, one tiny company had become two!

One of my representatives had approached me and said, "We really should look into the possibility of selling stocks." He had happened to talk with someone at First Marathon, which had a discount operation called Marathon Brokerage. Maybe we could make an arrangement with them, whereby they would do the stock transaction on our behalf? Then we wouldn't have to acquire all the administrative backroom setup to handle it.

I met with a fellow from Marathon, and he told me what the company was involved with. At that time I knew next to nothing about brokerage or stocks, but soon, we were allowed to tie ourselves to their brokerage house to handle the backroom, or the trading, side of our operation.

What I had stumbled onto, interestingly, was something that had never been tried before: up to that time, there had never been a mutual fund dealer in Canada who had wished to become a "correspondent broker." We were breaking new ground.

It was hardly merely signing a piece of paper. I had to purchase a seat on a Canadian stock exchange. After all, First Marathon was a full brokerage house; Fortune Financial was not. And the Securities Act insists that a correspondent broker must be a member somewhere. With a seat on an exchange, I'd have the right to buy and sell in the stock trading business, and would be able to use the backroom of First Marathon.

I knew that neither Vancouver nor Alberta had exchanges with much credibility at that time. The only ones with the needed credibility, of course, were in Toronto and Montreal, and I chose the latter because of the functional cost. Instead of having to spend close to $150,000 to own a seat on the Toronto Stock Exchange, I was able to land one on the Montreal Stock Exchange for only $30,000.

This did not happen overnight. Firsts rarely do. Our lawyers had never heard of such a thing, so they had to approach the osc and the stock exchange to find out how it could be done. And those people, in turn, had to speak with their own lawyers about how to accomplish this. But I knew it would happen. The Securities Act was clear on the possibility of such a thing; it was simply that no company had tried it before. It was really just a case of going through the process of explaining to everyone what I was attempting to do.

Still, the matter was complicated in other ways not first suspected or considered. What made the whole question even more difficult than its lack of precedent was the very structure of Fortune Financial. After all, our structure was very different than that of other brokers; our offices were all independent, while the other brokers' offices were all owned by their head office, with expenses paid by head office. Brokers were treated like employees, while Fortune Financial associates were considered independent businesspeople.

I wanted all my offices of Fortune Financial to be independently owned by the managers, I explained to them. This way, I could control costs. I reminded them that most mutual fund dealers — especially Tillcan — went out of business soon after the crash of 1987 precisely because they did not control their expenses. I was positive that, if I could control my expenses, the chances of Fortune Financial surviving would be much greater.

The other distinction between Fortune and other firms, I explained to both the Montreal Exchange and Ernst & Young, was that *I did not want to build an organization with hundreds of employees.* I was building an organization with *hundreds of entrepreneurs.* Entrepreneurs who were constantly encouraged, inspired, assisted, informed. I wanted Fortune Financial to be a giant umbrella made of money and love and trust and many hundreds of successful businesspeople. In a similar way, I hope to see Destiny Health Solutions take off through the entrepreneurship of thousands of men and women, too.

It was really nothing more than being a responsible parent: letting the kids be in charge of their own destinies, through giving them duties, an allowance, whatever. *"I will support you — but, better, you are on your own. Start budgeting, and keep track of it!"* Which is what I was doing at Fortune. True, my managers got a higher commission payout than most of my competitors were providing. But they were not necessarily taking home a whole lot more money, and in some cases less, due to the expenses they incurred and had to control. And the mere fact that they were in charge, took the responsibility away from me and the company and put it on their shoulders — just as good parents should attempt to do with their teenagers.

A further distinction between Fortune and other companies, during that remarkable decade of the '90s: if I did treat every single individual in this company as a businessperson with his or her own rights, I, therefore, had to help each one to become more successful in business. So whereas most companies treat their people as employees, even though they may provide a good environment in which to prosper, the employees still owe their lives to the company. ("I owe my soul to the company store," as Tennessee Ernie Ford used to sing in "Sixteen Tons.") And, as noted earlier, if employees chose to leave the nest, every firm would take them to court and sue them for all they were worth. *Talk about condescension! Talk about flawed capitalism.*

So, where the vast majority of companies were saying to their employees, "You are tied to me. Leave my apron strings and I'll threaten you, and if necessary, sic lawyers on you," I did quite the opposite; I told my reps how great they were, and treated them as if they were great. If I treated them as special, it seemed more likely that they would want to stay with me and be close to me and treat me as a friend, because they felt comfortable around me. I made it easy for them to leave — if they wanted to leave — but I worked my fingers to the bone to give them every reason *not* to leave. I treated them with respect, created the most incredible working environment for them, made sure I was doing everything possible to help them succeed — to make them the best businesspeople that they could be. I let them decide if I was doing enough. And if they decided that I was not, and they wanted to leave, they should have felt free to go — and if they did leave, I was determined to keep them as friends.

I just came across another "love letter," this one from a young financial consultant in Kitchener, about an hour's drive west of Toronto. His name is Ross Bauer, and I'll only quote a few lines from his November 5, 1997 letter: *"I joined Fortune near the end of 1996. This has been, without doubt, the best decision I've ever made. Since joining Fortune, my calendar year income has increased over 300 percent and there is nearly two months left in the year! . . . I have never felt this level of confidence and motivation ever before, and I owe it all to you, David. Without you, there would be no Fortune. Without Fortune, I don't think my life would have gone through this transformation."*

95

Lest you think I tried to create some kind of Nirvana at Fortune Financial, it's only fair to acknowledge that in the first half-dozen years, I had to either terminate, or saw leave, some 160 people. In the cases of termination, it was usually for low production. But in every case we remained on good terms. We encouraged those people to go on, made it easy for them to move on, and gave them their former clients and all the support we were able to.

GROUPS, GROUPS, AND MORE GROUPS

The companies kept on being created. Our initial existence as a mutual fund dealer, Fortune Financial Group, was quickly joined by a second firm, Fortune Financial Corporation, in 1990. The first could sell only mutual funds; the second was a securities dealer, selling stocks and more. In 1989, we also created Fortune Financial Management, as a holding company. Then, in 1992, I started another firm, Fortune Financial Estate Planning Group, when I recognized the opportunity to provide estate planning services to wealthy clients — putting together wills, planning smooth transition of assets after someone passes away, and more. Handing an estate from one generation to another had become an increasingly important financial planning tool, and the older our population grew, the more complicated our tax system got.

The goal, as you can readily see, was to create a further umbrella — a network of companies with which we could provide a full range of financial services to our growing clientele, through all these different operative companies.

Then, in 1993, we established Fortune Financial Retirement Service, to manage RRSPS, and RRIFS, among others, using the Toronto Dominion Trust Company as our trustee, along with several other related companies.

There was always a sense of integration behind the way I built Fortune. I am a very strong believer in building relationships with people, and I felt that if I could build Fortune Financial along the same lines — having strong relationships with people who have the resources and skills which I lack — I call this "strategic alliance" — it would give me the opportunity to provide all the financial services which our clients might require.

From that very first day in early December, 1988, we were consistent in this outlook and plan. We knew that we would let all the branches be responsible for their respective destinies. The managers of all the branches were partners of mine, as opposed to being employees of Fortune. I would visit each manager in each branch across the country and tell that individual, "We are partners in this. You run your business at the branch level out of the commission payout you will receive. And I will run my head office on the portion that I receive. *But we are partners! Let's build this together. You are working under the Fortune name, it's true, but you still have your own business.*"

This was one of the main reasons that clients belonged to each financial planner, and not to the head office. How could I tell people that they were their own businesspeople, if their clients belonged to me? Once again, consistency was central to my philosophy, and one of the secrets of Fortune's spectacular growth.

Does this sort of attitude lend itself to greater productivity? In many cases yes, but not in every case. Some people find it helpful to have a big brother looking over their shoulder, and they can be very productive under those circumstances. Not every follower is a loser and not every leader is a winner, of course. But many others don't need someone watching over them to produce effectively, even brilliantly.

This, then, was how I was different from my competitors. I insisted upon treating Fortune as if it were a large business, managing a slew of other businesses — over 700 "companies" at its peak, in fact. This led to that strategic alliance I spoke of earlier — with all of my branches and all of my hundreds of representatives.

SOME THOUGHTS ABOUT FORTUNE AND ITS EDUCATIONAL DRIVE — AND RECOGNITION

When we started Fortune, there was a single-minded focus on doing whatever it would take to help each one of our people become more and more productive every year. This was achieved through yearly "Strategies for Success Conferences," which entailed most of our reps attending a series of lectures on everything from the quality of various mutual funds to the best ways to assist their clients in growing their money.

At various self-help meetings, from Alcoholics Anonymous to Gamblers Anonymous, men and women are encouraged to stand up and admit their addiction and their determination to beat it. I admit mine here, and in writing: *I am drunk on the power of knowledge, and the need to share it.* (See my

Wealth, Health and Happiness sections, below!) A psychiatrist might point to my youthful recognition, back in Canal #1, that "*if I don't get educated, I'll never be able to escape this farm!*" And, indeed, it was my studies which allowed me to teach in the jungle, and later, to gain the business degrees in Canada which helped me become a successful financial planner, and eventually found Fortune Financial.

But the reason for my addiction is not really that important. What is essential is that my determination to make my fellow workers at my financial planning firm as wise and knowledgeable as possible not only led to great monetary rewards (for myself and hundreds of the reps), but also extraordinary recognition from the province and even the entire country.

And so, Fortune Financial was chosen as one of Canada's Top 50 Best Managed Private Companies, as announced just before Christmas 1994, in *The Financial Post*. Chosen by the accounting firm Arthur Andersen & Co. along with Canada's daily financial newspaper and Canadian Airlines, this honour became all the more precious to me (and our then 500 fellow Fortune folk) when we realized that over 600 nominations were received for what was the second annual award, and 175 finalists had been visited and evaluated. And we were even more pleased to discover that we were number nine in that Top 50 — not bad for a firm which, exactly six years earlier, had not yet seen the light of day, and lacked a five year plan when it set out on its entrepreneurial journey!

For the next two years, we received the same honour — of being one of Canada's 50 Best Managed Private Companies — three consecutive years, in all.

Since Fortune was my baby, I was deeply flattered; after all, it was hundreds of men and women who earned that award for the company we had been building together. But I was *personally* thrilled to receive the Ontario Premier's Award in 1995. Here is a brief excerpt from a letter I received from the Minister of Education and Training at Queen's Park, just before Christmas, 1995:

Dear Mr. Singh:
    To mark the 25th anniversary of Ontario's Colleges and Applied Arts and Technology in 1992, a new set of awards was launched by the province to honour outstanding graduates of the system. The

Premier's Awards is an annual series that recognizes individuals from each of the four areas of study: applied arts, business, health sciences and technology.

In total this year, 54 graduates were nominated for their overall achievement. Selecting the finalists from this deserving group was extremely difficult. On behalf of the province, it is my great pleasure to inform you that you have been chosen as the recipient of the 1995 Premier's Awards for the outstanding graduate from the field of Business. [Their emphasis] The career success and commitment to community demonstrated by this year's nominees is truly remarkable and you can be proud to have been selected to exemplify this fine group of individuals.

Since the nominating committee of George Brown College was kind enough to bring my name forward as a possible contender for that award, I soon decided to pay back what they had done for me. So, I created a financial planning program for the college which was quickly approved by the Canadian Securities Institute. When students complete that program at George Brown, they receive a two-year diploma in financial planning, with 240 hours of work-related experience.

The degree was immediately successful, with nearly 300 students enrolling in the first two years. The college was enthusiastic, and the Minister of Education of Ontario promptly began to promote the program across the province as the "David Singh" program. Why? Because it met the needs of the real world. Most programs of the past had been based on what academics thought the real world needed. What we did with this Diploma Program in Financial Planning was to exclaim, *"Look, you don't know what we need! Let us tell you what we need. We're in business, we're in the trenches. We know what we need!"*

Of course, it didn't hurt that I went knocking on doors across the province, hitting financial institutions, banks, phone companies, and others, and was able to raise $145,000 to fund the program for the first year. After that, the province took over. And a half-dozen years later, diplomas are still being earned and awarded at George Brown College — where I later became a member of the Board of Governors.

A good way to close this chapter is to quote from an interview I gave for *Advisor's Edge* magazine, in 1997.

> What gets me excited about this business is education. I plan to differentiate myself from everyone else by being more proactive in educating the public. I want to teach people how to fish as opposed to giving them a fish and saying buy this fish because look how great a fish it has been — in other words, look how great this investment has done over the year. For the most part people are investing on that principle. My goal is to give them the power — to teach them to fish.

Note my words of a half-dozen years ago: "education," "educating the public," "teach people." Yes, I admit it: I still am *"drunk on the power of knowledge, and the need to share it."* And now, in 2003 and beyond, I have moved into the health field, with Destiny Health Solutions, where I can do the same thing.

CHAPTER NINE

FORTUNE PEAKS, AND FORTUNE FALLS
(WHILE REACHING "INFINITY" ALONG THE WAY)

The ancient Greeks defined "tragedy" as a play in which someone reaches great heights and then comes crashing down to earth in the closing scene. After the poverty, hunger and brutality I witnessed in my birthplace of Guyana, I am reluctant to describe what happened to me and my business career in the last few years of the 1990s as "tragic." After all, here I am, a half-dozen years later, with a wonderful, supportive new woman in my life, a beautiful, healthy new daughter, and three older daughters of great integrity, beauty, talent, and goodness. Hardly the stuff of tragedy!

But those years were certainly traumatic, and often emotionally devastating to me, and I have learned life-affirming and probably life-saving lessons from the big mistakes I made during the closing years of the 20th century; ones which I am already applying to my entrepreneurial rebirth in a new business — Destiny Health Solutions.

The peaks were so many in 1997 and 1998, I hardly know where to begin. One telling example: in the latter year, as Fortune Financial advisors and offices continued to spread across the country, Marty Weinberg, the president of Assante, another thriving financial planning company (and today, one of the largest in Canada), actually came to my suburban Toronto home and placed a cheque on my coffee table.

It was for $50 MILLION dollars!

"I want to buy Fortune Financial, its reps, its clients, and all its offices," he told me.

I thought back to the years of hunger and endless, hated farm work in Canal #1, and the $20 which nearly burned a hole in my pocket as I flew to Canada as a young man, just two decades earlier. Twenty dollars to $50 million, I noted; not bad. "I want to think about it," I told him.

Within days, he flew me to his head office in Winnipeg, along with two of my top financial advisors. "Take it!" one of them told me. "Take the money! Sell Fortune!"

We arrived in the capital of Manitoba, and I studied the business plan of Assante. I quickly came to the conclusion that anything that Assante Corporation was attempting to do, I could do bigger and better. (I opened the Toronto phone book just now, as I am writing these words, and I found "Assante Capital Management," "Assante Estate and Insurance," "Assante Financial Management," and many other offices — in that city alone. They have grown just like my Fortune Financial companies had blossomed, just a few years earlier.)

The sports announcers on radio and TV love to talk about "20/20 hindsight" and "Monday morning quarterbacking," regarding what a team should have done during the big game.

And, in hindsight, of course I should have taken the money. But how could I have imagined to what depths I would fall, what problems Fortune would encounter, what disasters would cripple a new family of mutual funds I was then considering?

No, the reason I did not cash that $50 million cheque was because I still had a clear vision of what I wanted to build with my group of companies. My commitment was there; I was ready; I was eager to continue to place trust in all 750 of my representatives (although in that latter desire, I made one of my biggest mistakes of judgment); I was in the process of growing my beloved creation into an even greater force of quality investment, education, and more. *So why sell?*

No, it wasn't just "hubris" — the excessive pride of a vain, tragic hero. It was a merely a strong belief in myself and what I and so many others had already accomplished in the first decade of Fortune's existence, which had not been challenged up to that date. Why should anything go wrong?

THE FIRST CHALLENGE: ONE OF MY MOST SUCCESSFUL PLANNERS RUNS INTO "MIS-FORTUNE"

Shortly before I was offered that handsome cheque for Fortune Financial, my company had begun to get some sharply negative publicity in the print media of Canada, as a result of the actions of one of my advisors, Paul Tindall. He was one of the first to join me at our fledgling firm, along with his wife, Anne Louise. He quickly became astonishingly good in his work, and a leader in sales.

Yet — to be fair to Paul — he was drawn into a private investment scheme which had been created by an uncle of his wife, who lived in Detroit. The investment turned out to be a brilliant hoax — a pure fraud, in which Paul Tindall and his wife (close relatives to the evil genius behind it) were duped out of hundreds of thousands of dollars — and, sadly, several dozen of Tindall's clients each lost $25,000, $50,000, $100,000, even more, in their hopes to get rich quick.

One would think that this would be merely a case of lousy luck, leading to Tindall alone being sued by those who were bamboozled along with him. But not so. Paul Tindall worked for Fortune Financial; he was one of its top salespeople; and, as we all know, one bad apple can spoil an entire bushel. By late 1997, several of my top advisors and representatives approached me pleading: "*Get rid of Paul Tindall! You have to fire this guy!*"

I refused to do so, and not merely out of friendship with the man, and the fact that he, more than most, had helped me turn Fortune Financial into a giant in its field. (Indeed, about this time we had brought on board 175 new representatives from Brian Costello's wildly successful THE Financial Planning Group. Fortune was booming during this period.)

No, the real reason why I did not "cut bait" from Paul Tindall was based on a personal philosophy of mine. When I had started the company nearly a decade earlier, one of the things I always talked about was "how important it is to treat the advisors at Fortune as my clients, and then, their clients as their clients. As I've noted above, this was a concept which was unheard of in the financial planning industry at the time. Even brokers who chose to leave a bank were sued, if they wanted to take their hard-earned clients with them!

That was the way Investors Group had treated me, and I disliked that unfair treatment. I had vowed to myself that if I ever started my own firm, I would change that. This led me to an inevitable, and ultimately, near-fatal decision: Paul Tindall was my client, and his clients were his clients. And the most important thing in my life was to treat my clients (which included Paul, of course) with care and respect. I was there, in the capacity of president of Fortune Financial, to help my "clients" become successful, to be there when they needed me. I treated all of these hundreds of men and women with great respect, got to know them, became close with their families, took them on trips, went with them to conferences all over the world, had them at my home for giant barbecues — treated them all as if they were family. Which really, they were.

"Look," I told the growing number of financial planners who were beseeching me to "dump Tindall," "I can't do that. When I began this company, I was well aware that we offered no products which customers could not get anywhere else: mutual funds; GICs; life insurance; stocks and bonds. Sure, the compensation I was paying for each sale was a tiny bit more than other companies, but any of them could have chosen to match that. No, I made promises to all of them when they climbed on board Fortune's tiny ship: nobody would care for them more than I would; no one would ever spend more time training them and making them more educated, better, more helpful reps; no one would ever be more committed to their success than I would be." I reached for the phone on my desk.

"Call any of our 700 plus agents. Ask them about me. Ask them if I have delivered on those promises I made. I made these commitments that no one would be there faster to support them, in time of need, or in difficult situations. Well, Paul Tindall is facing a tough time now, and I have to make a decision as to whether I'm going to stick with him, when things are rough. Paul himself has often told me that the reason why he came to Fortune was because of that trust, that love."

A pretty speech, and from the heart. But as we all know, the heart can sometimes go astray, when it's not firmly backed by clear thinking. True, I didn't know all the details at this time in late 1997; all I knew what that several of Tindall's clients were in an uproar over some investment or other; it could have been an ill-chosen mutual fund or stock which had dropped precipitously. I simply felt that *you don't abandon friends when they run into trouble.* Isn't that precisely the time when we must stand firmly next to our friends, with our arms clasped around their shoulders in support and sympathy?

Not in this case. I think back at how I raised my daughters from infancy; there were some times when, no matter how difficult it was, I had to show what is often called "tough love." That's what I should have done with Paul Tindall. I should have drawn the line, and boy, did it turn out to be a giant mistake!

Interestingly, in the summer of 2001, I was invited to be the keynote speaker for a fine organization of students at Wilfrid Laurier University, about an hour west of Toronto. This was a couple of years after I had to sell Fortune and the other highly successful firm I had set up in the late '90s: Infinity Mutual Funds. The organization was called ACE — the Association of College Entrepreneurs, full of bright young men and women who will become the business leaders of tomorrow. After I finished telling them the highs and lows of my financial planning career, one of the students asked the obvious, but still painful, question: "*Would you handle the Tindall situation differently, if you encountered it again?*"

"I don't know what I would do differently," I admitted. "But I can tell you how I would manage the situation this time around. How I would do that is, *I would never put myself in the situation where I have to make such a decision!*"

This may sound flippant — the kind of answer you would expect from an elusive politician. But let me clarify what I meant; now that I've created a new company, Destiny Health Solutions, and I still run things, and support everyone who works with me, I have made Albert E. D'Souza the President of DHS — not myself. I still love my co-workers; I still care about them and their families. But now, I will not have to make the agonizing decisions, as I was forced to make (and chose not to make), in the case of Paul Tindall. I have learned from the "fire/don't fire" dilemma I encountered in 1997/98 with that financial planner, that I should delegate some of the authority which helped to destroy the reputation of my great company.

There was something else going on at this time, directly related to the Paul Tindall affair, and I'm sure it had some effect on my response to the painful decision which I kept putting off, until it was almost too late. This has to do with the profoundly moral, trustworthy nature of Fortune Financial, and how much it stood above most other firms in the same industry at that time, and since.

Let me explain. The reality of the financial industry is that millions of men and women put their trust — and their money, often their life savings and their monetary future — in the hands and judgment of their advisors, brokers, insurance salespeople. And every single day of the year, each and every financial institution around the world is faced with similar moral dilemmas and challenges: brokers recommend a bad stock (in order to gain a larger commission); a company uses insider trading to make a fortune; a planner here or a rep there moves their clients' money around — possibly for the best of motives — but without those clients' knowledge or consent.

A brief look over the financial pages of the first years of the 21st century will show exactly what I mean: a major brokerage house on Wall Street is fined $1 billion; CEOs sell off hundreds of millions of dollars worth of their shares of financially-doomed companies before the public discovers the ugly truth; accountants cook books on behalf of their billion-dollar bosses; financial planners are sent to jail after stealing a fortune. I could go on and on.

To be blunt, and at the risk of sounding like a child crying "he hit me first!" I must note that there were events which were taking place every single day in Canada, at the time that the Paul Tindall case began to garner headlines, which were far, far worse. A dozen times worse than what he so foolishly did.

The presidents or CEOs of the companies who those men and women worked for, in most cases, were never mentioned in the press! You would read, "Joe Schmoe of Financial Magic Inc. caught with hand in till." But were the names of the heads of those briefly smeared companies ever splattered with the mud of their irresponsible employees? Never.

Not so with Fortune Financial and Paul Tindall. Every few days another article would appear about my troubled financial planner, and "David Singh, president" was inevitably noted. I couldn't figure out why the two of us were forever linked, like Rodgers with Hammerstein or Sacco and Vanzetti. Why was I dragged into it, when no one else in my position ever appeared to be?

What further angered me was that, not once in its nearly decade of existence, had one penny — a single cent — disappeared from Fortune Financial's bank or trust accounts. Yet many brokerage houses could hardly claim that money never went missing — sometimes in the hundreds of thousands of dollars — from various clients' accounts; we know this, because every year, many brokers around the world are charged with major fraud, actually having stolen money from their clients! Yet in all these cases, to this very day, the situation is reported once or twice in the press, the institution is allowed to continue on, and the head of the company is rarely, if ever, mentioned in the article. And not only that: the number of times "the Tindall Affair" was described in the newspapers of Canada was astounding. Yet in Paul's case, he had never stolen money from any of his thousands of clients. He had made a few bad investment recommendations, one of which turned out to be a fraud which had fooled even him.

THE "INFINITY" THAT EVENTUALLY MADE MY COMPANY OWNERSHIPS TEMPORARY

Interestingly, it wasn't Paul Tindall, and my reluctance and refusal to fire him — by the summer of 1998, he was gone at last — which forced me to sell Fortune Financial, which I reluctantly did, in 1999. It was the very thing which I hoped and believed would make Fortune Financial even more substantial, more impressive, more respected, more permanent: the creation of a family of six mutual funds which we called Infinity.

The idea behind Infinity was inspired, and I'm still proud of what we did: in 1997, I and several others took the philosophy of the world's most successful investor, Warren Buffet of Berkshire Hathaway of Omaha, Nebraska, and used it as the *raison d'etre* behind a group of mutual funds. This philosophy can be conveniently summed up in two words: *buy* and *hold*.

It's more than that, of course, but at core, it's amazingly simple. If anyone wishes to make good money in investing, he or she should not trade in and out of investments, and try to "time the market," but, rather, choose a handful of good quality, reliable companies, buy them (and when you purchase a stock or security, you're buying a tiny chunk of that company, are you not?), and hold them for very long periods of time.

Buffett knows, and every intelligent investor knows, that every business will have good times and bad times; every firm will have its good and bad years, in which it makes or loses money, or is simply not as profitable as the year before.

You don't go and sell a business (or shares in it) simply because it's had one or two bad years. Do we throw our children out of the house if they keep acting up? If we did, our streets would be littered with homeless teenagers! Bill

Gates of Microsoft, for example, has most of his net worth in the company he co-created. And while the stock price of his great software empire has done very well over the decades, it's had some lousy quarters, even some losing years. But he did not sell his shares every time things were rough. In fact, since Gates was recently named the world's richest man (beating out Warren Buffett, who usually follows Gates on the wealthy lists), this suggests something about the importance of not turning your back on a company in difficult times.

You don't sell off a great bank either, such as Canada's Royal Bank or Toronto Dominion. Both have had years when they lost money; but few businesses are profitable every single year! Yet they are great institutions; companies which will last, probably for centuries. And you can't make money by panicking or racing for the exit every time a firm looks like it's on a losing streak. Do that, and when the company turns around and becomes profitable again, and its stock starts rising once more, you'll lose out, often on major profits.

It was Warren Buffett's philosophy of "buy and hold great companies" which we placed at the core of our new mutual fund firm called Infinity. Indeed, I and my friend Richard Charlton, who was in the forefront of creating our new fund family, co-wrote a book about this kind of financial thinking: *Invest and Grow Rich*. People clearly bought into it; Infinity funds became very, very successful, reaching a billion dollars in sales in the shortest period of time of any mutual fund in Canadian history!

But as the late, great American novelist Joseph Heller once famously wrote, "There's always a catch — Catch-22." The catch in our case was almost comical, in retrospect, even though it's what brought both of my empires (Fortune Financial and Infinity) tumbling to earth, moving me to sell them both. The Catch-22 was this: when you create a mutual fund which is highly successful, you are penalized for that success!

Let me explain: the way the mutual fund industry works is, you have to pay agents and brokers something called "up-front commissions." In other words, no one will sell your product — in this case, Infinity Mutual Funds — unless they get paid! And the more of the funds you sell, the more you must pay this money "up front." Then, in later years, the owners and operators of Infinity would receive revenue from "management fees," which the investors pay.

But what about the time between those up-front commissions and when the management fees start rolling in? It's a long time. So, while Fortune Financial continued to go from strength to strength — in spite of the Tindall dilemma — and Infinity took off with singular success — there was this new, huge demand for gigantic amounts of money to pay our salespeople and other brokers.

Just starting up Infinity led to the borrowing of a significant amount of money. I began, like most promising entreprenuers, by raising money from individuals. In this case, I managed to raise several million dollars from about 150 men and women, most of whom bought small shares in the birthing of the firm. CIBC then loaned us $10 million to create the funds, and National Bank had loaned us another $25 million, and we naturally had to start repaying those major debts.

Now, thanks to the "penalized for success" aspect of those up-front commissions, we found ourselves needing another $25 million from CIBC. But that fine institution was not prepared to lend us any more, unless we paid off some of what we had borrowed! This led us to create a product which was very popular in the markets at that time, called Income Trusts. (It's intriguing that these have become the hottest product on The Street again, a half-decade later.)

Income Trusts were so popular that year, they had become the vehicle of choice to raise money. So, Infinity created one of those income trusts, to allow us to go out and raise $15 million. But it was not to pay those up-front fees, which had shaken us so. No, we were going to use that $15 million to repay CIBC its earlier loan, and in turn borrow more from the same bank.

Bad luck — at the time that we brought our Income Trust to market, their popularity had started to taper off, and there wasn't very much interest from investors in this product. So, we were having difficulty raising the $15 million, and this put our earlier loans from the banks, and any future loans, into jeopardy.

Then, in the spring of 1998, Jeff Lipton, the chief portfolio manager and President of Infinity Mutual Funds, phoned me from Florida, where he was vacationing. "David, I'm not only your friend, but I'm also a securities lawyer. And I think I've found a way for us to raise the balance of the money we need from that Income Trust, to be able to close it. Infinity is legally allowed to purchase up to ten percent of the offering of the Trust."

I was delighted. Since the offering was $15 million, this meant that Infinity Funds would be able to purchase up to $1.5 million, which would be sufficient to wrap the project up, pay off the earlier debts to the banks, and obtain new ones. "Jeff," I told my buddy, "let's get on a conference call with our lawyer." We did so, and he agreed with Lipton that this would be perfectly legal. We then met with lawyers for the underwriting group, as well as the president of a major securities company, talking this over, debating it, and coming to the same conclusion that Lipton had reached, days earlier: Infinity would purchase $1.5 million worth of the Income Trust.

We were saved. We had closed the Trust, and we would now be able to pay off our earlier bank loans and take out a new one, so we could keep paying the fine men and women who had been selling the Infinity Funds so brilliantly to the public! Indeed, when we approached CIBC, they did their due diligence to lend us more money, declared that they were happy with Fortune and happy with Infinity, and wanted to be a partner with us; they were eager to lend us more money.

In the last month of 1998, CIBC approved us for another $25 million loan. We were on top of the world.

Then, on December 11, 1998, a shock came upon us with the impact and deadliness of an avalanche; as lawyers were sitting in the boardroom of Fortune Financial, completing this vital transaction — with a cheque for that much-needed last piece of the puzzle, the $25 million loan from CIBC, lying in the centre of the table — the phone rang. Someone wanted to speak with one of my lawyers. He excused himself and went out to take the call.

It was from the Ontario Securities Commission, informing us that there was to be a hearing in two days, concerning the Income Trust that Infinity Mutual Funds had created to save its bacon. "You may have done something which broke our rules," the caller told my attorney.

When I was called out of the meeting and informed of this, I felt as if a giant pit had opened below me, and I was falling through the floor. I didn't feel betrayed by the possible bad advice I had been given by everyone around me (the president of Infinity, my lawyers, other lawyers); no, not yet. What I felt was a complete sense of helplessness; of drowning; of a fear that any negative press at all could cause the collapse of Infinity, my gloriously successful, rapidly-growing family of mutual funds. Just moments before, I had been staring at that cheque in front of me, thrilled that I would be able to sleep peacefully through the night for the first time in many weeks ; after all, I had been fighting insomnia over the fear that with all the success of Infinity, we still lacked sufficient money to pay all those commissions — my horrible catch-22.

True, Fortune Financial had continued to grow by leaps and bounds; we had recently bought Keybase Financial, run by my old Guyana chum Dax Sukraj, bringing a further 125 agents into our family. But one law had always been clear to everyone: no money from Fortune could be mixed with Infinity's money; that was definitely out.

The company's lawyers were quickly notified of the threat from the osc, and we debated back and forth until midnight, at which point we agreed to break until the next morning. When we reconvened, we once again discussed the situation in great detail. Finally, the cibc's lawyers suggested that we "all just sit tight for a week," and wait to see what kind of fall-out there would be in the media, from this upcoming osc announcement.

It was absolute torture for me; naturally, some publicity did hit the media, and it was brutal: apparently, unknown to every "expert" with whom I had consulted, it was not acceptable for Infinity to have purchased that ten percent of our Income Trust, in order to close that $15 million deal. I had been given not only incorrect advice, but advice which threw my entire dream into a nightmarish position.

The results were gut-wrenching. The Ontario Securities Commission wanted the president and chief portfolio manager of my wonderful family of Infinity Mutual Funds, Jeff Lipton, to be suspended for six months. They also wanted me to be suspended for three months. There were fines, as well: $12,500 to be paid by Jeff Lipton, and $12,500 to be paid by me, as well as $12,500 fines for both Fortune and Infinity.

Fifty thousand dollars in fines, and brief suspensions, over an honest attempt — so we thought — to borrow $25 million? It seemed like a pittance in comparison, but, of course, that was hardly the worry. We were making tens of thousands of dollars every few days, in the runaway sales of our Infinity mutual funds.

And so, the great debates continued: what impact would this have on Infinity? How badly would the publicity harm our still-fledgling funds? We were hardly concerned with running the business for a few months without Lipton as its head; being suspended was not such a big deal, especially with our buy and hold philosophy: our President had long since purchased the bank and other financial stocks, and the equities of several of Canada's most impressive companies, and was letting them steadily grow in value, as they had been doing for years.

No, the concern was with the bad publicity — just like we had over the Paul Tindall fiasco with Fortune Financial. Finally, I made a judgment call — in retrospect, a bad one: "*People, we cannot let the public read in the press that the portfolio manager of Infinity Funds has been suspended for six months! That will simply kill the funds!*" Who, I had thought to myself, would leave their money in a young mutual fund, when the very man who ran it was forbidden to operate in his position, for half a year? Many clients would have seen this in the same way they would view our hiring a drunk to drive a school bus for class trips.

I went before the osc and pleaded with them: "We can't let you do this!" I exclaimed. "This will kill Infinity!"

"Make us an offer," replied the members of the Ontario Securities Commission.

"Okay," I told them. "I'll be the fall guy. I'll take the six month suspension in place of Jeff Lipton. Furthermore, fine me the full amount of $50,000."

And that's what happened. Jeff ended up with a three-month suspension and no fine, and I, as president of Fortune Financial, was suspended for six months, and hit with the total of the original fines.

The logic behind my decision was obvious to me at the time: it would be more beneficial all around, and certainly to Infinity, if I were penalized the most; after all, Jeff was president and portfolio manager of the fund family, and had to look the least hurt by the punishment.

As I've noted throughout this book, we all must make decisions through life; some small, and some large. What seemed so right for me and my companies at the time turned out to be one of the biggest errors of judgment of my life. The next day in the *Montreal Gazette*, thousands of Canadians read, "KING SINGH FINED $50,000." Nothing about the suspension. The *Victoria Times-Colonist* ran a similar headline on the same day: "SINGH FINED $50-GRAND."

In the eyes of the public, this young immigrant from South America was a criminal. After all, I had been fined this hefty sum; I must have done something wrong. Alas, that's how the media often work; most people read the headlines alone, and, at most, skim the rest of the article. Jeff Lipton, who had given me this wretched advice, along with so many of my lawyers, got buried deep in the story. This worked to the benefit of Infinity, as I had hoped, so I was proven right, at least, on that point.

My decision had killed David Singh, in the eyes of the business and investment community. I received no recognition and no appreciation from my shareholders for what I had done. And, in hindsight, once again (as with my too-gentle handling of Paul Tindall), I did it all wrong. If I could have done it over again, I would not have chosen to be the sacrificial lamb.

The date was mid-December, 1998. CIBC phoned and told me, "Look, David, we really do not know what kind of impact this is going to have on Fortune or Infinity. Why don't we all just go off on holidays, and we'll get back together in the second week of January, 1999."

As you may imagine, it was not a very pleasant holiday. For years, I had been traveling to our place in Florida with my three daughters, then all in their teens. It was a most depressing Christmas, since all I could think about was the possibility that Infinity could be dying, while I tossed and turned in the heat and sun.

There were some withdrawals from Infinity over this difficult period, but surprisingly few. And when we met with the bank on January 11, 1999, I heard the words that I was dreading would be spoken: "We have instructions from senior management at CIBC that we are not to lend Infinity any more money, due to all the negative publicity regarding your fund."

Now what? I was at the point where I had no money to pay all those up-front commissions for the brokers and sellers of Infinity. I became overwhelmed with personal health fears. It had been weeks, possibly months, since I had slept through the night, and I was going to bed with a towel next to me, because I would frequently wake up either sweating or freezing.

Yet there were no problems with Fortune Financial, my beloved planning firm, and all its many component parts. That older company had sorted out all of its difficulties, even coming to a settlement with the OSC about Paul Tindall. So, during this same month of Infinity horrors, Fortune was still blooming like a rose. It had no financial problems, regulatory problems, or compliance problems. Fortune was continuing on its merry way, doing what Fortune had always done, except larger and wealthier than ever before.

But Infinity had no money! I couldn't take it anymore, and in that same agonizing month — January, 1999 — *I decided to sell everything* — both companies which had so enriched over a thousand of its reps and other employees, and the financial portfolios of so many hundreds of thousands of clients in every province, with its fine selections of stocks and mutual funds.

If I had to do it again, I would have sold only Infinity, because that mutual fund company, for all its brilliance and grand success, was causing me all the pain. I was getting continual stomach cramps, and feared that I was developing an ulcer. My health has always been important to me — see the Health chapters, below — and I quickly came to the conclusion that all this suffering was not worth it; these were not the reasons why I got into the building of Fortune Financial and Infinity Mutual Funds.

I created those firms because I wanted to have fun, and I did have fun. I made countless good friends. I always enjoyed what I was doing. But it was no longer any fun; it was an endlessly stressful experience. It was simply too painful, too unhealthy, too unsatisfying, to continue to run them.

Having made this rather precipitious decision to leave the financial industry entirely, I began to contact several major firms and their presidents, as possible purchasers: Michael Lee-Chin, the gifted creator of AIC Mutual Funds, which had so inspired my own Infinity family; Ray Chang of CI Funds; Mark Bonham of Strategic Value; Jim O'Donnell from O'Donnell Investments, the man who had turned Mackenzie Funds into a giant of Canadian investment firms — and others. I also met with Ned Goodman, the highly respected president of Dundee Securities Corporation, with whom I felt the most comfortable. He seemed to have the organizational framework which would best swallow both Fortune and Infinity. (He also had many families of mutual funds under the name of Dundee, now called Dynamic Funds; today, he calls my Infinity Funds by the name of Focus Plus.)

And so, I had my fire sale of my two major financial firms: I sold Infinity Mutual Funds to Ned Goodman at Dundee for $53 million, and Fortune for $35 million, for a total of $88 million. I knew that I was almost giving them away, because not long before, I had met with CIBC Wood Gundy, to discuss how I wished to create a new company called Destiny Financial Group. The plan was to fold Fortune and Infinity into Destiny, and take it public on the Toronto Stock Exchange. At that time, the bank had put a combined value of $250 million on the firms! And here, just a few short months later, *I was sell-*

ing everything for barely over a third of that sum.

On August 31, 1999, I closed the deal; my two babies would be raised by someone else. A condition of the sale — this is normal practice in many mergers and sales of firms — was that I agreed to stay out of the financial planning business for two years. It's called a non-compete clause, and it was understandable and acceptable to me.

I had just gone through one of the most painful periods of my life. When I closed the deal in the Dundee offices, over 50 floors above the Toronto Stock Exchange, at the corner of King and Bay, I took the elevator down to the Concourse level, walked into the nearest barber shop, and asked to have my head shaved bald.

I had not planned this, but thinking back, it was clearly symbolic: I wanted a clean start. I wanted to leave all the garbage, all the pain and suffering behind me, and start anew. It was like stripping myself naked, and beginning the struggle to be reborn.

SOME THOUGHTS ABOUT THE YEARS THAT FOLLOWED

If you had met me on the day that I sold Fortune Financial and Infinity, I would have undoubtedly told you, "It can never get worse than this; I am now at the lowest depths of my life and career."

But not so. After all, if you are capable of even stating such a thing — of getting the words out of your still-functioning mouth — then you could always be worse off than that. And so it was. For one thing, I have never seen a dime of the $88 million I "received" from Ned Goodman and his fine organization, Dundee. You see, several of the clients who were burned by Paul Tindall's investments read that Fortune had been sold for tens of millions of dollars, and they assumed that they might be able to recover some of their losses.

Since the Ontario Securities Commission had jurisdiction over both of my companies, they insisted that we put all of the assets of Fortune and Infinity into a regulatory escrow account, pending the outcome of those claims. (It's fair, in a sense; imagine buying a house for $500,000; if you discover that a bank has a lien on it for $200,000, you are hardly going to shell out the full amount, but rather wait to see what it's really worth.)

It's been nearly four years since I sold the companies, and I have yet to see any money from the sale, as that lawsuit continues to drift through the Ontario courts. But I have kept my fingers crossed that some day I will get some money out of what I had built so carefully, and with such focus, direction, and love.

Meanwhile, I retreated to my house down in Florida with my fiancée. The plan was clear: to spend a long time there, trying to come to grips with the extent of my loss, and how to confront the future.

Yet after only two weeks, I was ready to come back to Toronto, and start again. I could not help it. I have always been the type of person who has pushed myself, endlessly and mercilessly, seven days a week, forever working extremely hard. I just couldn't sit around and do nothing.

I returned to the North, and decided to write a book, to give good financial advice to the Canadian public (always the teacher, whether in the jungles of Guyana or the boardrooms of Toronto), and to expose many of the things which I felt were wrong about the industry which I had loved and laboured in for so long.

It was a tough call to make, because that meant criticizing a business in which I worked for nearly two decades. What motivated me was not revenge, I don't think; it was, rather, as I've noted, that I had always treated my hundreds of advisors as if they were my own personal clients, and I expected them to treat their clients with the same kind of respect. I feared that respect was not always there; that many planners had not been working in the best financial interest of their customers, and that this trust had been broken.

I felt betrayed, and I wanted to share what I had learned with the general public, so I wrote a book called *Take Control of Your Financial Destiny*. Some of its key points about investing, insurance, tax planning and estate planning, are shared in the section called Wealth, below. (The book is still available, if you wish to contact me to purchase it.)

I briefly tried my hand at several businesses, which need not be discussed here. Then, I met the impressive and wise Albert E. D'Souza, and decided to create Destiny Health Solutions, to develop and sell quality health products. (It all fits together, as you'll see; I have always wanted Canadians to take control of their financial situation; now, I am moving toward urging those same Canadians — nearly half of them overweight or even obese — to do the same with their health. It's all about education, control, and choice.)

And so, I thought that 1998 and 1999 had been the worst years of my life. After all, I saw my dream, my determination, my vision, my passion, all reach their depths. In many ways it got worse, as the calendar changed to 2000, then 2001, then 2002. It seemed as if the roots had been cut out from the beautiful trees that I had planted in my chosen land.

I had made many people millionaires; I changed the lives of many thousands more. I took young people straight out of universities and made them hugely successful both financially and emotionally. So I never imagined that the years following the collapse of my dream would be as bad, and as challenging, emotionally and financially, as the peaks and depths reached in 1998 and 1999.

In retrospect, I should have taken those two years off. I recall a phone conversation I had with my dear friend Jim O'Donnell, a few months after my sale of Fortune and Infinity. "David, whatever you're doing now," he told me, "I have just one piece of advice for you: take off those two years of non-competition against Dundee, and simply relax. Clear your head; think; don't do anything."

But being the stubborn, pig-headed person that I am, I ignored Jim's advice. I felt that I just had to return to the real world. So, I wrote a book; I started a few small businesses which went nowhere, and, yes, I met a lot of unpleasant people who tried to take advantage of a once-successful man who was clearly down on his luck.

I had another setback during these few very tough years: I kept agonizing during 1999 and beyond over what I felt was incompetent legal advice I'd received, regarding the purported "legality" of Infinity purchasing ten percent of its own Income Trust. Finally, in the year 2000, I decided that I really had to achieve some kind of closure, some measure of justice. So I decided to sue my law firm for $100 million.

Then, something interesting happened. I contacted my lawyer, who told me that he could not partake in such a case; he had a conflict of interest with that major firm. But he offered to find me another lawyer to take on the firm. Six months went by, and we were unable to find a single lawyer in all of Canada who would take on the litigation. As soon as they discovered who the defendant would be, they'd call back and say, "I'm sorry, but we have a working relationship with that law firm. It can't be done."

I found it distressing and upsetting that in Canada, the system is designed in such a way that you have no difficulty finding a lawyer to take on a case in public, when the public is involved. But to get a lawyer to take on a case to sue other lawyers, or a law firm — impossible! I ended up dropping the case, because I couldn't find anyone to handle it for me.

I was bitter; very bitter. Bitter about the way I had been treated in the media; bitter because, even in hindsight, I still don't know how I could have handled the entire Infinity situation any differently. I had a president who was a trained securities lawyer who had told me that the purchase was legit. I had a major law firm — to whom I paid a quarter million in fees over the years — advise me it was legal; another lawyer from another large firm even declared the same thing.

Then the Ontario Securities Commission came along and told me, "No, it's not okay." How interesting that our investment of $1.5 million remains in that Income Trust to this day, in spite of its apparent illegality. The OSC never requested that it be taken out. What a world.

Of course, we can learn from experiences, learn from our mistakes. And boy, have I done plenty of both.

What I learned most from the glorious rise and ignoble fall of Fortune and Infinity is that as you embark on new ventures in life, you are going to encounter challenges that you never anticipated. If we could predict what lies ahead, then people would never make mistakes, or get into these situations, because they would always be expecting, and hence, planning for them.

But we simply cannot anticipate every possible scenario, so we try to plan as best as we can for all possibilities. That's why we take out car and house and life insurance (and critical care, if we're smart; see my section called Wealth, below).

As difficult and as challenging as my life has been, over the past half-dozen years, many good things happened. Although my relationship with my partner, Lori, was often strained, we now have a beautiful, bright little girl, Julia. Lori has been a true pillar of strength to me, and has kept me going through all this.

All told, I witnessed the sale of my two great creations, Fortune Financial and the Infinity family of funds, on the last day of August, 1999; the death of my father just a few months earlier, on April 13, 1999; and the birth of my fourth daughter, on April 14, 2001.

But some things remain the same: I am still strongly committed to learning, reading on average three or four books every week. This is because I still firmly believe that knowledge is power, and I must continue to feed my mind with quality ideas. It is only a matter of time before some of those seeds start growing and bearing fruit. It hasn't always happened exactly like I thought it would, or wanted it to, but that's the way life is: unpredictable.

What I see now, as I write these words in the first months of 2003, is that the newest seeds in my life have been sewn, and that many of them are coming to fruition.

The other thing I've learned in my first half-century is that when you are going in a particular direction, and you believe firmly in the journey on which you have embarked, and in the destination you have set for yourself, then you are going to get there. Oh, there will be detours, and you won't always end up going down the same road you had chosen. But you will get where you are going.

And here I am, after all the glories and the heartbreak of Fortune Financial and Infinity Mutual Funds — and I have never been more committed to continuing to strive to become a better person — to push myself — and to take hundreds, even thousands, of others along with me on this very exciting ride into the future. A future which now has a new name: Destiny Health Solutions.

SECTION
TWO

WEALTH:

PRACTICAL, REALISTIC MONEY
MANAGEMENT STRATEGIES

MONEY-MANAGEMENT
STRATEGIES FROM SOMEONE
WHO HAS BEEN THERE

Now that I have shared with you some of the highlights — and lowlights — of the first half-century of my life as a Third World child and First World entrepreneur, this is the ideal place to discuss what I have learned from several decades of working in the insurance and financial planning fields. You may be surprised to read some of the things I'll share with you in the following chapters, since many of them might seem to fly in the face of the work I did. But like any intelligent person, I have tried to learn from my mistakes.

What I have learned during my years in various aspects of financial planning — ranging from investing to insurance, tax planning to estate planning — can be summed up with some brief initial thoughts:

- We are all drowning in information, but actually starved for real knowledge.
- The financial services industry tends to care more about their success (mutual funds sold, insurance policies "closed") than the success of the people that they are purportedly serving.
- The majority of Canadians are either under-insured, or have the wrong type of insurance.

- Canadians can significantly (and legally) reduce the amount of taxes they pay.
- Stockbrokers and analysts are wrong more often than they are right in their stock-picking ability.
- Canadians — all people, in fact — need to be educated about the proven fact that the only investment strategy that works over time is to invest in "indexes" (such as the Standard & Poor 500 or the Toronto Stock Exchange 300), and to hold, not trade, their investments.
- Hard-working men and women do not have equal opportunity in the financial marketplace, since they face a structure-bias that is based on wealth.
- A new form of democracy is required in the financial world to create equal opportunity for all of us.
- By providing our citizens with the right financial knowledge and tools, families will once again be able to re-start their "dream machines" and have hope for the future.

Talking about the world of wealth creation and wealth management is worthy of dozens of books, and, indeed, I wrote one a few years ago, called *Take Control of Your Financial Destiny.* But since the book you are presently reading is dedicated to several topics — my own life in business, as well as the goals of Health, Wealth and Happiness — I will attempt to condense my major recommendations into MONEY MANAGEMENT STRATEGIES. These can be divided into four parts, and each deserves a chapter of its own.

CHAPTER TEN

INVESTMENT
PLANNING
STRATEGIES

Next to interpersonal relationships, money is probably more misunder-
stood than anything else in the world. I am not about to play
psychologist, but I do know one key thing about the dollar, and how to make
it grow: INVESTING CAN BE SIMPLE! Warren Buffett, the world's most successful investor, once said, *"There seems to be some perverse human
characteristic that likes to make easy things difficult."*

How right he was.

The first thing you should do to simplify the investment process is to
acquire a good understanding of the various investment vehicles available:
bonds, GICs, mortgages, gold and other precious metals, real estate, stocks,
and treasury bills.

Avoid complicated concepts such as hedging, derivatives, mean reversion,
portfolio optimization, risk-adjusted returns, and standard deviation. *These
are wonderful in theory, but meaningless when it comes to how you invest your
money.* Investing does *not* have to be difficult. Finance professionals use all
these big words the way medical doctors love to use Latin to describe the
problems their patients suffer from — in order to keep us common folk in
the dark. (By the way, if you ever hear two doctors conferring and mumbling

that your illness is "iatrogenic," that means it's "doctor-caused." *No wonder they like to use Latin!*)

It's a way for money managers and financial advisors to keep you out of the loop, making sure that you'll have to depend upon them — the experts — for assistance and guidance, you poor fool, you.

My goal in these four chapters is the exact opposite: *I want to show you how surprisingly simple it is to create and follow a very successful investment strategy.* In these pages we employ the same concept that Bill Clinton used during his first presidential campaign: "K.I.S.S." — "Keep It Simple, Stupid!" We are not, of course, suggesting that you, the reader, are stupid; rather, that *it's stupid to make simple things complex.*

Our educational system has done a remarkably good job of taking simple things in life and making them complex. We all went through this in our youth, especially in high school or university. Warren Buffett, who was a student and friend of Benjamin Graham, the great, late scholar of value investing, once noted that Graham's theories are seldom included in college curricula today because they just aren't difficult enough. Instead, schools teach more difficult, less useful theories.

The business schools, too, reward complex behaviour over simple behaviour, even though simple behaviour is usually far more effective.

The investment industry is also to blame. Over the years, we have seen, over and over again, how investment analysts, stock brokers, and mutual fund salespeople have used complexity to confuse the public into believing that these money men have some kind of supernatural power to predict the future.

As Jack Trout, the author of *The Power of Simplicity,* writes, "Everything we have learned in the Industrial Age has tended to create more and more complication. I think that more and more people are learning that *you have to simplify, not complicate.* Simplicity is the ultimate sophistication!"

We agree.

DON'T BELIEVE EVERYTHING YOU READ

I am sure that you have seen on numerous television channels, and read in countless magazines, newspapers and newsletters, items on topics such as these:

- "The old formulas for evaluating stocks are no longer valid, because this is the New Economy!" Again and again, through 1999 and early 2000, we saw hundreds of companies, most of them "hi-tech," which had huge losses, no earnings, no profits, and maybe no chance to ever achieve either of the latter two, become suddenly worth billions of dollars as investors rushed to buy their equities.

- Then, when the Nasdaq dropped 50%, we saw hundreds of these hi-tech stocks drop precipitously by 60–90%, and heard these same analysts, brokers, and mutual funds salespeople quickly (but belatedly) tell the public that "the market is far too high" and "these tech stocks are overpriced." (Funny how a stock trading at $600 a share early in 2000, and projected by these "experts" to hit $1,000, suddenly became "overpriced" according to the same experts when it dropped 50%, 80%, even 95% . . . Why didn't they warn us about this "overpricing" *before* the stocks collapsed?)

- Dozens — no, hundreds — of "marketing geniuses" warned investors to stay away from the stock market in the early 1990s, fearing that it was going up too quickly, too universally, too frantically. Of course, the early 1990s marked the beginning of the longest "bull market" in world history, when countless investors around the world became wealthy by putting their money into stocks and equity mutual funds. One wonders how many people missed out on that glorious explosion of growth and profits, which continued into early 2000, because of the professional chicken littles?

What is the answer, then? Maybe the best statement, once again, comes from the wise and witty Warren Buffett, who writes, *"Investment must be rational; if you can't understand it, don't do it!"*

Powerful words. But how does one go about gaining an understanding of investment so one can plan properly?

A good start is to read these chapters on money management strategies very, very carefully. With some basic knowledge about investments, you can usually do a lot better than you will by getting "advice" from these so-called "experts." As Buffett has also observed, "You don't need to be a rocket scientist. Investing is not a game where the guy with the 160 IQ beats the guy with the 130 IQ."

Indeed, it's often the exact opposite. One needs simple knowledge, not a high IQ, to be able to invest wisely and successfully.

TIPS FOR SIMPLIFYING YOUR INVESTMENT PLANNING

Here are some important concepts that can help simplify the investment planning process.

1. **Remember: Knowledge is power.** In my earlier book on financial planning, I listed dozens of important — and simple — concepts, such as compound growth, debt management, dollar-cost averaging, index investing, IPOs, leveraging, market timing, mutual funds, RRSPs, RESPs, RRIFs, the Rule of 72, and systematic withdrawal plans. My two decades of experience in this industry (coupled with all the business mistakes that anyone could possibly make) have taught me that nothing is more valuable to an investor than being informed and knowledgeable.

2. **Avoid actively managed mutual funds.** They make money for mutual fund firms, not people. Do yourself a favour: stop reading those full-page ads for particular mutual funds. The information you receive is almost guaranteed to make you fail at your investments.

The mutual fund companies win when you buy into their products, and their countless salespeople win when they sell them to you — but you almost always lose. Above all, avoid getting suckered by the past performance of actively managed mutual funds. Arguably, the biggest investment mistake people make is focusing on last year's mutual fund performance, rather than on what really drives returns. As John Bogle, author of *Common Sense on Mutual Funds*, writes, "I do not believe that investment advisors can identify, in advance, the top-performing managers — no one can! — and I'd avoid those who claim they can do so." *Invest in index funds, and avoid actively managed funds as if they were poison ivy.* (More on recommended Index Funds, below.)

3. **Do not try to time the market.** Accept the proven fact that market timing does not work. It never has and it never will. If you choose to purchase individual stocks, then choose great businesses, and hold their shares for long periods of time. You cannot lose this way — not over many years. Recall Warren Buffett's inspired words: "If you're at a baseball game and you only pay attention to the scoreboard, you are going to miss the plays." Surely it's what's happening on the playing field — the hits, the strikeouts, the home runs, the pitching, the stolen bases — that is worthy of interest, not what the constantly moving numbers on the scoreboard tell you. You shouldn't care at all about those numbers. If you watch the game, you'll know who wins, all right.

If you don't feel that you have the ability or knowledge to select shares of great businesses, then simply invest in a few stock indexes, which follow the movements of dozens, even hundreds of the most successful firms in the world. Most of the world's greatest investors agree that index funds are the best and safest way to grow your money — since those indexes are always growing and compounding and gaining in value over the long term.

You will be wise to heed the advice of author Larry Swedroe in his superb *What Wall Street Doesn't Want You to Know:*

- There is an overwhelming body of evidence to support the view that believing in the ability of market timers is the equivalent of believing astrologers can predict the future.
- We have two classes of forecasters: those who don't know and those who don't know they don't know.
- Trying to time investment decisions doesn't work, because most of the action occurs over brief, and unexpected, periods of time. Unless investors are always fully invested, they are highly likely to miss out on much of the market's gains.
- Active fund managers do not protect investors from bear markets.
- If the advice of market timers had any value, they would make far more money following their own advice than selling it.

- Treat "expert" opinion as entertainment.

Powerful insights!

4. **Choose your advisors carefully.** When it comes to investing, this is one area that I am probably more qualified to talk about than almost anyone else in Canada, and the reason is simple. As you just read in the first section of this book, I built one of the largest financial services organizations in Canada, with some 750 financial advisors. My experiences taught me that *investment strategies are doomed to fail as long as you are getting your advice from a poorly trained, commission-motivated salesperson.* Believe me, the vast majority of so-called advisors in this country fall into this category. I wrote at length on this dilemma in my study of financial advisors, in my last book, *Take Control of Your Financial Destiny.*

5. **Start investing early.** The earlier you start putting money away in your life, the easier it will become to get into the "investing habit," and the more time your money will have to grow. Time may be the enemy of our faces and waistlines, but it is the friend — the best friend — of every investor. *A long-term approach to investing will inevitably benefit you.*

6. **Invest regularly.** Dollar-cost averaging is a powerful wealth accumulation strategy. By investing regularly ($75 one month, $400 another, $150 another), you take advantage of the inevitable ups and downs of interest rates, stock prices, mutual fund evaluations, and indexes. Let market fluctuations — like time and compound growth — be your friend.

7. **Look continually for higher returns.** The charts in my earlier book on finances prove the importance of maximizing the return on your invest-ments: even a one percent difference could mean many thousands of dollars to you over a long period of time. Here is a snapshot example:
- **The value of a $10,000 investment after 25 years, if it is earning an annual 10% return, will be $108,347.**
- **The same investment with an 11% return: $135,854.**

The difference of $27,508 is all because of a one percent increase! Think of all the clothes, the vacations, the pleasures that amount of money could buy — all from that seemingly tiny one percent! By the way, the phenomenal impact of merely one percent a year is one more reason why it is best to go the Index Fund route, since the annual charge to handle these funds is far below all other mutual fund purchases. So, you are *already* ahead of the game with these funds.

For the highest returns over a long period, let *equity investments* become the cornerstone of your investment strategy. (By equities, I mean stocks. Index Funds are made up of the most important, successful stocks listed in the index of each stock exchange.) Here is some clear evidence: The end value of a $10,000 investment over a 30-year period — June, 1970 through June, 2000 — is as follows:

- **If invested in treasury bills: $115,583.**
- **If invested in bonds: $228,923.**
- **If invested in equities (based on the U.S. Stock Total Return Index): $815,186.**

Which return would you rather have?

8. **Diversify your investments.** In the discussion of asset allocation in *Take Control of your Financial Destiny,* I stressed how essential it is to *diversify.* Your portfolio should be diversified by countries and sectors. This, too, is accomplished by all Index Funds, by their very nature; the indexes of every stock market are made up of the finest equities in every sector there is.

9. **Pay as little tax as possible.** Taxes are probably the largest expense that investors incur — even greater than management fees or commissions — so *plan your investments in such a way as to avoid or minimize taxes payable on your profits.* Here are some helpful hints to remember:

- Active fund management imposes a large negative impact on aftertax returns. As the famous mutual fund genius John Templeton once stated, "For all long-term investors, there is only one objective — maximum total return after taxes."
- Past tax efficiency of active managers is *not* a predictor of future tax efficiency. (Ever notice how professional sports teams, even with the same players and coaches, *rarely* win the championships year after year?)

- Investors in actively managed funds can receive taxable distributions even during years when the values of their funds fall. This is a lose-lose situation!
- Capital gains taxes, when combined with transaction costs and fees, make investing in indexes the only logical investment strategy. (See chapter 12 of this Wealth Section, below, on tax planning strategies.) It isn't what you *earn* as much as what you *save* that counts in the long run.

10. **Prepare a plan — and stick with it.** Decide on an investment strategy, prepare a plan, write it down — and stick with it. Make sure that you review your plan every six months, just in case you need to make any changes. Remember, no one ever plans to fail. But people *do* fail to plan. As a witty commentator once noted, "If you don't know where you're going, you'll probably end up somewhere else."

Investing is not an exact science. The challenge is to construct a model that addresses the uncertainties we face. *My goal is to demonstrate how investments, and the market, really work, and thus provide you with the understanding necessary to make wise investment choices.* The end result will be that you will have the specific knowledge needed to build a portfolio that meets your unique situation.

A POWERFUL BUY & HOLD INVESTMENT STRATEGY: THE INDEX ADVANTAGE

Index Funds are a straightforward, and low-cost way to invest in Canadian and international markets. This method of investing has become one of the fastestgrowing choices of the world's major pension funds and some of the world's greatest investors.

While traditional mutual fund, stock, or bond investing generally tries to "beat the market," *index investing is different.* It emulates the performance of a particular market index, or benchmark, such as the Toronto Stock Exchange (TSX) 300 in Canada, or the Standard & Poor (S&P) 500 Index in the United States. This is achieved by holding the same securities as the index, or a representative sample, in the same proportions.

This so-called "passive" approach is what sets index funds apart from conventional, actively-managed mutual funds. There is *no attempt* to out-perform the index by using traditional, active money management techniques that try to identify promising stocks, industry sectors or geo-graphic regions. Nor is there any attempt to time the market by increasing or decreasing cash positions.

The underlying assumption of indexing is that markets around the world are becoming increasingly efficient, as stock and bond prices absorb and reflect news and information at a much faster rate than ever before. The more efficient a market, the more difficult it is to gain an edge through the search, purchase, and sale of "under-priced" assets. So, *over time, it is less costly and, in many instances, more profitable, to index.* And because stock index funds track the performance of major stock market indexes, these funds are also one of the least complicated to follow. Open a newspaper; if the market is up, your stock index fund is probably up, too.

Indexing — The Right Idea at the Right Time

Indexing emerged over 25 years ago from academic research known as "Modern Portfolio Theory." *The academics found that one of the best ways to maximize return and to minimize risk was to "own the market" itself.* By doing so, investors could earn higher rates of return by holding a broad basket, or index of stock, rather than by choosing a select few.

U.S. Corporations and large pension funds were the first to embrace an indexing investment strategy in the early 1970s. In 1976, index funds were introduced to the American public, and came to Canada in 1985. Today, indexing is one of the fastest-growing segments of the mutual fund industry, and with good reason.

REASONS TO USE THE INDEXING STRATEGY

Simplicity and Transparency

Indexing strategies are transparent and totally unambiguous; what you see is, quite literally, what you get. An index fund allows you to focus your atten-tion on, and dedicate your energy to, the risk return trade-offs of different asset classes, instead of trying to second guess the investment styles of many different managers, whom you are always paying big bucks to do this "favour" for you.

Stop wasting your time on the useless exercise of trying to figure out the styles of countless money managers, and listening to countless salespeople whose ability to pick the "right" fund is as good as fortune telling!

1. Lower Fees

It may surprise you that the lower fees charged by index funds actually translate into higher returns! Active money managers incur higher commissions, higher management fees, and higher bid/ask-spread costs.

One estimate shows that the trading costs for active portfolios are about six times greater than they are for passive investing.

One reason for lower fees with the index strategy is that index managers, by the very nature of their work, do not need the large staff of research analysts and portfolio managers that are inevitably required by actively traded funds. Have you ever wondered why you are paying such large amounts of money over the years — through management fees — to have analysts give you their favourite predictions? (In other words, "wild guesses.") Actually, those thoughts usually end up being as profound as "There is a 50/50 chance that our market might go up."

2. Tax Efficiency

Taxes are sometimes left out of the investing equations, but they are an essential part of determining your real return. Investing in an index fund can significantly reduce taxes.

3. Effective Diversification

With an indexing strategy, you can create a well-diversified portfolio of bonds, cash, stocks, and more, and this diversification helps you to reduce risk. For example, if you want to diversify within your stock portfolio, you can choose from among the following U.S. indexes: The Dow Jones Industrial Average Index, The Standard & Poor, and The Nasdaq, as well as The Canadian TSX 300 Composite Index and the TSX 60. There are also International indexes, European indexes, Japanese indexes, and many more — over 250 around the world.

4. Performance

Study after study has shown that indexing consistently outperforms active management — which is, in many cases, merely an attempt at market timing with a college education. As your parents probably taught you years ago, "Why pay for nothing?"

5. Increased Foreign Diversification

Many Canadian investors understandably wish to diversify their investments beyond our borders, but current rules for registered tax-deferred plans limit foreign content. RRSP-eligible index funds, however, offer an alternative approach that provides real exposure to foreign market indexes, and the federal government still accepts these as Canadian content for tax purposes.

In brief, indexing should certainly be a major part of any intelligent, knowledgeable investor's portfolio.

But don't just take my word for it. Think about the following:

What some of the World's Greatest Investors Have to Say About Indexing

- *Warren Buffett (who is the second richest person in the world):* "If you do not have the ability to pick great companies to invest in, then your next best choice should be to invest in the INDEXES."
- *Charles Schwab (Founder and Chairman of a world-renowned money management firm):* ". . . 75% of my personal money is invested in the major INDEXES. . . ."
- *Ted Cadsby (Author of* The Power of Index Funds," *and* CEO *of* CIBC *Investments of Canada):* "If you want to increase the odds of investing in a 'winner' and more importantly, reduce the odds of investing in a loser, then indexing is the way to go."
- *Fortune Magazine:* "Building a portfolio around an index fund isn't really settling for average (or a little better). It's about refusing to believe in Magic."
- *John Bogle (Author of* Common Sense on Mutual Funds *and the Founder of the world's largest mutual fund company, Vanguard Investments):*
  "The idea that a bell rings to signal when investors should get

135

into or out of the stock market is simply not credible. After nearly 50 years in this business, I do not know of anybody who has done it successfully and consistently. I don't even know anybody who knows anybody who has done it successfully and consistently. Yet market timing appears to be increasingly embraced by mutual fund investors and professional managers of fund portfolios alike. Index funds will always outperform most actively managed funds because investors, as a group, can do better than the market — collectively, we are the market."

Are you convinced? Even if you are, there are other worthwhile investment vehicles to consider. Here is a list:

Another Alternative to Mutual Funds: Segregated Funds
This is a further investment strategy that can give you safety, security, and peace of mind. First things first:

What Are Segregated Funds?
Segregated funds offer many of the same benefits as mutual funds, such as professional management, diversification, convenience, and the ability to transfer between funds. But they have many attractive benefits that mutual funds do not have.

Maturity Guarantee
Most segregated funds give you the option to guarantee 75% or 100% of your principal (less withdrawals and fees) at maturity, ten years from the date of contract issue.

Death Guarantee
If the owner of the fund dies within the ten-year period, the beneficiary of the investment will receive either the current market value or the original investment, whichever is greater.

Lock in Your Gains
Another very attractive feature of a segregated fund is that it allows you to

lock in your gain with the "reset" option. By resetting your guarantees, both the Maturity Guarantee and the Death Benefit Guarantee, if there have been any gains in your investment, you will replace all existing guarantees in that account with the new, higher amounts. Note: different Segregated Funds have different restrictions on the frequency of your ability to use the "lock in" and "reset" options.

Creditor Protection
Should you declare bankruptcy, your segregated fund will be shielded from your creditor's reach, as long as the fund was purchased a year ago and you have a named beneficiary.

Probate Fees Exemption
By naming a beneficiary to receive the death benefit under the policy, an investor may be able to bypass probate fees.

Insurance Protection
To the extent that the Maturity and Death Benefit Guarantees of segregated funds are applicable, these same amounts are covered up to $60,000 by Comp Corp., the Insurance Company Protection Association.

Tax Benefits
Income made by a segregated fund is allocated monthly, so you don't have to pay taxes on gains that arose before you owned units, as you would have to do with mutual funds.

Also, if a segregated fund loses capital in a given year, the unit holders can claim capital gains made on other investments. Taxation rules allow the allocation of capital gains or losses without cashing in units held. Mutual funds do not have this ability.

Lower Fees
Management Fees on most segregated funds are lower than many mutual funds.

Greater Investment Options

Investors have a wider selection of investment opportunities with segregated funds when using the preferred strategy of "passive" vs. "active" investing for their RRSP.

BENEFITS OF THE GUARANTEES

- **Provide you with exposure to unlimited growth potential of index-based mutual funds while safeguarding your principal**
- **Reduce the overall investment risk and volatility of your portfolio**
- **Enable you to invest worry-free**

Now, before we move on to Insurance, Tax and Estate Planning Strategies, I have one more powerful suggestion for your Investment Planning:

A PROVEN SUCCESSFUL INVESTMENT ALTERNATIVE TO STOCKS: EXCHANGE TRADED FUNDS (ETFs)

ETFs, or Exchange Traded Funds, almost always referred to as iUnits or iShares, combine the advantages of stocks with those of Index Funds. Like stocks, they are liquid, easy to use, and can be traded in whatever number of shares one wishes. Like Index Funds, they provide diversification, market tracking, and low expenses. ETFs also behave like stocks, in that their prices will fluctuate, and there is no assurance that ETFs will meet the investment objectives of their underlying indexes.

ETFs trade on major stock exchanges the same way as shares of any publicly held company. It's easy to buy and sell these products through any brokerage account — indeed, discount brokers are recommended. They can be traded any time during normal trading hours, using all the portfolio management approaches associated with stocks.

But ETFs are *not* shares of a company; they are shares of a portfolio which is designed to closely track the performance of any one of an array of market indices. Here are several that I recommend highly, that are listed on the Toronto Stock Exchange (TSX) and major U.S. stock exchanges. In the case of the former, Canadian ones, they are all 100% RRSP eligible:

ETFS LISTED ON THE TORONTO STOCK EXCHANGE (TSX)

NAME OF ETF	OBJECTIVE	TICKER SYMBOL
iUnits S&P/TSX 60 Index Fund (i60 Fund) (Large cap Canadian Equity)	i60 Fund seeks to provide long-term capital growth by investing in shares of the 60 companies that make up the S&P/TSX 60 Index.	XIU
iUnits S&P/TSX 60 Capped Index Fund (i60C Fund) (Large cap Canadian Equity)	i60C Fund is an index fund that seeks to provide long-term capital growth by investing in shares of the 60 companies that make up the S&P/TSX 60 Capped Index in the same proportion as they are reflected in the Index.	XIC
iUnits S&P/TSX Canadian MidCap Index Fund (iMidCap Fund) (MidCap Canadian Sector)	iMidCap Fund is an index fund that seeks to provide long-term capital growth by investing in shares of the 60 companies that make up the S&P/TSX Canadian MidCap index in the same proportion as they are reflected in the Index.	XMD
iUnits S&P/TSX Canadian Energy Index Fund (iEnergy Fund) (Canadian Energy Sector)	iEnergy Fund is an index fund that seeks to provide long-term capital growth by investing in shares of the companies that make up the S&P/TSX Canadian Energy Index in the same proportion as they are reflected in the Index.	XEG
iUnits S&P/TSX Canadian Financials Index Fund (iFin Fund) (Canadian Financial Sector)	iFin Fund is an index fund that seeks to provide long-term capital growth by investing in shares of the companies that make up the S&P/TSX Canadian Financials Index in the same proportion as they are reflected in the Index.	XFN

NAME OF ETF	OBJECTIVE	TICKER SYMBOL
iUnits S&P/TSX Canadian Gold Index Fund (iGold Fund) (Canadian Gold Sector)	iGold Fund is an index fund that seeks to provide long-term capital growth by investing in shares of the companies that make up the S&P/TSX Canadian Gold Index in the same proportion as they are reflected in the Index.	XGD
iUnits S&P/TSX Canadian Information Technology Index Fund (iIT Fund) (Canadian IT Sector)	iIT Fund is an index fund that seeks to provide long-term capital growth by investing in shares of the companies that make up the S&P/TSX Canadian Information Technology Index in the same proportion as they are reflected in the Index.	XIT
iUnits S&P/TSX Canadian reit Index Fund (ireit Fund) (Canadian Real Estate Income Trusts)	iREIT Fund seeks to provide income and long-term capital by investing in real estate income trusts (REITs) that make up the S&P/TSX Canadian REIT Index in the same proportion as they are reflected in the Index.	XRE
iUnits Government of Canada 5-year Bond Fund (iG5) (Mid-term Government of Canada Bond)	iG5 Fund seeks to provide interest income and capital gains potential by replicating as closely as possible the performance of a bond issued by the Government of Canada with a five-year term to maturity.	XGV
iUnits Government of Canada 10-year Bond Fund (iG10 Fund) (Mid-term Government of Canada Bond)	iG10 Fund seeks to provide interest income and capital gains potential by replicating as closely as possible the performance of a bond issued by the Government of Canada with a ten-year term to maturity.	XGX

NAME OF ETF	OBJECTIVE	TICKER SYMBOL
iUnits S&P 500 Index RSP Fund (i500R) (100% RSP-Eligible US Equity)	The i500R fund seeks to provide long-term capital growth by matching to the extent possible the return of the S&P 500 Index, while remaining fully RSP-eligible. To achieve this goal, the i500R Fund primarily invests in exchange traded futures contracts based on the S&P 500 Index and in high-quality short-term money market instruments.	XSP
iUnits MSCI International Equity Index RSP Fund (ilntR Fund) (100% RSP-Eligible International Equity)	The ilntR fund seeks to provide long-term capital growth by matching to the extent possible the return of the MSCI EAFE Index, while remaining fully RSP-eligible. To achieve this goal, the ilntR Fund primarily invests in exchange traded futures contracts based on the stock market indices of countries that are included in the MSCI EAFE Index as well as high-quality short-term money market instruments.	XIN

ETFS LISTED ON MAJOR U.S. STOCK EXCHANGES

iSHARES S&P INDEX FUND SERIES

iShares S&P/TOPIX 150 Index Fund	The iShares S&P/TOPIX Index Fund seeks investment results that correspond to the performance of the Japanese equity market as represented by the S&P/Toyko Stock Price 150 Index.	ITF

NAME	OBJECTIVE	TICKER SYMBOL
iShares S&P 100 Index Fund	The iShares S&P 100 Index Fund seeks investment results that correspond to the performance of U.S. large-cap stocks from a broad range of industries, as represented by the S&P 100 Index.	OEF
iShares S&P 500/Barra Growth Index Fund (IVW)	The iShares S&P 500/BARRA Growth Index Fund seeks investment results that correspond to the performance of U.S. large-cap growth stocks, as represented by the S&P 500/BARRA Growth Index. This index consists of those companies with the highest price-to-book ratios within the S&P 500 Index.	IVW
iShares S&P 500/BARRA Value Index Fund	The iShares S&P 500/BARRA Value Index Fund seeks investment results that correspond to the performance of U.S. large-cap value stocks, as represented by the S&P 500/BARRA Value Index. This index consists of those companies with the lowest-price-to-book ratios within the S&P 500 Index.	IVE
Shares S&P 500 Index Fund	The iShares S&P 500 Index Fund seeks investment results that correspond to the performance of U.S. large-cap stocks, as represented by the S&P 500 Index.	IVV
iShares S&P Europe 350 Index Fund	The iShares S&P Europe 350 Index Fund seeks investment results that correspond to the performance of stocks across a broad range of industries in continental Europe, as represented by the S&P Europe 350 Index.	IEV

NAME	OBJECTIVE	TICKER SYMBOL
iShares S&P Global 100 Index Fund	The iShares Global 100 Index Fund seeks investment results that correspond to the performance of global large-cap stocks in leading transnational companies, as represented by the S&P Global 100 Index.	100
iShares S&P Global Energy Sector Index Fund	The iShares S&P Global Energy Sector Index Fund seeks investment results that correspond to the performance of companies in the energy sector of the S&P Global 1200 Index as represented by the S&P Global Energy Sector Index. Component companies include: oil equipment and services, oil exploration and production, and oil refineries.	IXC
iShares S&P Global Financials Sector Index Fund	The iShares S&P Financials Sector Index Fund seeks investment results that correspond to the performance of companies in the financials sector of the S&P Global 1200 Index as represented by the S&P Financials Sector Index. Component companies include: major banks, diversified financial companies, insurance companies, real estate companies, savings and loan associations, and securities brokers.	IXG
iShares S&P Global Healthcare Sector Index Fund	The iShares S&P Global Healthcare Sector Index Fund seeks investment results that correspond to the performance of companies in the health care sector of the S&P Global 1200 Index as represented by the S&P Global Healthcare Sector Index. Component companies include: health care providers, biotechnology companies and manufacturers of medical supplies, and advanced medical devices and pharmaceuticals.	IXJ

iShares MSCI Index Fund Series

NAME	OBJECTIVE	TICKER SYMBOL
iShares MSCI Australia Index Fund	The iShares MSCI Australia Index Fund seeks to provide investment results that correspond generally to the price and yield performance of publicly traded securites in the aggregate in the Australian market, as measured by the MSCI Australia Index.	EWA
iShares MSCI Austria Index Fund	The iShares MSCI Austria Index Fund seeks to provide investment results that correspond generally to the price and yield performance of publicly traded securities in the aggregate in the Austrian market, as represented by the MSCI Austria Index.	EWO
iShares MSCI Belgium Index Fund	The iShares MSCI Belgium Index Fund seeks to provide investment results that correspond generally to the price and yield performance of publicly traded securities in the aggregate in the Belgian market, as measured by the MSCI Belgium Index.	EWK
iShares MSCI Brazil Index Fund	The iShares MSCI Brazil Index Fund seeks to provide investment results that correspond generally to the price and yield performance of publicly traded securities in the aggregate in the Brazilian market, as measured by the MSCI Brazil Index.	EW7
iShares MSCI Canada Index Fund	The iShares MSCICanada Index Fund seeks to provide investment results that correspond generally to the price and yield performance of publicly traded securities in the aggregate in the Canadian market, as measured by the MSCI Canada Index.	EWC

NAME	OBJECTIVE	TICKER SYMBOL
iShares MSCI EAFE Index Fund	The iShares MSCI EAFE Index Fund invests in most of the same stocks listed in the MSCI EAFE Index. The Index was developed by Morgan Stanley Capital International Inc. as an equity benchmark for international stock performance. The Index includes stocks from Europe, Australasia, and the Far East.	EFA
iShares MSCI EMU Index Fund	The iShares MSCI EMU Index Fund seeks to provide investment results that correspond generally to the price and yield performance of publicly traded securities in the aggregate in the European Monetary Union (EMU) markets, as measured by the MSCI EMU Index.	EZU
iShares MSCI France Index Fund	The iShares MSCI France Index Fund seeks to provide investment results that correspond generally to the price and yield performance of publicly traded securities in the aggregate in the French market, as measured by the MSCI France Index.	EWQ
iShares MSCI Germany Index Fund	The iShares MSCI Germany Index Fund seeks to provide investment results that correspond generally to the price and yield performance of publicly traded securities in the aggregate in the German market, as measured by the MSCI Germany Index.	EWG
iShares MSCI Hong Kong Index Fund	The iShares MSCI Hong Kong Index Fund seeks to provide investment results that correspond generally to the price and yield performance of publicly traded securities in the aggregate in the Hong Kong market, as measured by the MSCI Hong Kong Index.	EWH

NAME	OBJECTIVE	TICKER SYMBOL
iShares MSCI Italy Index Fund	The iShares MSCI Italy Index Fund seeks to provide investment results that correspond generally to the price and yield performance of publicly traded securities in the aggregate in the Italian market, as measured by the MSCI Italy Index.	EWI
iShares MSCI Japan Index Fund	The iShares MSCI Japan Index Fund seeks to provide investment results that correspond generally to the price and yield performance of publicly traded securities in the aggregate in the Japanese market, as measured by the MSCI Japan Index.	EWJ
iShares MSCI Malaysia Index Fund	The iShares MSCI Malaysia Index Fund seeks to provide investment results that correspond generally to the price and yield performance of publicly traded securities in the aggregate in the Malaysian market, as measured by the MSCI Malaysia Index.	EWM
iShares MSCI Mexico Index Fund	The iShares MSCI Mexico Index Fund seeks to provide investment results that correspond generally to the price and yield performance of publicly traded securities in the aggregate in the Mexican market, as measured by the MSCI Mexico Index.	EWW
iShares MSCI Netherlands Index Fund	The iShares MSCI Netherlands Index Fund seeks to provide investment results that correspond generally to the price and yield performance of publicly traded securities in the aggregate in the Dutch market, as measured by the MSCI Netherlands Index.	EWN

NAME	OBJECTIVE	TICKER SYMBOL
iShares MSCI Pacific Ex-Japan Index Fund	The iShares MSCI Pacific ex-Japan Index Fund seeks investment results that correspond to the performance of publicly traded securities in the Australia, Hong Kong, New Zealand, and Singapore markets as represented by the MSCI Pacific ex-Japan Index.	EPP
iShares MSCI Singapore Index Fund	The iShares MSCI Singapore Index Fund seeks to provide investment results that correspond generally to the price and yield performance of publicly traded securities in the aggregate in the Singaporean market, as measured by the MSCI Singapore Index.	EWS
iShares MSCI South Korea Index Fund	The iShares MSCI South Korea Index Fund seeks to provide investment results that correspond generally to the price and yield performance of publicly traded securities in the aggregate in the South Korean market, as measured by the MSCI Korea Index.	EWY
iShares MSCI Spain Index Fund	The iShares MSCI Spain Index Fund seeks to provide investment results that correspond generally to the price and yield performance of publicly traded securities in the aggregate in the Spanish market, as measured by the MSCI Spain Index.	EWP
iShares MSCI Sweden Index Fund	The iShares MSCI Sweden Index Fund seeks to provide investment results that correspond generally to the price and yield performance of publicly traded securities in the aggregate in the Swedish market, as measured by the MSCI Sweden Index.	EWD

NAME	OBJECTIVE	TICKER SYMBOL
iShares MSCI Switzerland Index Fund	The iShares MSCI Switzerland Index Fund seeks to provide investment results that correspond generally to the price and yield performance of publicly traded securities in the aggregate in the Swiss market, as measured by the MSCI Switzerland Index.	EWI
iShares MSCI Taiwan Index Fund	The iShares MSCI Taiwan Index Fund seeks to provide investment results that correspond generally to the price and yield performance of publicly traded securities in the aggregate in the Taiwanese market, as measured by the MSCI Taiwan Index.	EWT
iShares MSCI United Kingdom Index Fund	The iShares MSCI United Kingdom Index Fund seeks to provide investment results that correspond generally to the price and yield performance of publicly traded securities in the aggregate in the British market, as measured by the MSCI United Kingdom Index.	EWU

As you can see, I've listed over three dozen ETFs (iShares). This may seem like a large number, but each of them represents *hundreds* of quality companies from around the world. How much better than picking and choosing a handful of stocks, often from only one country or sector — always unsure of which are the best. I can assure you — after three decades in the financial planning business — that *Index Funds, Segregated Funds, and ETFs, are the most sensible ways to invest.*

CHAPTER ELEVEN

INSURANCE PLANNING STRATEGIES

Insurance planning is one of the most important aspects of wise money management. After all, don't we *all* want to protect the future of our family? If we truly do, then I urge everyone reading this book to purchase *low-cost* Life, Disability, and Critical Care Insurance. That is what this brief chapter is about.

To begin, forget what you know, or what you think you know, about insurance. Ignore what you've heard from insurance agents. Put aside your biases. Perhaps for the first time in your life, you are about to hear the *truth* about insurance — including a number of things that your insurance agency would rather you didn't know. No matter what you've been told, *there is one reason, and one reason only, for buying insurance:* **to protect against a financial loss.**

If there is no potential for financial loss, you simply do not need any insurance. Financial losses can occur if you die, if you are injured, or if you become sick. They can also be incurred if your property is damaged, destroyed, or stolen, or if you get sued. You *must* protect yourself financially if any of these events occur. And the best way to do this is by purchasing insurance to protect the amount, or value, of the asset that is at risk.

THE BASICS

Before you ever get caught in the morass of the insurance industry, always ask yourself three basic questions:

1. *Why do I need insurance?*
2. *How much insurance do I need?*
3. *What type of insurance should I buy?*

Once you've answered those questions (and don't worry if you're not sure about the answers right now — I'll help you gain the knowledge you need to determine the answers) you'll know what you are looking for.

All insurance is not created equal. For this reason, always work with an independent insurance agent or broker. As I insisted upon with my financial planning company, "independent agents" represent many carriers (whether mutual funds or insurance offerings), so they are free to shop the market for the best policy for you and your needs. *Never use an agent who represents only one company!*

Life insurance plays a very important role in your financial life. While many people find it confusing, the concepts are really not difficult. The hard part is winding your way through the maze of different deals available, and making sure you get what you need — *no more and no less* — and for the best price possible. And speaking of price . . .

HOW ARE INSURANCE RATES DETERMINED?

This is a crucial issue that you should understand, before we proceed. Most insurance companies use three factors to determine how much you pay for life insurance:

Mortality rates — the number of people who will probably die
 at each specific age.
Investment returns — the profit that the insurance companies
 receive by investing your premium over the years.
Operating expenses — the cost of running their business.

Although the first two factors have worked in favour of the public during recent years (people living longer; the stock markets doing remarkably well through most of the 1990s), these benefits have not been passed on to the public to the extent that they should be. I'll show you why this is true, in the next few pages.

TYPES OF LIFE INSURANCE

There are two basic different categories of life insurance: **term insurance** and **permanent insurance.** Let me save you a large chunk of money, possibly many thousands of dollars, with a single recommendation: *avoid the latter.* Under most circumstances, *term insurance is all you will need.* Here's a look at both kinds:

    Term Insurance: sometimes called Temporary Insurance, this covers you for a specific period of time. Like neapolitan ice cream, it comes in three flavours:

1) *Annual Renewable Term,* the cost of which can go up each year as you grow older (although this is not always the case, because of savings to insurance companies, discussed above).
2) *Level Term,* which locks in the cost for a specific period of time, or until you reach a specific age, such as 65 or 80.
3) *Decreasing Term,* which is probably the least attractive of all, since your coverage is reduced over time while the premium remains fixed.

Permanent Life Insurance is one of the least attractive products in the insurance industry. Here, too, there are three types:

1. *Whole Life,* which insures you, as the name implies, for your entire life. *Avoid this type of insurance at all costs!*
2. *Universal Life,* which was created by the insurance industry to combine insurance coverage and your investments. This type of insurance is appropriate for a small number of people.
3. *Variable Life,* which allows you to invest your "excess" premium in mutual funds.

"Whole Life" Insurance is usually defined as life insurance that remains in force during the entire lifetime of the insured, while building a savings element ("cash value"). "Universal Life" policies contract for a certain amount of life insurance coverage, but also include additional premiums to "invest" in a portfolio within that policy. In other words, Universal Life has two components: term insurance and an investment side. Naturally, the value of the latter depends on how well those investments perform.

HOW MUCH DO YOU NEED?

Or how little? Here is a simple form to help you determine how much life insurance you might need. Just fill in the blanks, then add them up to get the total:

Funeral Expenses, etc.:	_____
Final Expenses:	_____
Mortgage:	_____
Other Debts:	_____
Emergency Fund:	_____
Education Fund:	_____
Adjustment Period:	_____
Charitable Gifts:	_____
TOTAL:	_____

WHAT WILL IT COST?

To give you an idea of what term insurance costs, I've created a chart for your reference. The following assumes that you are in good health and a non-smoker. If so, and if you are paying much more than these rates, shop around. You can learn much from using the Internet, at least at the start.

Annual Premium for Ten-Year Renewable Term

Amount of Coverage

at age	$300,000	$500,000	$1,000,000
30	$209	$295	$515
35	$218	$295	$565
40	$241	$385	$745
45	$340	$550	$1,075
50	$523	$855	$1,660
55	$766	$1,200	$2,315
60	$1,190	$1,920	$3,770
65	$2,220	$3,650	$7,225

GETTING QUOTES AND PURCHASING THE POLICY

Once you have determined how much life insurance you need, you can obtain quotes by contacting your insurance agent and making sure that he or she sells you the insurance you need. Finally, if you determine that you no longer need life insurance coverage, you should cancel your policy as quickly as possible, much the same way as you would cancel your car or house insurance if you sold either of those assets. *Why pay for what you don't need?*

DISABILITY INSURANCE

You don't have any, do you? I have just two words on this subject, before I begin: *Christopher Reeve.* (Once the actor who flew through the air as *Super-man* in the popular movies of the same name — now a quadraplegic because of a fluke fall from a horse. Of course, none of us drive cars, or ever cross a street, do we?)

We often joke about catching a cold or the flu, and laugh at the old uncle who is always complaining about his aches and pains and the dozens of pills he downs every day. But becoming so ill that we are disabled is no laughing matter. You may be surprised to learn that *your largest financial asset* is not your house, your cottage, your car, even your company pension. Rather, *if you are working, your largest asset is almost certainly* <u>*your ability to produce an income*</u>. *Thus, the most important type of insurance one can purchase is disability income insurance.*

EVERYONE NEEDS DISABILITY INSURANCE

You actually need disability insurance *far more* than any other kind of insurance: more than life, health, home-owners, or even auto insurance. Yet most people do not purchase this kind of insurance. There are two main reasons why, and it's informative to look at them both:

Reason #1: It Won't Happen To Me!

Oh? Read these statistics, and if you don't weep, then at least shudder a bit: *Forty-eight percent of all mortgage foreclosures on houses in Canada are caused by disability.* After all, with no income, a family cannot make its mortgage payments. Furthermore, according to recent research, *about 90% of all families in which a disability occurs suffer from a marriage break-up.* (So much for "in sickness and in health.")

There are actuaries who make their living from figuring out things like how long smokers will live on average, what percentage of sisters of victims of breast cancer may be struck by the same disease, how long someone in their mid-60s with poor health is likely to live, and so on. The results of their research into the chances of disability are quite shocking. For instance, *the chances of someone becoming disabled for at least three months before the age of 65 are one in eight.* The chance of someone's house burning down is less than one in a thousand. But guess how many people have fire insurance on their homes? *Close to 100%.*

How many have disability coverage? *Only about one in seven!*

Actuaries have discovered other shocking facts as well. For instance, over one-third of any group of men and women between the ages of 45 and 65 will get diabetes, over 40% will contract heart disease, and 70% will experience hypertension during their lives. (Good luck to anyone who wants to purchase even term insurance after the illness is discovered.) And yet *over 85% of Canadians never purchase disability insurance!*

Reason #2: It's Way Too Costly

It is true that disability insurance does not come cheap, especially compared with term life insurance. The reality is, one really cannot afford to live without it.

GROUP DISABILITY INSURANCE

Many people who do have disability insurance acquired it because their employer provides it. These group insurance plans have a few problems that you should be aware of:

The cost of the coverage can increase.
- Your employer has the right to cancel it at any time.
- If you leave that employer, you lose your benefit.
  (Of course, you *never* lose the chance that you will become disabled during your lifetime.)

FACTORS AFFECTING DISABILITY INSURANCE

You may need some help from a trusted insurance advisor to help you find the best possible disability coverage. Remember to shop around. I cannot stress enough, however, that with disability insurance, unlike with life insurance, cost should not be your only consideration. There are several *other* questions that you should take into account:

How does the policy define "disability"? The concept of life insurance is simple: you die, they pay. Disability insurance is a little less cut-and-dried: there are all kinds of interpretations of what constitutes disability. For example, if you are an accountant and you lose a finger, are you disabled? Maybe you could find a job as a math teacher. It's important to check things like this carefully, before purchasing a policy.

What is your occupation? The more dangerous your job, the more likely you'll be hurt, and thus, the more expensive the disability policy. Professional mountain climbers, beware!

Does the policy include inflation protection? Inflation is the silent financial killer of the world economy. Check to make sure that your payments are indexed against inflation. This means that they should increase as the cost of living index increases.

What is the waiting period? You can set the length of time it takes for your benefit payments to start: 30 days, 60, 90, etc. Naturally, the shorter the time, the more expensive the premium.

Does your protection increase as your income grows? Look for a disability policy that will let you increase your coverage to keep pace with your increasing income.

What is the length of period for which benefits are paid? Try to ensure you get a policy that pays benefits to the age of 65.

Will the policy pay a partial benefit if you are partially disabled? If you are injured and your doctor wants you to work no more than a few hours a day or week — as opposed to your usual work week — you may not receive any benefits from your coverage! Again, check this out carefully before you buy a policy.

Is your policy both guaranteed and non-cancelable? Guaranteed means that the cost of the policy cannot rise. Non-cancelable means that you are covered for as long as you can pay your premium.

THE TRUTH ABOUT LIFE INSURANCE

At the opening of this chapter, I asked you to "forget everything you think you know about insurance," because there are a lot of widely-held misconceptions out there — and a lot of important facts that are relatively unknown. The following facts and suggestions will help you sort out the myths and hoopla from the reality. *These few paragraphs could save you many thousands of dollars, so read them carefully!*

Don't believe the nonsense that term insurance should be avoided because it is "only temporary insurance." Isn't insurance on your car temporary, until you renew it each year? And how about the insurance you pay annually on your house? *Buy insurance for a specific purpose, and for a specific period of time. Don't pay for something you may never need!*

Avoid mortgage insurance! Why would you want to pay a fixed premium on a constantly reducing amount that you owe? As your outstanding mortgage reduces, the amount of insurance also reduces, but your premiums stay the same! Shop around for life insurance the same way that you shop around for car or house insurance. There is no difference.

A REAL LIFE LESSON: BE RESPONSIBLE; IT COULD HAPPEN TO YOU

Because the insurance industry has not done a very good job of educating the public, far too many Canadians either lack adequate life insurance coverage, or are not insured at all. This is too bad, because, for an *amazingly* small monthly premium, you can protect your spouse or children in the event of your untimely death. Don't leave your loved ones in need — and don't pay more than you should for protecting them!

The following true insurance story has to do with planning and taking one's family responsibility seriously. Someone that I know — a male, age 34, married, with three children under the age of 11 — suddenly found out that he was suffering from lung cancer. There was only a 50/50 chance that he would live, and he would never be able to purchase life insurance in the future. A consultant I know met with him, and during their discussion, discovered that the young father had no disability insurance. Since he was self-employed, he had no group coverage. He had no life insurance, either!

Please learn a lesson from this true-life situation. If you have *any* dependents, or if you have any financial risk that you will have to cover, take the time to sit down and share the simple instructions in this brief chapter. *Find out how much insurance you really need, and go out and buy the cheapest version of that policy you can, to protect your loved ones.* This gentleman — who is a non-smoker — could have easily purchased a half-million dollars' worth of term insurance for less than $30 a month! What a dreadful situation for his wife and children — and it could have been avoided, for such a tiny amount of money.

CHAPTER TWELVE

TAX PLANNING STRATEGIES

PAYING OUR DUES

It seems as if they're everywhere, and there is nothing we can do to escape them: there's income tax — federal, provincial, and sometimes even municipal. Then there's the GST (which we vaguely remember the Liberals promising to get rid of a few years ago; whatever happened to that political promise?), not to mention gas taxes, surtaxes, capital gains tax, tax on dividends, tax on interest — and on and on.

It seems as though every single time our governments need more money — too often due to mismanagement — they find new ways to tax us and new things to tax. The average Canadian pays more than half of his or her income in various kinds of taxes. Each year, somewhere around the middle of July, the media loves to remind us of the day "when you can start keeping your own money." Before that date — over halfway through each year — every single penny is going to one government or another in some form of tax.

There is no denying that taxes have an enormous effect on our lives. For this reason, *it's crucial to consider the tax implications of your investment decisions.*

We have no control over what taxes the government chooses to charge us. We do, nonetheless, have *some* control over the amount of tax we pay, and I am eager to help you legally avoid at least *some* of the potential tax hit on your finances.

PLANNING IS KEY

Despite the modest proposals for tax reduction often made by our federal and provincial governments, for most Canadian families, income tax remains the largest single annual cash outlay. It significantly erodes disposable income and the wealth of most families. *By implementing a variety of tax-planning strategies, a family can minimize the effects of a potentially large tax burden and maximize personal wealth.*

Tax-saving opportunities, contrary to public perception, are not just for the wealthy. Dozens of strategies for tax deferral and tax reduction are available to the average Canadian family. Saving as much as possible from the tax man should be a key element of any financial plan. And never think that the difference will be too small to be worth the trouble.

Remember that regular investment, even of small amounts, can combine with compound growth, to increase your wealth surprisingly quickly. Let us say, for example, that through careful planning you were able to save $1,000 every year. If you took that thousand dollars and invested it in the U.S. Stock Total Return Index (see our discussion of Index Funds in the first Chapter of this Section, above), then *after 30 years at current rates of return, your $1,000 yearly savings would be worth $509,611.* That's quite a bit of money to *not* have to give to our governments. As I love to point out, it isn't what you earn so much as what you save that counts in the long run.

In this chapter, I'll take you through the maze of tax planning step by step, giving you the knowledge you need to make wise decisions in this most crucial area of your financial life. I'll look at family-related tax-planning strategies, your retirement, general tax-planning strategies for your investments, strategic advice for the self-employed, and, yes, the unpleasant but necessary subject of taxes related to death.

FAMILY TAX PLANNING STRATEGIES

With proper planning, there are several ways your family can end up paying a lot less in taxes. Here, I will try to clarify and explain the various options that are open to you. Let me begin with a simple thought: *love them enough to not waste their money!*

Keep the tax breaks described below in mind, not just at tax time but throughout the year, and you could save thousands of dollars — dollars that you can put to excellent use by investing them according to the advice given in my Investment Planning Strategies at the beginning of this section.

Tax Credits

Take full advantage of any **tax credits** available to you. A dollar in tax credit is actually worth *more* than a dollar. How is this possible? It's easy; tax credits are subtracted from the amount of basic federal tax that you are required to pay. Since your provincial taxes and federal surtaxes are calculated based on these basic federal taxes, this means that each dollar of credit can actually save you as much as $1.50 or more in taxes. Not a bad deal.

Income Splitting

Income splitting can save you a great deal of money, and it's perfectly legal. In essence, it means that you can arrange your family affairs in such a way that the tax burden is divided up among the various family members, so as to reduce the amount of taxes that must be paid. Here are some possible income-splitting strategies:

- Contribute to a spousal RRSP if your spouse is — or will be — in a lower marginal tax bracket when the funds are eventually withdrawn.
- Make gifts to children aged 18 and over. This will enable them to earn sufficient income to absorb their deductions and credits, and to pay for certain expenses that you would ordinarily pay out of your after-tax dollars.
- The higher-income spouse should pay most of the household expenses, so that the lower-income spouse can save; both can then invest more of their incomes.

- Invest your child's tax benefit payments in the child's name, because the attribution rules will not apply to income earned on these funds.
- Apply to share Canada Pension or Quebec Pension retirement pension payments with your spouse. This, too, can save you on your tax bill.

Charitable Donations

You can save yourself a lot of tax dollars as you support your favourite cause(s). Your tax or estate planning advisor can show you numerous ways in which charitable donations can become a win-win-win situation: for you, for the charity or charities you respect and want to support, and even for the government. Suppose that you support a women's shelter, for example; the money you donate will assist that worthy cause, lower the amount of tax you must pay, *and* make it less necessary for the government to donate its own funds to such a charity.

Here are a couple of tips on how you can maximize the tax benefits of your charitable donations:

- If you typically make large charitable cash gifts, and *also* plan to sell securities and realize capital gains on these, consider *gifting the securities instead,* to reduce your taxes.
- Maximize your tax credits by claiming all donations made by you and your spouse on one tax return, preferably the one sent in by the lower income earner.

Saving Through Schooling

Take the time to understand how tuition and education credits work, and take full advantage of the carry-forward provision. You can carry forward indefinitely any unused portion of a student's tuition credit until he or she has sufficient income. And 17% of thousands of dollars of tuition as a personal tax credit can save you a lot.

Medical Expenses

Combine claims for any medical expenses across the family. The spouse with the lower income should make the claim, so as to maximize the tax credits.

Pension Income Credit

If you or your spouse is aged 69 or over and you are not making use of your **pension income credit**, consider purchasing an annuity or RRIF. This will generate annual pension income. If your pension qualifies, you can save 17% of up to $1,000 in non-refundable tax credits.

Lower Taxes Through Politics

If you contribute to the campaign of a candidate for election to the House of Commons, or to one of the registered federal political parties, you are eligible for **a political contribution credit** of up to $500. The credit available is 75% of the first $200 in contributions, plus 50% of the next $350 donated, plus 33 1/3% of contributions in excess of $550. The maximum credit is reached with a donation of $1,075.

Buying a Home with Tax-Sheltered Funds

The **Home Buyers' Plan** permits first-time home buyers to borrow up to $20,000 from an RRSP without suffering tax withholding, if the money is used to finance the purchase of a home. (You are considered a first-time home buyer if neither you nor your spouse has owned a home or lived in one as your principal place of residence in any of the five calendar years preceding the date of the withdrawal.)

If you withdraw funds from your RRSP under this plan, you must purchase a home by October 1 of the year following the year of withdrawal. The withdrawn funds must be repaid to your RRSP over a period that does not exceed 15 years. This 15-year repayment period begins in the second calendar year after the withdrawal of the funds.

Tax-Free Schooling

The **Lifelong Learning Plan** works in a similar way, but to fund educational opportunities. It allows you to withdraw up to $20,000 from your RRSP, on a tax-free basis, to finance full-time education or training for yourself or your spouse. A maximum of $10,000 can be withdrawn annually. RRSP withdrawals under this plan are generally repayable, in equal installments, over a ten-year period, with the first repayment due no later than 60 days after the fifth year following the first withdrawal.

Child Tax Benefits

Under the **child tax benefit** system, a base benefit and a **national child benefit supplement** are available to help lower-income families with children. Those who meet the income test are eligible to receive a non–taxable payment for each child under the age of 18. If you deposit a child tax benefit in a bank account, or invest it in the name of the child, the income it earns will be taxed as the child's. The child tax benefit is eliminated for families with one or two children once family income reaches approximately $70,000.

TAKE CONTROL OF YOUR RRSP

It is my strong belief that the Registered Retirement Savings Plan (RRSP) should be renamed simply Registered Savings Plan (RSP). An RRSP is usually defined as a CCRA/Revenue Canada-approved savings program that allows tax-deferred savings towards one's retirement. But *I see it as so much more.*

It is true that our friendly government in Ottawa, when the RRSP was introduced, wanted us to save for that distant idea of "retirement." But what *is* retirement? If you had enough money at the age of 40, and wanted to spend the rest of your life doing other things, would you retire? Why limit RRSPs to vehicles for our "retirement years" when many of us plan to work — in one way or another — until the day we die?

My point is this: there are some common rules that we should all follow when it comes to managing our financial affairs. *An RRSP can be used very successfully as an investment and tax-planning strategy, without any consideration of retirement.*

Here's an example for you: Mr. Ted Jones is 30 years of age, and recently married. His wife, Sally Jones, is also 30. Both of them have great jobs, and are in a 35% tax bracket. The Joneses are planning to start a family, with Sally staying at home to raise the children until they are of school age. Sally Jones will, therefore, have no income for several years.

This is a marvelous opportunity for smart planning! The Joneses should contribute the maximum possible into their RRSPs when they are both working, even if they have to borrow money for this. Then, they should withdraw the proceeds from Sally's RRSP when she, as a stay-at-home mom, is in a much lower tax bracket. The young couple will then be able to invest those proceeds

outside her RRSP, and reap many benefits. (Notice how the word "retirement" never came up in this example?)

There are two key components to an RRSP: tax savings, and investment. Let's look at each one individually.

TAX SAVINGS BENEFIT

Every Canadian who opens an RRSP will get this benefit — and it's a good one. The dollar amount of the savings depends on your marginal tax rate (that is, your tax bracket). If you are earning $50,000 a year and your marginal tax rate is 35%, then for every $1,000 you put into your RRSP, you will save $350 in taxes that year.

If you *really* want to maximize the value of your investments, add that tax refund (of $350) to the $1,000 you've already put into your RRSP account. You can see what's happened: your $1,000 has miraculously turned into $1,350 — a 35% increase in the value of your RRSP, in just minutes! That's pretty good financial planning. Now, who needs an advisor, when you now have the knowledge to get this kind of mileage out of your hard-earned income, all by yourself?

INVESTMENT BENEFIT

This is the component of the plan in which the majority of Canadians get short-changed. This is a shame, because this aspect is the single most important consideration when it comes to RRSP planning.

Here is an idea that could change the way you manage your RRSP significantly: *treat the funds in your plan the same way that you would a portfolio **outside** your plan.* Ask yourself the exact same questions: "What kind of returns can I expect?" "What investment risks are involved?" "Is the investment strategy I'm considering a proven and successful one?"

According to recent research, most of us do not think about our retirement at all — especially in our youth, or even in our middle years. Hence, this terrifying statistic: *82% of Canadian women over the age of 65, and 54% of Canadian men over the same age, rely on government cheques as their only source of cash.*

Here's where an RRSP comes in. When you register one with the federal government, you are taking advantage of quite a marvelous tax-savings deal. You are agreeing to put money away into this plan for use "in your retirement years," and not to touch it until then. (Although you may *well* choose to do so prematurely, for various reasons, such as to make a down payment on a house, or pay tuition fees for your children, or to make it possible for you to stay at home and raise a family.)

The government will be so touched by your foresight — and so eager to see you saving money that will eventually keep you off the welfare rolls in your later years — that it will offer you a gift as its part of the deal: it will let the money you put into your RRSP grow tax-free, and it will give you a tax deduction each year for your trouble.

Here, then, to help you achieve the WEALTH part of your HEALTH, WEALTH, AND HAPPINESS, is . . .

EVERYTHING YOU EVER WANTED TO KNOW ABOUT RRSPS

1. **An RRSP is NOT an investment!** It's a strategy that allows you to save taxes, *and* defer the gains on your investment until you withdraw the funds.
2. When does it make sense to withdraw your funds? When your marginal tax rate is lower than it was when you made your contributions.
3. Don't just look at RRSPs as funding your eventual retirement. **Use them as a tax-planning vehicle as well.**
4. **Make sure you maximize the return on your RRSP funds.** Qualifying investments include, but are not limited to, bank savings accounts, GICs, T-bills, mortgages, and stocks. You can, of course, choose a mutual fund or segregated fund that invests in one or any combination of these. And you know, from chapter ten, that I urge everyone to consider Index Funds and ETFs before any other move.
5. **Make contributions early in your career, and contribute as much as possible every year.** Compound growth can work wonders in your portfolio every year.
6. **Consider making your contributions early in the year.** *Don't* wait until the deadline of late February or early March of the

following year, when all those advertisements fill the papers —
as most Canadians unfortunately do.

7. Your contribution limit is 18% of your earned income. There
   are some other factors that could affect how much you can
   contribute, and your current tax assessment will indicate your
   current allowable contribution amount.

8. Generally, if you contribute *less* than your RRSP deduction
   limit, you can carry forward the excess indefinitely (until the
   age of 69).

9. If you are married and your spouse's income is lower than
   yours, **consider making a spousal contribution.**

10. If you don't have the funds available, you should **consider
    borrowing to make your contribution.** Use your tax refund
    to start repaying the loan. And remember, the interest cost is
    not tax deductible.

**An RRSP is a powerful tax and investment-planning tool. Use it to your
advantage, before the government takes that money away in taxes.**

TAKING A LOAN TO MAXIMIZE YOUR RRSP CONTRIBUTION

Taking a loan to invest in an RRSP can sometimes be very beneficial. There
are several "loan programs" that are available to Canadians from most financial institutions.

SOME ADDITIONAL PLANNING INFORMATION

Timing of Contribution

You may deduct from this year's taxes all RRSP contributions made during the
year (minus any that were counted toward the previous year), or up to 60 days
after the end of the calendar year, subject to your annual limit. Generally, it's
advisable to make your RRSP contribution as early as possible, to take advantage of tax-free compounding. **Financial planning is like comedy; timing is
everything.** As I noted above, if you invest the year's RRSP contributions in
March of one year, and claim that deduction the following April, you can
gain over 13 months' worth of returns from your investment. If you wait until
the last minute like the vast majority of your fellow citizens, making most or

all of your contribution for each year at the last possible opportunity (around March 1st), you can waste a fortune in potential earnings.

Deduction Limits

Your RRSP deduction limit is the maximum amount of tax-deductible contributions that you can make in any one year. Your deduction limit is typically 18% of your earned income for the previous year, up to the following maximums:

- $13,500 in 2003
- $14,500 in 2004
- $15,500 in 2005

Your earned income for the purpose of determining RRSP contribution limits generally includes the following:

- employment income, as shown on your T4 or T4A;
- net rental income; and
- alimony and maintenance payments.

You can carry forward unused RRSP "room" from previous years. For example, if your RRSP deduction limit in 2001 is $12,000, but you make a contribution of only $8,000, you will be allowed to make an additional deductible RRSP contribution of $4,000 in future years. This provision can come in very handy should you get a windfall, inherit money, land a new job with increased pay, etc. Generally, you can carry forward excess contribution room indefinitely until you reach the age of 69, when your RRSP must be collapsed.

Any contribution made to your RRSP in excess of your deduction limit for the year is considered to be over contributions. Under the current rules, if the total RRSP over contributions exceeds $2,000, the excess is subject to a 1% per month penalty tax. That's a lot.

Additional Contributions

Retiring allowances that are received from your employer, either upon ordinary retirement, out of a retirement compensation arrangement, or for a loss of office or employment, can be transferred to your RRSP. The maximum transferable amount is as follows:

- $2,000 for each full or partial year, prior to 1996, during which you were employed by a company that was paying the retirement allowance; plus
- $1,500 for each full year prior to 1989 for which employer contributions to a registered pension plan (RPP) or deferred profit sharing plan (DPSP) have not vested.

Lump sum amounts received out of an RPP or DPSP may also be transferred directly to an RRSP.

Transferring Between Plans

If you wish to change the investments in your RRSP, or change the plan issuer, you can transfer your plan without triggering any taxes. However, you must be careful *not* to de-register the plan during the transfer process.

Withdrawal of Funds Before Retirement

As discussed above, you can use an RRSP as a tax-planning tool that goes well beyond retirement planning, because funds from your plan can be withdrawn at any time. The reason for the withdrawal will determine whether you must pay taxes or not. Here is a summary of withdrawal scenarios:

RRSP WITHDRAWAL SCENARIOS

Reason for withdrawal	Tax situation
To buy your first home (See Home Buyers' plan, discussed in **Family Tax Planning Strategies**, above)	No tax payable
To pay tuition fees (See Lifelong Learning Plan, also discussed in **Family Tax Planning Strategies**)	No tax payable
Maturity (See "When your RRSP matures," below)	Depends on what you choose to do with the "collapsed" RRSP
Cash	Amount withdrawn is fully taxed as income

If you make cash withdrawals before the plan matures for a purpose other than those allowed under the Home Buyers' Plan or the Lifelong Learning Plan, the amount withdrawn is taxable as income. The financial institution is required to withhold a portion of it to submit to the government directly; how much depends on the amount withdrawn and on where you live. (It's higher in Quebec than in the rest of the country.) Here is what is withheld by provinces:

Amount Withdrawn	Other than Quebec	Percentage Withheld Quebec
$5,000 or less	10%	25%
$5,001–$15,000	20%	33%
$15,000+	30%	38%

WHEN YOUR RRSP MATURES

Your RRSP matures at the end of the year that you reach the age of 69. This means that you must collapse it and move the funds to some other vehicle. Note that the deadline for final contributions is December 31 of the year that you reach that age, not the end of Feburary of the following year.

TAX PLANNING STRATEGIES FOR INVESTORS:
SHARE LESS OF YOUR PROFITS
WITH THE GOVERNMENT

One of the biggest mistakes people make when it comes to investing is to ignore the tax consequences of their decisions. If you are serious about getting real returns from your investments, I beg of you to please pay attention, and ask lots of questions about the impact of taxes on your investment returns. Remember, it is not what you make, but what you keep, that truly counts.

Here are a few aspects of *the world of tax planning for your investments:*

Interest Income
Any interest that you make from savings accounts, guaranteed investment certificates, bonds, treasury bills, or mortgages is fully taxable, just like your regular income from employment. Whether you received this income, or have left it to grow in the investment, you are responsible for including in your income tax any interest earned in the current year.

Interest-bearing securities are typically the worst investments. This is because, after adjusting your gains for taxes and inflation, your returns can be as low as zero — or can even venture into negative territory.

Dividend Income
Dividends get preferential tax treatment. Thus, they're *much* more attractive than interest income. Your non-refundable federal dividend tax credit, combined with the effect of that credit on your provincial taxes, will result in a combined tax credit of approximately 25% of the dividend received.

Here is a summary of how interest and dividend income are taxed at different levels of income:

Approximate Income Level	Tax Rate on Interest Income	Tax Rate on Dividend Income
Up to $29,000	27%	7%
$29,000–$59,000	41%	25%
$59,000+	50%	33%

Capital Gains and Losses

When you sell an investment, you incur a **capital gain or loss** equal to the difference between the **adjusted cost base** and the **net proceeds received.** Under current federal budget proposals, you must include in your income 50% of your capital gains for the year, net of capital losses.

Probably **the most attractive thing about capital gains income is that if you do not sell your investments, you pay no tax whatsoever.** Interest-bearing investments, on the other hand, pay their returns in the form of annual taxable income.

If you are serious about maximizing your after-tax returns on your investments — and why wouldn't you be? — then your best strategy is to *invest for capital gains* by buying stocks, equity mutual funds, and index funds, and *avoid interest-bearing investments,* to reduce the amount you must share with the federal government.

Capital Gains Reserves

This is a way to help defer taxes on major capital gains. If you sell capital property and take back a mortgage or note receivable from the purchaser, you may be able to claim a **capital gains reserve** for the proceeds, not due until a later date.

However, in most cases, you must include the taxable capital gain in your income over a period of five years, at the rate of 20% of the capital gain each year.

Loss Carry-overs

If your allowable capital losses for the year exceed your taxable capital gains, you can apply them against capital gains of other years. You may carry allowable losses backward up to three years, or forward indefinitely.

Allowable Business Investment Losses (ABIL)

If you suffer a loss on a business investment, you may be able to claim an **allowable business investment loss** (ABIL), which can reduce your income for tax purposes. In fact, although capital losses can be used only to reduce capital gains, 66 ⅔% of an ABIL can be used to reduce your total income from all sources.

Therefore, if you are a shareholder, or a creditor of a financially unstable private corporation, consider selling your shares, or debt, to an unrelated person before December 31 to realize an ABIL.

Capital Gains Exemption

Shares in a qualified small business corporation and qualified farm property are still eligible for a $500,000 **lifetime capital gains exemption**. (This exemption was universal only a few years ago.)

If you plan to use your exemption this year, and you have outstanding **Cumulative Net Investment Lost** (CNIL) as of December 31, you cannot claim the full exemption. If you are a shareholder of a private corporation, the quickest way to reduce your CNIL is to increase your investment income, in particular, the interest or dividend income you receive from the corporation.

We strongly recommend that you consult with a qualified tax expert for advice on how to use this strategy.

Investment Holding Companies (IHCS)

If you own a large investment portfolio, consider forming an **investment holding company** (this is what Warren Buffett did, with his multi-billion-dollar Berkshire Hathaway). There are a number of benefits, including the following:

- income and capital gains splitting;
- planning for probate fees;
- sheltering assets from U.S. estate tax;
- creating earned income for the purposes of RRSP contributions;
- reducing personal net income to preserve certain tax credits and social benefits; and
- converting what might otherwise be non-deductible interest into tax-deductible interest.

There are also some drawbacks to investment holding companies, however. We strongly recommend that you get help from a qualified tax professional before embarking on one.

TAX PLANNING STRATEGIES FOR THE SELF-EMPLOYED

If you own your own business, you want to be sure that the tax-planning side of your business is bringing you maximum benefits. To put it another way, why not move CCRA (Revenue Canada) lower on your payroll? I shall cover several important issues, but I strongly recommend that you obtain guidance from a qualified, trusted tax professional if you are self-employed. All accountants are not created equal.

Incorporation

There are many benefits to incorporating your business. From a legal point of view, the potential for liability for a corporation is limited to assets owned by the corporation. Your personal property is protected. From a personal point of view, many people find that separating business and personal activities results in a more efficient operation.

Incorporating a business also makes it easier for it to continue after the owner's death.

The major tax benefit of incorporating is tax deferral, obtained by qualifying to pay taxes at a reduced rate: 18–22%, which is much lower than what a salaried employee has deducted from each paycheque.

Shareholders' Agreements

If your corporation has more than one shareholder, be sure to establish a **shareholders' agreement**. This document can protect your rights as a shareholder, minimize disputes, and ensure a smooth transition in the event of a shareholder dying or choosing to withdraw from the partnership.

Corporate Loans

If you borrow money from your corporation, ensure that the loan is repaid by the end of the taxation year following the year in which the loan was taken. If you don't, the amount of the loan may end up included in your income and taxed at the personal rate.

Additional Tips

Here are some more assorted tax-planning tips for the self-employed:

- Pay yourself enough salary or bonuses, if you can, so that your earned income entitles you to the maximum RRSP deduction each year.
- Accrue any bonuses to reduce your corporate income to the small business deduction limit, which was $200,000 but has been increased to $300,000 phased in over four years.
- Remember that accrued bonuses must be paid out within 179 days of the corporation's year-end.
- Pay yourself enough salary or bonuses to reduce the minimum tax liability.
- If you think that your CNIL balance will affect your ability to claim your remaining capital gains exemption, pay yourself dividends rather than salary.
- To obtain a tax-free return of paid-up capital, pay down shareholder advances as an alternative to taking an income.
- Consider retaining in your corporation any income that is eligible for the small business deduction of $300,000; this will result in a welcome deferral of taxes.
- Consider employing your spouse and/or children, to take advantage of income-splitting opportunities.

There are plenty of other ways that the self-employed can realize huge savings through careful tax planning. Consult a trusted, qualified tax professional.

ONE ESSENTIAL IDEA TO SHELTER
YOUR EXTRA INCOME: START A HOME-BASED BUSINESS

As I have noted throughout this book, I have begun a new, promising business called Destiny Health Solutions (DHS), in which I am selling quality health products through network marketing. It is not by chance (and not without some vested interest!) that **I urge every reader of this book to consider creating a business in their home** — whether DHS, or another. The tax advantages are quite extraordinary:

- Any business, whether operated from your home or otherwise, must be carried on with a view to making profits. In other words, there must be a reasonable expectation of profit, for it to be acceptable to the federal government.
- Any expense incurred for this business can be offset against business income, providing it is legal, reasonable in the circumstance, and incurred for the purposes of earning income.
- If this business is operated from your home, you will be allowed a tax deduction for "home office expenses," which can be a reasonable proportion of all the expenses incurred in owning or renting a home.
- If the business is unincorporated, then the owner must include his or her business profit with his or her personal tax return for each year.
- If the operations of an unincorporated business result in a loss before the deduction of "home office expenses" for a particular year, then the taxpayer can offset his loss against his/her other income for that year.

Let me give you an example of how you can earn extra income and pay no tax:

Mr. Joe Destiny earns $45,000 from his full-time employment. He operates a home-based business on a part-time basis, consulting and training on software products to individuals and small business. He doesn't maintain any inventory of products, and he employs his 12-year-old daughter to do his record-keeping, answer the phone, and several other small duties.

Here is a possible Business Income Statement for the year 2002, for tax purposes:

INCOME

From Employment:	$45,000.	
From Home-Based Business:	$10,000.	
TOTAL:		$55,000.

BUSINESS EXPENSES

Advertising:	$1,600.	
Interest and bank charges:	$200.	
Wages (paid to daughter):	$2,000.	
Entertainment (50% of $1250):	$900.	
Office Expenses:	$1,900.	
Auto Expenses:	$1,200.	
Accounting fees:	$500.	
Telephone:	$900.	
CCA (depreciation) on Computer and Car:	$1,800.	
TOTAL:		$11,000.
NET PROFIT/ (LOSS):		$44,000.

What, then, is happening here?

First, Mr. Destiny earned $10,000 from his home-based business and paid no taxes on this attractive amount.

Furthermore, he also **reduced** his income from "outside" employment by $11,000, for tax purposes.

CHAPTER THIRTEEN

ESTATE PLANNING STRATEGIES

STRATEGIES TO PROTECT YOUR ESTATE

Your estate is the culmination of your lifetime achievement through hard work and careful investment decisions. *Estate planning is the continuous process by which you can attain your objectives while you are alive and give effect to them after your death.* Estate planning can benefit anyone who has accumulated assets during their lifetime. You and your spouse should clearly identify your wishes and objectives and a plan should be put in place to coordinate your actions and maximize the growth of your estate and to give effect to those goals. Careful consideration should be given not only to minimizing taxation, but also to accomplishing your goals through the proper distribution of your estate.

1. THE WILL

A Will states how you want your assets divided and passed on to those you wish to benefit.

An Executor is the person who will implement your instructions as contained in the Will. If you die without a Will, the laws of the province in which you reside determine how your assets are distributed. In Ontario, for example, your spouse will be entitled to the first $200,000 of assets, and the remainder will be divided as follows: one-third to the spouse and two-thirds to the children. Until the latter reach 18, the government is responsible for administration of their shares.

Dying without a Will may leave your heirs with substantial legal problems and costs, as well as tax burdens, such that your property may not be distributed as you had wished.

2. POWERS OF ATTORNEY

Powers of Attorney apply to your affairs while you are alive.

In the event that you become mentally or physically incapacitated, you would require someone to make decisions consistent with your thinking. A Power of Attorney for Property gives control of the management of your estate to an individual, subject to instructions outlining your wishes. The powers that you give to that person may cover all aspects of your financial affairs ("general"); or to specific types of decisions ("limited"). As long as you are mentally competent, you may revoke a power of attorney.

A Power of Attorney for Personal Care, sometimes referred to as a "Living Will," expresses your wishes for specific medical treatment to be administered or not, when you are incapable of doing so.

The government can intervene to make these decisions in the event that you have not set up these Powers of Attorney.

3. TRUSTS

A trust allows you to control how certain financial assets are to be used after you have given them away, by transferring them to the trust. Trusts may be set up during your lifetime ("inter vivos") or upon your death ("testamentary"). If you establish an inter vivos trust, you must remember that the assets in the trust no longer belong to you. Those assets will no longer be subject to attachment by your creditors, and the future growth of those assets will accrue to your beneficiaries.

The trust will pay tax on the income derived from the assets. The terms of the trust will stipulate how and at what age, the assets (or the income from the assets) will be distributed.

Testamentary trusts set up in your Will can ensure that assets will remain for the beneficiaries and the age at which they would receive some or all of those assets.

4. CORPORATIONS

In certain circumstances, the use of a corporation to conduct a business can result in a lower rate of taxation of "active business income."

The corporation can be used to limit the liability of the individuals who carry on the business. In addition, the ownership of the business can be divided between different persons, and can include different types of shares between the owners to achieve certain management and tax benefits.

Upon the disposition of the ownership of the business, certain capital gains tax exemptions may be applicable to the sale of the shares.

5. ESTATE FREEZE

An "Estate freeze," accomplished through the use of a corporation or a trust, can establish the value of the assets at the current value, and thereby establish the tax liability based on today's value. However, the tax payment can be deferred until the death of the taxpayer.

The future growth of these assets and the corresponding future tax liability attributed to this growth is passed onto the new owners of the common shares and those persons upon disposition would pay the tax.

Specific legal and tax advice must be sought to properly implement this strategy.

6. OFFSHORE INVESTING

Assets located outside of the jurisdiction of the place of residence at your death may not form part of your estate, and as such may not be subject to probate fees. In addition, these investments may be beyond the reach of your creditors.

However, in the event that you have failed to report such assets to Canadian taxation authorities, you may be subject to penalties and/or prosecution for "tax avoidance."

7. UNIVERSAL LIFE INSURANCE

Universal life insurance can provide a tax-free income upon one's death and can create one's estate. It provides the benefit of life insurance, the proceeds of which are tax-free to the beneficiary as well as the tax-sheltered accumulation of investment funds, which may be paid out directly to the beneficiary tax-free on death, thus also avoiding probate fees.

Another option is to have insurance proceeds payable upon the death of the remaining spouse so as to protect the capital accumulated in his or her estate of that spouse.

8. GIFTING & CHARITABLE GIVING

You have the right to give your property away before you die. However, certain gifts will attract tax from Revenue Canada. These gifts are deemed to have been sold by you at fair market value and you would be subject to capital gains tax based on that value.

If the item that you had given away would not be subject to such a tax, such as your principal residence, then no tax would be due. You may give away your cash without paying any tax, provided that you do not give it to your spouse, or your children or grandchildren, who are under the age of 18.

Planned giving is when a charitable gift is made in such a way that you maximize the tax and estate planning benefits. Life insurance as a form of charitable giving can be an excellent method to provide a large sum of capital for little expense. A person using life insurance as a charitable gift can either make the premiums deductible or the death proceeds deductible (through tax credits).

9. AVOIDING/REDUCING PROBATE FEES

Probate is the process whereby the Will and the terms thereof are certified by the Court. Many institutions will not release your assets to the Executor until proof of the validity of the Will is provided by means of a Certificate.

The cost for the issuance of said Certificate is based upon the total value of the assets included in your estate. The fees are $5 for each $1,000 of value up to the first $50,000; and thereafter $15 for each additional $1,000 or part thereof.

Items that pass to a beneficiary outside of your estate, such as designation of a beneficiary under an RRSP, RRIF, or deferred profit-sharing plan; or by operation of law, through joint tenancy, do not attract probate fees. However, you should carefully consider your overall plan of distribution of your estate, before you make decisions based solely on the avoidance of probate fees.

Careful and knowledgeable advice at each stage of the Estate Planning process should be sought, in order to ensure that your lifetime accumulation of assets is properly distributed in accordance with your wishes.

SOME FINAL THOUGHTS

As you can see, most money management strategies which can save you many thousands of dollars — even after death — need *not* be difficult or complex.

Like HEALTH (see below), investment, insurance, tax, and estate planning are all *long-term* programs. The sooner you start, the better for you — and for your loved ones.

The Money management strategies which I have discussed throughout this section, and the health advice I will presently discuss, should assist you in reaching the goal which all of us long for, and deserve on this earth: happiness.

SECTION
THREE

HEALTH

SECRETS FOR A LONG AND
HEALTHY LIFE

CHAPTER FOURTEEN

WHAT MAKES A HEALING REGIMEN?

"Health is a matter of choice.
Build it, one meal at a time."
—Steve Meyerowitz, author of
The Sproutman

There are many causes for the ugly explosion of ill health and disease in North America today. One in 20 women discovered they had breast cancer a generation ago; today, even as we are living longer and purportedly better, the number is closer to one in nine. Something has clearly gone wrong.

A few of the most serious health problems of today, which your grandparents, and maybe even your parents, did not encounter to the degree that you and I do, include the following:

- **Nutritional deficiencies and excesses**. The latter we all know about: from "super-sizing" too much of what we eat, to eating the wrong things, often both. But the former includes the lack of sufficient quality food — and even eating food that was *once* healthy for us, but is now grown on such inferior soil, it lacks many of the nutrients it contained only decades ago.
- **Environmental pollutants**. In mid-February, 2003, *Newsweek* ran a brief story about the explosion of cancer among children in a single town in the U.S. You don't need to smoke cigarettes,

or stand behind a city bus, to breathe in hundreds of chemical poisons in even the smallest towns and cities today.

- **Chemicals in foods**. Sadly, these are almost impossible to avoid. Which is why *I urge all readers to purchase organic fruits, vegetables, and yes, even meats and fish, whenever possible.* The U.S. finally has standards which have put some meaning behind the word "organic" — take advantage of them. Of course, organic foods usually cost more — but what's your health, and the health of your loved ones, worth to you?

- **Unsafe personal care products**. Toothpastes, shampoos, perfumes, make-up and more. You'd be surprised what quality consumer products are now available in even the smallest health food stores.

- **Unresolved emotional repression**. This can't be fully addressed in a book like this, but I sense you know what I'm talking about here. From carrying grudges against siblings to not forgiving our parents their mistakes, these emotions can kill, in the long run. At the very least, they can create continuing stress on your mind and body, which can lead to countless ailments.

- **Lack of spiritual direction or beliefs**. Religion may not be a cure-all, or compensate for lousy eating habits, but searching for meaning in one's life can add years to that life.

- **Medications**. With over 100,000 Americans (and untold Canadians) dying *every single year*, from mixing prescription medicines, or ingesting wrongfully-prescribed drugs, this is a growing problem, especially in our aging society.

- **Synthetic supplements**. All men may be created equal under the U.S. Constitution, but not all vitamins are. Experts agree that certain Vitamin C supplements, for example, which are made from natural sources and not from chemicals, can do much to avoid a cold or shorten a flu, whereas too much of even the finest Vitamin C leads to little more than very expensive urine.

- **Dental amalgam fillings**. There is disagreement among many dentists, but few will deny that the mercury in 95% of our fillings has the potential for leakage, and serious damage to our physical and emotional health. Some health plans will actually pay to remove your old, mercury fillings and replace them with others which lack this deadly material. Consider this, if you can.

- **Parasites**. These are always a problem, but one which can be lessened through eating organic fruit and vegetables, and a healthier diet.
- **Improper organ function**. This includes constipation and more.

The above can be captured in three major groupings:

1. **The Physical**. This would include everything from polluted blood to lack of oxygen; a clogged lymphatic system and more. *The solution? Eliminate toxins as much as possible; oxygenate your blood with diet, supplements (vitamins), exercise, and rest.* When I say "exercise," this can mean anything from walking up and down several floors at work every day (instead of taking the elevator), to 30-45 minutes of brisk walking in your neighbourhood; one need not jog or run, in order to achieve superior health through daily exercise. *And never forget*: it is most beneficial to exercise in fresh air and sunlight. (Yes, even in wintery Canada.) Quality sleep and daily naps are essential for energy and good health.

2. **The Emotional**. Unresolved emotions such as anger and fears can cause serious psychic damage. *The solution? Resolve major past emotional issues through close friends, psychotherapy, and meditation.*

3. **Spiritual Enlightenment**. *The solution? Follow a path of spiritual discipline.* Follow your heart-felt beliefs, without ever sacrificing your true self. Feeling connected to God, or to our higher self, enriches our life with moral order and a sense of purpose. This can even include volunteering in your community. There is an ancient Jewish expression that "Charity saves from death."

But this doesn't mean only monetary giving; actively caring for others, whether visiting the sick in nursing homes, or delivering meals on wheels, can save from death as well.

I must note here: this Health section will focus on the importance of diet as a key basis for creating health. (Understandably, weight loss or proper weight maintenance, both come, often automatically — if not overnight — with intelligent, conscious eating.)

CHAPTER FIFTEEN

THE LOW-STRESS DIET

"Optimal health is the birthright of us all."
—Nobel Laureate Linus Pauling, Ph.D.

There was a "healthy diet" book which was published over a decade ago that had an inspired title, even if I disagree with many of its theories about eating: *The Cure is in the Kitchen.*

That phrase doesn't say it all about what we should put on our plates and into our stomachs, but it *does* make a crucial point about the direct relationship between food and healing; *every bit of food we put into our bodies has a tremendous impact on how we feel, how we look, and our overall health.* What goes into our mouths will ultimately have a major effect on how long we'll live, and whether we'll fall prey to the countless diseases which are presently ravaging tens of millions of North Americans.

I often think about our bodies in a metaphorical way — as if they were automobiles. If you pour sugar into your gas tank, your car not only will not start, but its insides will rust and even be ruined by this foreign invader. Pump gas into the same tank, and your car will start, and run. It may run better on higher quality gas (organic fruit and vegetables, for instance, in the case of humans), but even with the cheapest fuel (rusting lettuce? mushy apples?), your car will take off when you put your foot on the accelerator.

Those who love to sneak junk food into their mouths, from cheeseburgers to chocolate bars to carbonated cola drinks, hate to hear or read the following words, but they are undeniable: *We can be nourished, energized, and physically and mentally balanced by the foods that we eat — or we can be poisoned and weakened by them.*

Here's another line which is proven a hundred million times daily: **The kinds of foods we put into our bodies, and the way we combine them can make or break us.** And I'm not exaggerating here; foods can make our health better, or they can break it down. This may take months or it may take years, but this is a proven fact. New research proves this almost weekly.

Indeed, let me make another powerful statement here; when you go to your family doctor, and she or he asks how you are feeling, checks your blood and urine, counts your pulse and takes your blood pressure reading, but *fails to ask about what you are eating,* he or she is being just as negligent as a financial planner who fails to ask about your total assets, your "risk tolerance" level regarding stocks and bonds, and the age you hope to retire! (There is my health and wealth link again — and it's never been truer.) *Doctors who don't ask about, or care about, what their patients are eating are failing their medical duty as much as any broker who pushes a client into a penny stock investment without knowing if he can afford to lose all that money.*

Is the cure *really* in the kitchen? Thousands of scholarly research papers published in such quality publications as the *Journal of the American Medical Association* to the *New England Journal of Medicine* (and dozens more of similar value and respect) are continually showing that a wide range of illnesses can be avoided or cured through proper diet: everything from diabetes to stomach disorders, hypoglycemia to acid reflux and ordinary low energy can be helped, even cured, by the foods we eat. You have a whole pharmacy waiting for you, just a few steps away from your living room, and it's called the kitchen. And unlike so many of the often wondrous "miracle drugs" which the pharmaceutical companies are forever creating, *there are no side effects from decent food.* Especially if the food is eaten in the right combinations with other well-chosen food.

Let me give you just two examples from today's newspapers and TV commercials: true, there are now excellent new drugs to help with acid reflux. But why reach for a prescription pill when you could avoid that painful, even dangerous problem by simply cutting out certain "food combinations" and poor eating habits?

My second example is even more shocking: *The New York Times* — considered the most trustworthy newspaper in North America (and in this case, it was quoting studies published in superior medical journals) — reported in the late 1990s that when a control group of people who were suffering from clinical depression swallowed several "fish oil capsules" a day, they had no need for Prozac, Zoloft, or Paxil. In other words, hundreds of thousands of men and women could be easily weaned off those "miracle drugs" just mentioned — drugs which often have a myriad of harmful side effects.

It's a well known fact that "sexual dysfunction" (that is, the inability for men to get erections and for women to orgasm) is an exceedingly common side effect of nearly every major prescription drug for depression! Now, without being vulgar about it, I sense that most of us would become seriously depressed if we were unable to enjoy sex, due to our taking a certain drug! Yet by swallowing a half-dozen or more top-quality fish oil tablets a day — or, in the case of most of us who do not suffer from serious depression, by eating fresh fish once or twice (or more) each week — we can keep our brains from sinking into that painful disorder. Which makes more sense? The miracle pills with dozens of side effects, or the contents of your fridge? North Americans tend to want "quick fixes," which can be understandable. But fish oil capsules cost a fraction the price of prescription drugs for depression, and have been proven to work just as well — with zero side effects.

It shocks many of us — and most of today's doctors, alas — that *almost all preventable health problems can be related to digestive disorders!* In other words, eat properly most of the time, and you can usually forget about 80% of the illnesses which ruined the last years, even decades, of your favourite aunt and your beloved grandfather. Here is just a partial list of what happens to the human body when it experiences "incomplete digestion" or "poor assimilation of food":

- **fermentation in your stomach**
- **putrification of what you've eaten**
- **mucus production**
- **constipation** (or would you rather take pills all the time?)
- **flatulance** (and it's no joke)
- **bloating**
- **acid rebound**

- **diarrhea** (lots of pills with lots of side effects, for that, too, unless you prefer to eat healthily)
- **nausea**
- and, yes, **various degrees of starvation** (If you think your teenager is actually thriving on those french fries and soda pops he or she lives on at school, you have another "think" coming. And our kids wonder why they get so exhausted in the afternoon, and have trouble concentrating.)

Alas, there is more: every one of the above problems — and who of us has not suffered from at least one or two of them in the last month, if not yesterday? — causes further damage to the body: *these digestive disorders can cause stress in other organs, and hamper proper body function.* In fact, if a person has any digestive upset after eating any meal or snack, they may be eating the wrong food combinations, or breaking other rules of correct digestion.

I would *never* urge all readers to give up coffee, or never touch another piece of fried chicken. What I'm doing here is listing foods and ways of eating which will help you towards the finest possible health, in the least confusing and complex manner. The following is not an "eat this and don't-eat-that-or-else" diet; **it's really a way of life, like being a decent human being, or a good neighbour**.

We will all backslide; we'll all have our good days and our bad days. Maybe the most committed Muslim will never, ever touch non-halal meat; the most Orthodox Jew will never bring pig or shellfish to his lips; the most faithful Hindu will never taste the flesh of a cow. But that's not what I'm after here, since those men and women are driven by a deep faith in their respective religions. I cannot expect such passion and dedication, when it comes to food and diet. I'm out to help you live longer and healthier — and this admirable goal does not have to be an all-or-nothing thing. Indeed, the products which I have formulated with Albert E. D'Souza for Destiny Health Solutions have been created precisely because 90% of us will *not* eat properly every day; there will always be those mornings when we grab nothing but a chocolate bar, since we're late for work; or find ourselves at a Christmas party or wedding where nearly all the food is "bad" for us.

By eating or using health food products created and sold by DHS (described in the following section), we can at least keep our bodies functioning well, whether we are consistently eating wisely or not.

A NUTRITIONAL PROGRAM WHICH YOU MAY WISH TO CONSIDER

There are two categories of foods on this nutritional program, which I call **low-stress** and **high-stress** foods. "Stress" refers to the impact which these kinds of foods put on our poor, over-worked stomachs.

Low-stress foods are to be eaten as much as possible. They are all low-mucus-forming, easily digestible, and give the body more energy than ever before.

1. **These foods** — you've probably already guessed that they don't include M&Ms and Mountain Dew! — **digest more easily and more quickly.**
2. **They leave little residue for the liver to detoxify.**
3. **They do not cause toxic build-up** (which eventually leads to countless diseases, so many of them easily avoided).

The gain is obvious; you conserve energy, which can be used to purify, re-build tissue, and greatly increase the energy you need to run your home, be a parent to your children, a loving partner, and a more alert and creative wage-earner.

These are low-stress proteins: chicken with the skin removed. Cottage cheese. Eggs (but not hard-boiled). Fish of all kinds. Sesame butter (also called "tahini"). Seeds soaked over night in water (such as flax, sesame, pumpkin, sunflower, etc.). Sprouts, tofu, miso, bee pollen, and spirulina.

These are low-stress vegetables: sweet potatoes, radishes, squash, green and red peppers, onions, peas, okra, celery, cabbage, broccoli, brussels sprouts, beets, string beans, artichokes, asparagus, chard, endive, kale, romaine, and red leaf lettuce. (This doesn't sound like your old school lunch, does it?)

These are low-stress oils: monounsaturated and polyunsaturated oils that have no effect on the insulin levels in the human body. Examples include canola, flax seed oil, olive oil (which is the best of all by far), guacamole, avocado, sesame butter (tahini), olives, mayonnaise, and — yes — coconut (for the "meat" and the "water" inside).

Low-stress carbohydrates: enter the bloodstream slowly, thus raising blood-sugar levels gradually, producing a moderate insulin response. These include cooked oatmeal, cooked grains beans, rice, and sweet potatoes. (In spite of the "sweet" in their name, they are *far healthier and less stressful on your stomach and body* than regular potatoes.) All grains and beans should be soaked overnight, then drained *before cooking*. This improves their digestibility greatly — to the point that you may never "break wind" again. Really.

Okay, fellow health lovers, here's the tough part. Yes, the so-called high-stress foods I am about to list probably include a dozen of your favourite snacks, if not more. Maybe you actually live on many of these evil foods. Well, you never promised me a rose garden, and I can't promise you eternal life. But the more you cut out or cut down on the following foods from your daily, even weekly, eating habits, the less stress you will put on your body, your energy, your blood, your actual health — yes, *on the very way you feel and act and think each day*. Imagine what goes through an alcoholic's mind whenever a drink is offered to him or her at a party, and ask a similar question to yourself, when tempted by poor food choices: *is this (soda/donut/candy bar) worth the momentary thrill on my tongue?* For the AA member confronted by a glass of whiskey, probably never; for those everyday food challenges of the rest of us — well, that's up to you.

High-stress foods are to be avoided as much as possible in anyone's diet, and for the best of reasons: *They all require a long digestion period, contain toxic substances, and may cause degeneration of millions of cells.* Unfortunately — but not surprisingly, since they taste so good — high-stress foods compromise the majority of foods that most North Americans eat on a regular basis. (No, it's not easy to give up all of the following. But what a difference you will feel, if you give up the vast majority, for most days of the week.)

Some examples of **high-stress foods** are:

- **Refined Foods**: white flour based products, prepared cereals, cakes and pies, macaroni, bread, pancakes, Jello, coffee, canned fruits and vegetables, commercial fruit juices (as opposed to far healthier ones that you can make quickly at home with even the cheapest juicer), candy, ice cream, and soft drinks.

The above list may horrify many readers, but please remember: one can replace these stressful, sugary products with fresh fruits, dried nuts, raw honey, maple syrup, and a remarkable, natural product called Stevia, available at any decent health food store, which is much sweeter than refined sugar, yet derived from a naturally-grown plant.

- **Fried foods**: these include donuts, potato chips, french fries, etc.
- **Citrus fruits**: all citrus fruits shift the body to an overly alkaline state. This does not mean that you should remove oranges and grapefruit from your list of good foods. What it does mean is *no processed fruit juices* — and especially, *none to be eaten with anything else.* (In other words, the "classic" breakfast of orange juice, cereal and/or eggs is out.) If you love citrus, enjoy it, but *eat the entire, freshly-peeled fresh fruit, alone, on an empty stomach, preferably first thing in the morning.* Otherwise, it's bad for you; in fact, drinking canned or bottled fruit juice is like mainlining pure sugar into your body! It tends to lead to fatigue early in the day.
- **Irritating Foods**: things like mustard greens and peppercorns are difficult to digest and irritate the mucous linings. The next time the waiter eagerly brings over that giant grinder and asks, "would you like some fresh pepper?" you'd be better off declining the offer.
- **Hydrogenated Fats**: such as hardened shortenings, like Crisco. Margarine is also a no-no — in spite of claims of "healthiness," most are high in saturated fats, and often contain rancid factors.
- **Seasonings**: such as ketchup, mustard, bottled sauces, prepared salad dressings. (You'd be surprised how easy — and cheap — it is to mix up your own oil, vinegar, garlic and spices to pour over your salads. Try it.)
- **Red meat and pork**: if you truly want to feel your best, and *not* tax your stomach, say goodbye to McDonald's, Burger King, Wendy's, Colonel Sanders, and all those foods we love too much, and whose television commercials are so darned catchy.

- **Soy products:** with the rare exception of miso, tofu, and soy sauce, soy products should be avoided; and even these three should be eaten sparingly. We're sorry to break it to the vegetarians, but soy is *not* very well digested by the body. There are other, far healthier, things to eat, which can replace meat, chicken, and pork.
- **Dairy products:** Cheese and milk are very mucus forming, in spite of what the dairy associations keep claiming in their witty "Got Milk?" advertisements. Cottage cheese and butter are okay, though. And, if you can find "raw" or "unpasteurized" milk and cheeses — the latter are abundant in good health food stores—then you will receive the full, enzyme-rich power of these foods. Unfortunately, almost all the dairy products you can buy in your local supermarket are *not* raw or unpasteurized, and add little value to a good diet.
- **Nuts and nut butters:** they are stressful on the human body; maybe squirrels might thrive on them, but we human beings do not.
- **Honey:** this is an extremely alkalizing food, and must be used in moderation.
- **Foods with additives and preservatives:** yes, that means almost any packaged foods that you love to grab and throw into your shopping cart: from breakfast cereals to frozen dinners. That's why they call them "pre-servatives": these often stomach-troubling chemicals are put into those lifeless products precisely because they allow the "foods" to sit on the shelf for weeks, even months and years. Health food researchers have two jokes about these: *"Additives are Badditives,"* and *"Read the list out loud from the side of the boxed and canned foods that you love to eat; if you can't pronounce the names of the additive or preservative, don't eat it."*
- **Head lettuce:** this common food — some call it iceberg lettuce — contributes to constipation, and actually contains an opium substance. Yes, we used to love it, too.
- **Canned foods:** see the above warning about "additives and preservatives." And more: *canned foods contain large amounts*

of salt, sugar, and hydrogenated oils, and are far less nutritional than their fresh counterparts.

- **Refined table salt:** this one may really shock you, but it's been known by health experts for years: "refined table salt" usually contains up to 25% sugar! Enjoy God's own sugar in fruits, certainly. But why over-sweeten your own foods, when you can't even take the tasting pleasure (or good health) from it? I urge you to *replace table salt with Celtic sea salt, or organic tamari, or various herbs.* Sure, this is more expensive, but your heart may thank you for the few extra decades of healthy life you are adding to it.

- **Coffee, sodas, and alcohol:** since Starbucks is a great corporate citizen and a wonderful place to work, it hurts me to say this, but I must; coffee is stressful on the body and the heart, and not merely because of the caffeine and the sugar they pour into our favourite frappa-cappa-chinos. *Cut down, or cut it out entirely.* As for sodas, from Coke and Pepsi to the store brands, they actually leech vitamins and minerals from your body. Drink water instead, as often as you can. Alcohol? It turns right into sugar; you may as well be pouring a liquid candy bar down your throat. (Although you can drive safely, after eating a candy bar; that, I must admit.)

- **Tap water:** this is such a problem — but such an easily-solved problem, that it deserves a listing of its own. Even the finest, most "purified" water in the best cities in the world, is filled with everything from lead and other dangerous toxins, to deadly chlorine. (Indeed, the towns and cities of North America use this awful chemical in order to detoxify their water, to make it "safe" for drinking. But it could be a lot safer. Whenever you drink water — and four to six glasses a day is about right — *make it purified water, whether via Brita, or bottled water.* These vary considerably in quality, but Coca-Cola's Dasani is one of the best, I'm forced to admit.) You can also purchase a purifier, preferably "reverse osmosis," to attach to your kitchen sink. I can hardly stress this enough. Our bodies are over two-thirds water; why pollute them more than we have to?

By the way, there are many good replacements for coffee, soda pop, alcohol, and tap water; try not only purified water, but fresh-squeezed, home-made vegetable juices. (This juicing need not be expensive or time-consuming, considering the health which comes from them. Herbal and green teas are also superb for your health.)

FOOD CATEGORIES

This is something they don't teach you in kindergarten. In fact, your mother and grandmother probably never knew this — nor, sadly, do most professional, university-educated dieticians who work in hospitals. (Have you seen the food they serve in those institutions recently? It's shocking and outrageous, considering that healthy, nutritious food is important to healing and optimum health! If I see one more sugary, gelatin dessert on the meal tray of a friend in a hospital, I may call the cops instead of the nurse.)

Here's the story: *How foods are combined* (on your plate and in your stomach) *can cause either easy digestion* (the goal) *or difficult digestive problems* (the usual result of what most of us eat, when we ignore the importance of food combinations).

There are three main food categories:

1. **Proteins**. These can be derived from animal or non-animal sources. Most people think that protein comes only from animal products, but it's not so; there is a ton of protein in vegetable juice and nuts. Protein forms the matrix of physical life, from the development of the embryo to our ability to ward off bacteria and viruses. Proper dietary intake of protein is essential for healthy life.
2. **Carbohydrates**. These include all grain products, such as wheat, breads, rolls, muffins, pastries, and rice. Carbohydrates are the molecules which our bodies can readily use for cellular energy or store for future energy requirements. Fruits and vegetables are self-explanatory, and should be the basis of all that we eat. They provide vitamins, minerals, enzymes, water, and fibre, which are all necessary for our health.

4. **Lipids or fats**. These are food substances found in seeds, vegetables, and other plant and animal sources.

Before we move on to the importance of what foods we eat together, I must confront a difficult issue, which I have referred to, only in passing, but which belongs here, just below the list of the four major food categories:

THE ORGANIC QUESTION, AND ITS ANSWER

The idea of eating organic fruits, vegetables, meat, chicken and fish, is essential. After all, it's been on the cover of both *Newsweek* and *Time* recently, and has even been the cause of major new rules and guidelines from the U.S. Food and Drug Administration.

If the above recommendations to give up coffee and soft drinks haven't been enough to send you screaming to your nearest fast food restaurant, I would be remiss if I did not look closely at this very important subject.

You have probably read and heard about some of the key reasons for switching to organic foods whenever possible. (Sure, it's awfully difficult to eat organic all the time; most of us go out for dinner occasionally, and can't avoid those Sunday dinners with our parents now and then.) Let me list a few of the best reasons:

-   Eating organic helps you avoid the consumption of artificial colours, flavours, preservatives, herbicides, pesticides, and other agricultural chemicals. Even fruit labelled "organic" cannot guarantee to be 100% pesticide-free: winds blow across many farms, most of which use toxic sprays. But even 50–80% *less* herbicides and pesticides on what you put into your precious body is worthwhile, is it not?
-   BGH (bovine growth hormones), and many others which are shot into cows, and oodles more which are fed to and injected into chickens and pigs, to make them grow faster and fatter), can be kept out of your system by eating organic meats.
-   Genetically-modified organisms (GMOS) can be almost entirely avoided by eating food labelled "organic."

- Other non-natural substances can also be eliminated from your diet, if you insist on purchasing, and eating, organic fruits, vegetables, meats and fish, as often as you can.
- Organic fruits and vegetables have actually been found to be more nutritious — ounce for ounce, kilogram for kilogram — than their commercially-grown counterparts. Indeed, recent studies have shown some mineral levels of organic foods to be double, even triple, those found in the same amount of non-organic foods. Yes, organic foods and products are more expensive; I cannot deny that. But when you purchase a pound of, say, organic bananas, or organic apples, you will nearly always be getting far greater quantities of nutrients (per ounce and per kilogram) for your money. Consider that, at the very least.

No one can deny that we live in a chemically-laden era. We depend upon a few thousand gigantic farms across North America (instead of the millions of small, independent farmers who put food on the tables of your parents and grandparents). These agri-businesses are not evil — but they do have to use tons of pesticides on their crops, in order to feed a growing population. This is inarguable.

Please — purchase organic fruits and vegetables as often as you can, aiming for 85–100% of your intake of those cleaner, healthier foods. How wonderful that a growing number of supermarkets across Canada and the U.S. are carrying larger selections of foods with organic labelling. This book is too brief to cover the endless questions which always arise about meat, poultry, pork, and fish, so let me sum up these "organic thoughts" with just a few points:

- Our hunting and gathering ancestors ate primarily wild game meat. If you can purchase meat of this kind — venison, buffalo, ostrich, etc. — do so. But if you cannot, or want variety, all beef, poultry, and pork should be free-range; in the case of beef, grass-fed as well. (Those chemicals pumped daily into old Bessie are truly vile.)

- Eat plenty of liver as well — if you can get it from organically-raised, free-range animals. Many people hate liver; it's almost a joke of eating, like broccoli. But, to quote one brilliant researcher, "uncontaminated liver is one of the most nutritious foods available, and was eaten by all meat-eating" ancestors of ours.
- Canned, and even fresh tuna is often filled with mercury, since our oceans have become increasingly polluted over the past few decades. But wild, or organically-farmed salmon is available in most supermarkets (as well as many health food stores). Sadly, most of the salmon you find in your neighbourhood stores is commercially farmed and fed antibiotics.
- One more thing, which may make many coffee fanatics feel a bit better: both tea and coffee are available in organic varieties. Sadly, much of commercial coffee and tea crops is heavily treated with chemicals before it is harvested. If you were trying to support over 10,000 Starbucks and another 100,000 independent coffee shops around the world with enough coffee beans to go around, you would probably be forced to use pesticides and herbicides, as well.

To sum up, *As many of the foods you put into your body as possible should be organic, for maximum nutrition and minimum toxicity.* Seems fair to me.

Recently, I came across a fine list of those vegetables and fruits which are the "least likely to be contaminated" by pesticides and herbicides, created by medical doctors and researchers with doctorates. I find this extremely helpful, because it could be a good reminder of when to "risk" eating non-organic foods, and when to avoid those non-organic produce altogether. The following are listed is order of "least likely" to be contaminated, down to "most likely" to be carrying toxins.

Vegetables:
Broccoli, brussels sprouts, cauliflower, onions, and green onions, are the safest vegetables to eat, even if not labelled "organic."
- Potato, pumpkin, squash, sweet potato/yams. As you can see,

all of these are root vegetables, so they're less likely to be contaminated with pesticides and chemicals. Still, none of these should be eaten too often, since they were rarely found in our ancestors' hunter-gatherer times.

- Artichoke, asparagus, beets and beet greens, cabbage, carrots, collard greens, dandelion greens, eggplant, endive, kale, kohlrabi, lettuce, mushrooms, mustard greens, parsley, parsnips, peppers, radish, rutabaga, seaweed, squash, swiss chard, tomato,turnips, turnip greens, and watercress are moderately contaminated by toxins.
- Here are the vegetables which are most likely to be contaminated: bell peppers, celery, cucumbers, and spinach. Consider organic varieties of these vegetables as often as you can.

Fruits:
Avocados, bananas, grapes (grown in the U.S.), plums, and watermelon, are the least likely to be contaminated.

- Blackberries, blueberries, boysenberries, cassava, cranberries, figs, gooseberries, grapefruit, guava, honeydew, kiwi, lemon, lime, lychee fruit, mangoes, nectarines, oranges, papayas, pomegranites, raspberries, rhubarb, star fruit, and tangarines, are more likely to be sprayed with chemicals, but are not the most dangerous to eat "non-organically."
- The following are fruits which are most likely to be heavily contaminated with toxins; in these cases, reach for the ones labelled "organic" in nearly every possible situation: apples, apricots, cantaloupe, cherries, grapes (from Chile), peaches, and strawberries. Like celery, cucumbers, and spinach, try to avoid these, at all cost and at all times, unless they are organic.

PUTTING THESE THOUGHTS TOGETHER

1. Eat your food as fresh and as "close to the source" as possible. If it comes from a can, a box, or is frozen, then *it is not fresh.* For example, try to make your own pinto beans, by soaking

and cooking dry beans, rather than buying the canned form.
2. Switch to whole-wheat flour products, instead of white flour products.
3. Reduce your sugar and dairy intake, especially milk and cheese.
4. Reduce wheat flour products, including breads, rolls, cookies, crackers, etc., and substitute for those such just-as-pleasurable foods as rice, potatoes, sweet potatoes and beans — such as lentils, pinto beans, garbanzo beans, etc.
5. Use conventional forms of cooking. Do not heat or warm your food in a microwave. Thousands of studies have shown that this often destroys the nutritional benefits of your food.

Preparation guidelines
1. Microwave ovens should be avoided on any program dedicated to improving your body's health, as "nuking" destroys the molecular structure, and enzyme and vitamin content, of the food.
2. Only olive and canola oil should ever be used for cooking. These oils can be heated to a higher temperature, before they convert to cancer-causing substances. For raw use, such as salad dressings, olive oil is always the best.
3. Do not cook with aluminum or Teflon-coated cookware. There have been numerous studies which show serious problems with both of these.
4. Rinse all raw vegetables. Wash all raw produce thoroughly with a "vegetable wash" available from any health food store, even if the vegetables are organic. (Remember those pesticide-filled fields, often right next door to many organic farms.)

Now, at last, a chapter on that often neglected concern of good health — how we combine foods in our bodies (and how we should not).

CHAPTER SIXTEEN

FOOD COMBINATIONS

"Mankind's food supply has changed remarkably inrecent years,
but his digestive apparatus has not."

— Dr. Abraham Hoffer, Canadian medical giant who has cured thousands of
schizophrenics with food and supplements, in his book,
Guide to Eating Well for Pure Health

It is commonly thought that the human stomach should be able to digest any number of different foods at the same time. However, digestion is governed by physiological chemistry, not by what we want to believe. Remember, *it's not what we eat that is crucial to our health; it's what we digest and assimilate into our bones, cells, and blood.*

Here are two essential words which are not generally parts of our vocabularies: **digestive enzymes**. These are secreted into our stomachs in very specific amounts and at very specific times of the day and night. Different food types require different digestive secretions.

So, carbohydrate foods require "carbo-splitting enzymes," while protein foods require "protein-splitting" ones. This knowledge of the digestive process has led many practitioners to urge efficient food combining. Let me share some of the rules of this wise practice:

1. **Carbohydrate foods and acid foods should never be eaten at the same meal**. (Recall my warning about "eating raw citrus in the morning, away from other foods.") Do not eat bread, rice, or potatoes with lemons, limes, oranges, grapefruits, pineapples, tomatoes, or other sour fruits. Why? Because the enzyme ptyalin in the saliva acts only in an alkaline medium. In fact, it is actually destroyed by the mildest acid.

Fruit acids not only prevent carbohydrate digestion; they also cause fermentation. As you can see, stomach upset and flatulence can be explained scientifically, and without any Ph.D. in biology. A simple example of the power of these acids — there is enough acetic acid in a single teaspoon of wine vinegar to completely halt salivary digestion. To quote Dr. Percy Howe of Harvard Medical School, "Many people who cannot eat oranges at a meal, derive great benefit from eating them 15–30 minutes *before* the meal."

It really has to do with misplaced blame; men and women who complain that they "cannot eat oranges and grapefruit because they give me gas!" may be falsely accusing the fruit. No, the problem may lie with the escape of starches, and the body's release of pancreative juice and intestinal enzymes to break them down. In a sentence: *An acid process (gastric digestion) and an alkaline process (salivary digestion) cannot be carried on at the same time in an ideal way in the human stomach.* Eventually, they cannot proceed at all, as the rising acidity of the stomach soon stops carbohydrate digestion entirely. The highest efficiency in digestion, then, demands that we eat in such a way as to offer the least hindrance to the work of digestion.

2. **Do not eat a concentrated protein and a concentrated carbohydrate at the same meal.** Examples: Don't eat nuts, meat, eggs, cheese, or other protein foods at the same meal with bread, cereals, potatoes, sweet fruits, cakes, and so on. In fact, candy and sugar greatly inhibit the secretion of gastric juices, and delay digestion greatly. If consumed in large quantities, sugar can depress all stomach activity. (I don't mean to put down the traditional "meat and potatoes" diet of England, of

which my native Guyana was long a colony. But they really were not eating wisely, in terms of digestion.)

3. **Do not eat two concentrated proteins at the same meal.** So, avoid combinations of nuts and meat, or eggs and meat; cheese and nuts, cheese and eggs, meat and milk, eggs and milk, or nuts and milk, at the same meal. Milk — if it is to be drunk at all — is best taken alone. Once again, the reason for avoiding these combinations is that each protein requires a specific character and strength of digestive juice to be secreted. Eggs require different timing in stomach secretions than do meat or milk.

4. **Do not eat fats with proteins.** Avoid using cream, butter, oil, etc., with meat, eggs, cheese, and nuts. Fat depresses the action of the gastric glands, by delaying the development of appetite juices, and inhibiting the release of proper gastric juices needed to digest meats, nuts, eggs, or other protein. Shockingly, fats may lower the entire gastric action by over 50 %.

5. **Do not eat acid fruits with proteins.** By this, I mean that oranges, tomatoes, lemons, and pineapples should not be eaten with meat, eggs, cheese, or nuts. Acid fruits, sadly, seriously hamper protein digestion, which results in putrefaction. Milk and orange juice — in spite of the TV commercials which so often show them together, are not a good combination; even worse is orange juice with eggs. Tomatoes should also never be combined with starchy foods. They may, however, be eaten with leafy vegetables and fat foods.

6. **Do not consume starch and sugars together.** Jellies, jams, fruit, butter, sugar, honey, syrups, and molasses should *not* be spread on bread or cake, nor shared at the same meal as cereals, potatoes, or cereal with sugar. Once again, fermentation occurs.

7. **Eat only one concentrated starch food at any meal**. This rule is more important as a means of preventing over-eating, than as a means of avoiding bad food combinations.

8. **Do not consume melons with any other foods**. Watermelon, muskmelon, honeydew, cantaloupe and all other melons should always be eaten alone.

9. **Milk is best drunk alone — or let alone entirely**. Milk is the natural food of baby mammals. But each species, from whales to humans, produces milk precisely adapted to the needs of its young. Naturally, babies take in their breast milk alone, and not in combination with other foods. Milk does not digest in the stomach, but in the duodenum. This means that *in the presence of milk, the stomach does not respond with the proper secretion*. However, the use of acid fruits with milk does not cause any trouble, and doesn't conflict with its digestion.

10. **Consume purified water — either reverse-osmosis, or distilled**.

By the way, if the majority of fruits, vegetables, and, yes, dairy products, are eaten raw and uncooked, the body will be sufficiently hydrated as to not need as much water as it usually does.

Here is a good plan of eating three meals a day, each with the proper combinations, to prevent stomach upset, reflux, diarrhea, flatulence, and more:

Breakfast
Fruit. Any fruit in season may be eaten (although I continue to urge you to *eat organic as often as possible*). Most experts suggest that not more than three fruits be eaten at any meal. A good combination would be grapes, well-ripened bananas and an apple. In season, melons may make up your breakfast. In winter months, one or two dried fruits, such as figs, dates, raisins, or prunes, may be substituted for fresh fruit.

Lunch

A large salad of lettuce, celery, and one or two other raw vegetables, plus avocado and alfalfa sprouts, or nuts and seeds. A good alternative is a vegetable salad (omitting tomatoes), one cooked green vegetable, and a starch.

Dinner

A large, raw vegetable salad (if nuts or cottage cheese are to be used as the protein, then tomatoes may be used in this case), two cooked, non-starchy vegetables, and a protein.

Fat meats, sour apples, beans, peanuts, peas, cereals, bread and jam, or hot cakes with honey or syrup, are notoriously slow in digestion, and often are the source of discomfort and putrefaction.

A growing number of researchers believe that *if the reserves in every human body are carefully observed, more and more of us can live beyond the 100-year mark, with youthful enthusiasm and well-being.* Tragically, the depletion of those reserves is one of the most common calamities of modern life. It is sad to say, but so much of the modern, fast food diet, so often served in awful food combinations, robs our bodies of reserves, weakens our vital resistance to disease, and sooner or later produces a state of physiological collapse. Of course, there will always be those who can eat garbage and live long and relatively healthy lives; some people are "blessed" with better genes than others. But why take the chance?

Here are some straightforward rules about food combinations:

1.   **Never combine pure fats (butter, cream, bacon fat) with high starches (potatoes, bread, cereal, sweets) at any one meal.** It's simple to understand, much like wise financial planning with Index Funds and Segregated Funds, rather than risky stock-picking and foolish market-timing. In a sentence, *if you're having high carbs at a meal, avoid fats; if you're eating fats, avoid carbs.* Simple, indeed, even if it flies in the face of every hotel brunch I've ever encountered! If you're eating bacon for breakfast, skip the cereal or bread. And if you're having potatoes for lunch, along with a sweet desert, don't put butter on the potatoes, or any cream in your coffee.

2. **Don't combine acids and carbohydrates**. So, don't have but-
    termilk, orange juice, lemon juice, grapefruit, or any vinegar
    at a meal which also includes high starches and sugars.

    Finally, good news for most people: if you have trouble
    drinking orange juice (or eating it's healthier complete coun-
    terpart) because "it gives me an acid stomach," it's for a
    reason; the orange juice is usually drunk at breakfast with
    cereals, toast, or other carbohydrates. Just drink the orange
    juice or eat the oranges alone; this way, you'll get the taste
    pleasure and the sugar fix, without the side effects on your
    digestion.

3. **Do not combine high proteins (such as meat, fish, poultry,
    eggs or cheese) with high starches (potatoes, cereals,
    breads, pasta, and sweets) at the same meal**. To review the
    evidence, assuming you wish to be healthy and feel well: pro-
    teins require acid for their digestion in the stomach. But
    carbohydrates require alkalines for their digestion in the
    small intestine. It's that simple.

And that's it! Of course it's not easy. What's easier, of course, is grabbing a
donut and cup of java as you race into the office, and then topping it off with
a Happy Meal at lunch or dinner. But as we are always admonishing our children (when they think they can ace a test without studying), *easy isn't always
the best way to succeed.*" We're talking about a long life of good health and a
strong sense of physical and emotional well-being here, and not just a little
test which will be long forgotten after a few months. So, without further ado,
and at the risk of some repetition, which may well be necessary, here goes:

DIETARY RULES FOR GREAT HEALTH

I'll begin with a general rule: **always be sure that you eat enough of the vital
food elements (organic is best!), and be sure that you eat these foods in the
right combinations**.

1. Eat all kinds of meats, fish, poultry, eggs, leafy vegetables, cit-

rus fruits (and carbohydrates, if you just have to) as the safest way to avoid any dietary deficiencies. Once again, organic is always best.

2. Do not combine pure fats (butter, cream, or bacon) with high starches (potatoes, cereals, breads, pasta, cakes, or sweets) in any one meal.

3. Do not combine acids (citrus juices, vinegar, buttermilk) with high starches at any one meal.

4. Do not combine high proteins (meat, fish, eggs, cheese) with high starches at any one meal.

5. Eat fats freely with proteins and acid solutions.

6. Be sure you get enough of each of the following, essential nutritional elements, as follows:

    a. Meat and eggs: one serving of each, or two servings of either, each day, with butter or other fat. Fish or poultry may be substituted for meat and eggs.

    b. Milk, buttermilk, or cheese: two glasses of milk or buttermilk, or 2.5 ounces of cheese a day — or, one glass of milk or buttermilk, plus an ounce or more of cheese. Raw dairy products are always far healthier than pasteurized dairy. Try them and you'll see what an awesome difference you'll feel, in well-being and vigour.

    c. Raw, low-starch fruits and raw green and yellow vegetables: two servings a day, or one large salad bowl-sized servings each day.

    d. Supplement the above daily with one or two tablespoons of flax seed oil, or its equivalent in other fish liver oils, or their concentrates in capsules. You'll be stunned by the effect this will have on you.

SOME SUGGESTED BREAKFASTS, LUNCHES, AND DINNERS, FOR OPTIMAL HEALTH

The predominantly protein breakfast
- Coffee or tea with cream but no sugar (organic everything, please).

- Citrus, preferably as whole fruit, eaten several minutes before the protein.
- Eggs with butter, eggs with bacon or ham, or an omelette. (Fish or meats may be substituted for eggs.)

The hard part: no toast, no bread or crackers, no cereals, no sweets. You've outgrown Coco-Puffs and Fruit Loops by now, haven't you?

If you have been eating like most of us have eaten over the past few decades, and wish to achieve maximum detoxification of the fast-food poisons you've been gleefully shoveling into your mouth; and if you wish to reach the peak of nutrition and energy, begin every day with fresh-pressed vegetable juice (organic), using a quality juicer, such as Green Star.

A morning drink of this kind provides *all* the necessary vitamin-enzyme mineral supplementation necessary for excellent health.

Here is a sample recipe for the above Green Drink:
- 2 stalks of celery
- ½ of a cucumber, peeled, if not organic
- a handful of parsley and/or spinach
- 4 carrots
- 1 apple, seeded
- 1 slice of lemon
- Store the excess in a glass jar, and drink as a midday boost. You will thank me, and Destiny Health Solutions, for the rest of your (very long) life.

The Predominantly Carbohydrate Breakfast
- Any whole fruit — but no citrus juice!
- Remember that oranges and grapefruit may be taken with a carbohydrate meal, but not their juices. When the whole fruit is eaten, the chewing you must do tends to make you salivate, thus partially neutralizing the acid. When juice is drunk, too much of the free acid reaches the stomach that way. This is what millions call "an acid stomach," and it's so easy to avoid!
- Cereal, preferably whole grain — with milk, not cream
- Toast or bread or crackers, preferably whole grain, with jam,

marmalade or honey — but no butter
- Sweet milk or tea or coffee, with sugar but no cream
- No fats, no acid solutions, no high proteins

The Predominantly Protein Lunch or Dinner
- Any thin soup or broth
- Meat, fish or eggs (poultry is considered a meat)
- Liver, kidneys, sweetbreads, tripe
- Leafy vegetables (such as cabbage, spinach, brussels sprouts, asparagus, dandelion or beet greens)
- Raw, leafy salads, (watercress, escarole, chicory, romaine, dandelion, green pepper, lettuce, cabbage, celery, carrots, and tomatoes)
- Oil and vinegar dressing
- *Dessert* — limited to any three of the following:
- Cheese
- Gelatin with cream
- Citrus fruit or other low starch fruit
- Buttermilk, because it is acid, may be taken with the meal — but not sweet milk
- Tea or coffee, but no sugar (if desired, but best would be to drink this before eating)
- No high starches; no sweets

The Predominantly Carbohydrate Lunch or Dinner
- Thick or thin soup (meat soup is acceptable with a carbohydrate-type meal, since the broth is principally the mineral extract of the meat)
- Any vegetables (including high starch veggies such as potatoes)
- Baked beans
- Macaroni or spaghetti (a cheese or tomato sauce may be used for flavouring)
- Any vegetable or fruit salad (I should note: when these are eaten "plain," and well-chewed, they develop a wonderful flavour in the mouth, but adding a bit of Celtic sea salt and pepper is okay

- Any sweet or starchy dessert (yes, here's your chance to eat pie and strawberry shortcake — but no whipped cream!)
- Milk (sweet) or coffee or tea with sugar, but no cream
- A low-fat ice cream or ice is permissible
- A cocktail, highball, wine, or beer is quite permissible, if desired

Avoid These Combinations in Any of Your Meals:
- Bread with butter (use jam or preserves instead; put butter on proteins)
- Potatoes with butter (quality potatoes really don't need butter; use salt and pepper)
- Rolls or toast with bacon (substitute fried tomatoes or mushrooms)
- Meat with potatoes and bread (the old stand-by, and one of the worst food combinations known to man
- Rolls and frankfurters
- Rich ice cream (if made with a lot of sugar and pure cream, beware)
- Whipped cream, or any cream, on starchy desserts (use jam)
- Pork with baked beans (pork may be cooked with baked beans, but for flavouring only; don't eat them together — another glorious tradition, ruined)
- Oil and vinegar dressings with starchy meals (although these dressings are very good with protein meals, don't forget)

The Following Combinations may be Eaten Freely:
- With meat, fish or eggs:
    Butter
    Bacon
    Buttermilk
    Vinegar and oil
    Jam sandwiches (including jelly, preserves or honey sandwiches)
    Tomato and lettuce sandwiches
    Cereals with soy milk or rice milk

213

Breads with milk

A glass of warm water with carbohydrate meals

Vegetable gelatin desserts with either protein or carbohydrate meals are also very good because they place very little burden on the digestive system, and contain amino acids. The latter are indeed protein, but they are already split up, and ready for absorption. Cheese instead of desserts is an excellent habit, with protein meals.

IN CONCLUSION . . .

What I have been describing in this Health section must seem like a diet from outer space for most of you — especially all the pointers about good and bad food combinations.

And, indeed, it was with the recognition that most North Americans will not be able to follow the above pages to the fullest extent, that Albert E. D'Souza and I formulated Destiny Health Solutions various products. If you can eat even 75% of your meals like the ones I've suggested in these pages, you may well not need extra supplements, or any of the excellent products which DHS has created.

At the risk of some repetition, let me conclude by listing some of the most important points I have made in this section:

- Proteins combine with vegetables only.
- Avoid combining two or more proteins at any one meal.
- Do not combine proteins and starches.
- Protein should never be eaten with sweet fruit.
- Protein and sugar is one of the worst combinations.
- Do not combine fats with carbohydrates.
- Starches combine with vegetables and other starches only.
- Fruits should be eaten alone — or with dairy products, avocados, nuts or seeds.
- Eat sweet fruits alone.
- Eat melons alone. (Unfortunately, when they are eaten with other foods, they begin to decompose, causing gas. And we know what that means.)

Some final thoughts:
- One food at a meal is the ideal!
- Fruit is the ideal food for the *first* meal of every day.
- A protein meal should be the *last* meal of each day.
- Milk is not recommended, unless it is organic and raw/unpasteurized. Goat's milk is preferable to cow's milk.
- Drink distilled or purified water. Often.
- Water dilutes digestive enzymes when taken with meals, however. So, keep your water intake to a minimum around meals, by leaving ample time before or after you consume food.
- Drink (non-tap) water copiously throughout the day, but

    15 minutes *before* meals;

    30 minutes *after* fruit meals;

    2 hours *after* starch or carbohydrate meals;

    4 hours *after* protein meals.

Are the above diets and food combinations (or lack of them) difficult to achieve and maintain?

They needn't be. And I am not about to beg you to follow every word of the above chapters. But everything here comes from medical doctors and researchers from around the world — some of them with over a half-century of experience in healthy and healing diets. This has all been tested on countless control groups. These guidelines are not fads — they are medically proven.

Few readers are going to run to the cupboard and throw out most of the non-nutritious things which we all have in our kitchens. But if you at least make a start on the above — drinking purified water, eating organic fruit and vegetables, cutting down on refined sugar, fried foods, and white flour products — these few actions would make an excellent beginning. Then, you may see the improvement in your general sense of well-being, energy and, yes, weight-loss — within days.

Give it a try, even if only a few, tentative baby steps towards better health.

Whether you do follow the advice that I've shared in this Health section or not, I have worked to create some very attractive, common-sense, and well-researched health products with my new company, DHS, which can only improve the way you look and feel today.

These products will be discussed in the following section on Destiny Health Solutions. But first, a look at how I created DHS, and a bit about the new president of my firm, Albert E. D'Souza, and his philosophies.

One of Canada's most respected physicians, Dr. Carolyn DeMarco, once declared, "*Most health problems begin right in our kitchen.*" To this, I would add a more optimistic addendum: *most health problems can be solved there, as well.*

In the meantime, throw away that donut, spill that coffee, and *always* think organic. Your children, and grandchildren, will thank you for it.

SECTION
FOUR

THE JOURNEY CONTINUES

THE CREATION OF
DESTINY HEALTH SOLUTIONS

CHAPTER SEVENTEEN

WHEN DAVID
MET ALBERT

One never knows just how or when serendipity occurs. The word means the "making of happy discoveries by accident." An almost comic example of serendipity occurred about a decade ago when pharmaceutical researchers discovered that the pill they were developing had an unexpected side effect; a large percentage of the control group kept getting sexually aroused! In their desire to improve blood flow to various parts of the human body, they found a serendipitous additional use, and Viagra was born. The drug had been used by over 16 million men — with nine tablets dispensed every second, worldwide. It is a multi-billion dollar industry, as anyone who has received a half-dozen spam emails every week is too well aware.

Call it serendipity, that I crossed paths with a gifted herbologist and researcher, Albert E. D'Souza, and created a firm called Destiny Health Solutions. (It should only take off like Viagra did!)

The background of our meeting is rather interesting. In 2001, I was putting together a new business called Destiny Money Solutions, based on my recently published book, *Take Control of Your Financial Destiny*. The objective behind my third financial planning book, and my new firm, was to focus on knowledge and education; to educate Canadians about their money, and how to maintain and grow it wisely. As you can see, my love of teaching and educating, so continuous at Fortune Financial, was still at the core of my being.

I gave many lectures on behalf of my fledgling company, based heavily on this new book, and there was one pleasant, bright woman named Nellie Ekudofia, who came to my Saturday morning talks religiously. I was very impressed with her; her interest, focus, and her thoughtful questions made her stand out among the 50–100 people who would come and hear me speak each weekend. She approached me after one of my seminars.

"David, I really think that you should meet someone I know. His name is Albert E. D'Souza."

"Why do you think the two of us should get together?" I asked her.

"Well, he's been my teacher and mentor for many years on several health issues, especially natural medicine." To be honest, I really had no interest in meeting this unknown individual; I was focused on my new financial planning company, and besides, the centre of my life for nearly two decades had been wealth management, not health management. While I had always been obsessed with good health for myself and my children, I didn't see why I should take the trouble to talk with someone who specialized in such a totally different field. But I liked Nellie a lot; she had such a passionate interest in my weekly talks that I could not bring myself to ignore her kind suggestion.

"Sure, Nellie," I finally told her. "Have this Albert give me a call, and I'll be happy to meet him."

Serendipity in action! Albert soon phoned, and came to see me in my suburban Toronto offices. He sat there, talking about his big dream which seemed at first only to rhyme with my own goal to teach Canadians about wealth — his goal was to educate Canadians about their health. I appreciated his adamant belief that men and women could be healthier if they ate better, took the right supplements and herbs, and in doing so "took control of their personal health destiny."

It was hardly love (or business) at first sight. But it didn't take more than a few meetings until I came to the conclusion that *we both had the same belief systems!* Albert cared profoundly (and studied endlessly) about health care and disease prevention and alleviation; I was similarly obsessed about financial services — wealth, and wealth management.

I consider myself a pretty good listener, but I found myself jumping in all the time, when Albert was speaking! "That's so interesting," I often said in reference to his ideas about health education, "because I feel exactly the same way about the financial industry!" On another occasion, I blurted out, *"You're on the health side, I'm on the money side!"*

Finally, it became clear that we could work together — but on what? I invited Albert to create a proposal for a company, in which we could join forces — for education, for public good — just as I had been working so hard to achieve with financial planning for nearly half of my own life.

Several weeks later, Albert returned to my office with a rather daunting plan; he wanted to actually manufacture products for health — quite a few of them — and we would form a new company which would develop, package, and sell these to the public, all the while educating consumers to live better, and ultimately, longer lives.

At first, to be frank, I wasn't quite sure if I wanted to go in this direction. I was still looking for ways to develop and grow my Destiny Money Solutions firm.

Finally, in the summer of 2002, I made a commitment to Albert E. D'Souza: "Okay, I've made my decision. I'll start paying you, because you'll have to quit your job and work full-time on this. Let's turn this plan into a reality, and start creating these new products, which seem so promising, and important."

In retrospect, in spite of my initial hesitation, it was a perfect fit; the more time the two of us spent together, evolving Destiny Health Solutions, and the more we spoke about developing entirely new health products the more understanding I gained as to how these products fit into a healthy lifestyle.

There were other far more remarkable connections, than our shared Indian heritage — Albert was himself from part of the same, huge subcontinent, on the other side of the globe. But what truly struck me was that Albert's business plan for Destiny Health included the creation of a "Destiny Health Solutions Institute" — a kind of college. Just a few years earlier, I had created a Financial Planning course for George Brown College, and I had been in the process of creating a Destiny Money Solutions Institute, as part of my new company, just weeks before I had met Albert! Here was a man who, for so many years, had been teaching herbal medicine and the importance of quality supplements to improve the health of his countless customers and students. And what had I been doing at Fortune Financial and with Destiny Money Solutions? The same thing — except in the world of finance.

But there were even *more* links. Albert is an avid reader in the fields of health and wellness; you already know about my own obsession with books, learning, and teaching. I thought back to how I had launched a magnificently successful group of mutual funds with Infinity; now I could take that knowledge and launch, with Albert E. D'Souza, a successful line of health products! As with Infinity, I would have to educate the public about how these new products would make them feel, think, and live better and longer. With my family of funds, I had to convince my financial advisors to recommend, and sell, Infinity products to the public; the same would have to be done with Albert's health care products; we would have to convince people to purchase them, and to distribute them.

When I looked around all I saw from the cover stories in newspapers and magazines, to items on TV was the stunning fact that half of North Americans are overweight — digging their graves with their forks — and succumbing to preventable diseases such as diabetes, heart disease, and cancer.

In fact, this growing media interest in health and disease prevention was reflected in the stock markets of the world, too. McDonald's Restaurants had its first losing quarter in its history, in 2002, closing down dozens of stores, and pulling out of countries where it had opened franchises. It became all to celar to me that people were killing themselves with sugary, fattening, unhealthy food while governments and social agencies were becoming increasingly fearful about obesity and disease, and the billions of dollars in inevitable health care costs which would result. Even as we speak, diet books are selling in the tens of millions, and people are trying to lose weight like crazy — even to the point of life-threatening operations — and more and more men and women are turning to healthier ways of eating and living (yoga, walking, jogging, juicing, eating only organic produce, becoming vegetarians or vegans, cutting down on refined sugars and white flour) — you name it; people are doing it. I didn't need to read about McDonald's falling on hard times to know that something was happening in North America in the first years of this new millennium, and it had to do with health, and health supplements.

CHAPTER EIGHTEEN

ALBERT E. D'SOUZA — HIS LIFE AND BELIEFS

Albert E. D'Souza was born in Mangalore, about 400 kilometres south of Goa, a Portuguese colony on the West coast of India, in 1957. He was the youngest of five siblings.

He had a strict upbringing, because his father was an inspector of police. His education started in a "hill station" called Marcara, or Coorg, in St. Joseph's Convent, which was run by nuns from England, Scotland, and Ireland, where he learned to speak English, which is always an important advantage in the modern world.

After D'Souza finished his early education, his father was transferred to Mysore, where he ran a police training college. This time, D'Souza was enrolled in the Good Shepherd Convent, and only returned to Mangalore after his father's retirement in 1970.

D'Souza eventually attended the University of Mysore, St. Aloysius College, in Mangalore, and earned a Bachelor of Science Degree, with majors in Chemistry, Botany, and Zoology, all of which fascinated him greatly.

He actually longed to be a pilot, and study in the Indian Defence Academy, but his father flatly refused. It was exceedingly difficult to get into that academy, but he passed their exams with ease; however when a father says "no" — at least in that culture — the answer is "no." D'Souza still longed to fly, and see the world.

He moved on to study to become a flight attendant in Bombay, took an airline tourism course, and graduated at the top of his class. He was selected by Air India for an interview, but encountered a real problem; the officer who interviewed him asked for 40,000 rupees as a bribe, to land the position! That was approximately $4,000, and he was incensed. "I want to land this job for what I am," D'Souza told him angrily, "and not by paying you off," and he walked out.

He applied next for a job as a Professional Services Representative for E.R. Squibb & Sons Inc., one of the world's largest pharmaceutical companies — certainly the largest in India, and was most fortunate to obtain employment there. Sadly, in India — a land of over a billion people — it is not by choice, but often by chance, that you get any job at all. (Well, chance, plus the occasional bribe.) It is a country teeming with well-educated men and women, but there are simply not enough jobs available to give them all work.

His job at Squibb was fascinating. He would meet with doctors and inform them about the latest developments in the medical field, while promoting Squibb's dozens of products. At that time, the giant pharmaceutical company was manufacturing over 120 different drugs. D'Souza excelled in his job, and was soon called to apply for the position of regional manager. He stood first in all of South India, but could not be promoted. "You're the baby of the company!" he was told, and therefore too young to land that important position.

D'Souza was in his early 20s, and working for one of the most powerful companies in all of India; he had peaked career-wise at an early age. He was consulting to pharmacies and medical doctors on drug therapy and regulations, advising professional staff on drug information and interactions, co-ordinating hospital and retail pharmacy services, dealing with wholesalers who were placing orders for prescription drugs, doing inventory control management of promotional products, and even training new representatives! There was really no other place to go that would offer him greater responsibilities and respect, and he was earning a good living.

But as I know from my youth in Guyana, there comes a time to move on and change directions, even countries. But D'Souza had worked in Coimbatore, and later in Ooty, a beautiful place which is called "the Switzerland of

224

Eastern India." How could anyone think of leaving?

But Squibb was owned by a wealthy family named Ambalal Sarabhai, and it ran into various difficulties. The great pharmaceutical company began to stagnate a bit, and he felt there was no more growth potential there.

By sheer chance — think of my meetings with Mike Lee-Chin, who urged me to leave the insurance industry and sell mutual funds — D'Souza was visited by one of his childhood friends named Roshan Pais. "Albert!" he declared, fresh from working in Kuwait, "What are you still doing in India? Get out of here! Go to another country! Why not Canada? You've got a brother there, don't you? (It was true; his eldest brother was there; and he was a genius.) Just go to Canada, Albert, even in your underwear, and stand in the airport. You'll be looked after — you won't have to worry!"

D'Souza thought it over, and applied at the Canadian Embassy. He was surprised that in only seven months, he had his papers to migrate to the New World. You may be interested to know that one could not take U.S. dollars out of India. Ironically, he was allowed to leave with only $20 — the same amount I had when I came to Canada. D'Souza was able to obtain more on the black market, which he did. So, he arrived at Dorval Airport in Montreal with $600 U.S. dollars. It was May 30, 1988, at exactly 5:30 p.m.

He was a bit frightened, but hardly worried; his brother picked him up at the airport, making his arrival a lot less intimidating than it would have been for so many other immigrants. His first response was, "This country looks deserted! There are no people! Everything is empty here!" One can under-stand his initial reaction as India is a land of wall-to-wall people! Imagine had he landed in the Prairies, and not in this country's second largest city! He may have panicked by the endless expanse of land, with so few people, and gone back to Southeast Asia!

D'Souza stayed with his brother for only a few days, just to get used to the weather, and then moved on to Toronto as he knew no French.

D'Souza was a lucky immigrant in more ways than merely knowing Eng-lish and having an older brother who was already established in Canada, within one week, he was hired by Shoppers Drug Mart, as a manager in late June, 1988. It was his first job in Canada and it was so very important; he gained a strong interest in health and healing, more than he had ever expe-rienced working for the huge Squibb company back in India.

He first worked at a store on Yonge Street in downtown Toronto, and had the good fortune of being there when his location became one of the initial stores to become converted to agressively health-conscious places. There was a wide selection of vitamins, minerals, and herbs available at that Shoppers, and because of his pharmaceutical background he started recommending products to customers. Many of them would return to the store, weeks later, saying, "I'm feeling so much better!"

That began to pull D'Souza toward natural health care — what we are now creating with Destiny Health Solutions. Before the summer of 1988, he hadn't read a single book on health and healing, but from those days onward, he started buying, and reading intensely: books on herbs; Chinese medicine, Indian Ayurveda medicine; in short, books on *anything* pertaining to this vital subject. Today, his library contains more than 700 books — and he considers himself fortunate to have been able to share his knowlege with thousands of customers at the several jobs he has held in Canada.

D'Souza had a family then — a wife and two young children; the latter are now in their late teens. As the sole breadwinner, he couldn't afford to go to college or university; he had to work full time to keep (healthy) food on the table. He remained at Shoppers for nearly three years, until 1991, specializing in vitamins, minerals and herbs, hiring new staff members, and imparting his growing knowledge of "complementary medicine" to the pharmacists.

His good luck continued; his next job was at Noah's Natural Foods, one of the earliest and finest health food stores in Canada, where he was soon operating the whole supplement business with an emphasis on the education and promotion of natural health products: how often to take them, and why; possible toxicities, contra-indications (yes, there are herbs which can be dangerous to take before an operation, and others with interact poorly with other herbs and prescription drugs), and more. He eventually became director at one store, and oversaw and expanded its operations into three stores, increasing sales by 120% in the newly-established branches. Albert was educating people about their health — and just a few kilometres away, I was educating people about their wealth!

D'Souza never studied herbal medicine formally, even though he would eventually lecture to the Canadian College of Naturopathic Medicine on the manufacture and quality control of natural medicines and give educational seminars for senior citizens on common ailments and their prevention with natural health products. He even trained fourth-year naturopathic graduates, concentrating on the protocols of nutrition. In Canada, the field of natural health care is not licensed or regulated. His philosophy became "*it's not a degree that is important — it's how much you know, how much you have retained, and how much you can put your learning into practice, by helping others.*"

What he has done for the past 15 years now, is to offer proper suggestions to thousands of men and women on their health regimen, their lifestyles, what supplements and herbs they should take to prevent ailments, and what not to take.

Along the way, D'Souza learned invaluable lessons aiding in the creation of Destiny Health Solutions. He began researching the manufacturing process of vitamins and minerals, as well as the raw materials that went into them. He soon discovered that 95% of all materials were supplied by the giant Hoffman LaRoche firm, and could learn much from the people there.

Through his employment at Noah's, he started getting calls from many of the supplement manufacturers; Jamieson invited him to visit their facilities, then Natural Factors, then Sisu, and others. He learned quickly about their manufacturing practices, raw materials, quality controls, and other factors which allowed him to recommend the best brands of vitamins, minerals, and herbs to his customers.

D'Souza remained at Noah's for a half-dozen years, until 1997, when he moved on to several other complementary health product manufacturers and retail stores, including Elements and Supplements Plus. Finally, in 2000, he became a Faculty Member at the Canadian School of Natural Nutrition, where he taught chemistry, biology, anatomy, pathology, nutritional symptomatology, lifecycle and preventative nutrition, advanced holistic nutrition, and, of course, interaction with prescription drugs.

But even though teaching was close to his heart, as it has always been for me, he had begun to formulate new supplements, as early as 1991. He studied glucosamine, wrote several research papers, and considered approaching various companies to manufacture this new supplement. He studied weight loss from the angle of how fat builds and breaks down in the body, and the physiology of weight gain and loss. He even created a formulation that would increase growth hormone release. And he discovered that no one in the industry in North America had created such formulations.

Then, we finally met. At first, he approached me hoping to discuss conducting health seminars, possibly to run parallel with my numerous lectures on money and money management (health joining wealth, if you will). But weeks later, after several animated discussions, I came out and asked him, "So, Albert, do you have anything in mind that we might do together?"

That's when he began to talk about the many formulations he developed over the years. "How can *we* formulate these products?" he asked me. "How can we manufacture them, sell them and market them to the public? Millions of people are suffering out there!"

It was, indeed, a true meeting of minds. D'Souza has a gift for sensing people's energy and he felt I had the right energy. We knew little about each other but we both felt there was something special about the other, and that we could work together. Within months we began work on Destiny Health Solutions.

At the time, he told me what I am about to tell you here; after nearly 15 years in the health food industry, he realized that — not unlike the world of financial planning — there was more "sell sell sell" than actual knowledge. Most of the employees in health food stores are in their early twenties, and they often have no clue about products. Customers who go into most health food stores seeking advice, do not get the proper information on which supplement will help them the most with their fibromyalgia or with their diabetes; with their high blood pressure, or high cholesterol; with their weight gain, or weight loss concerns. Unfortunately, just like in my world of finance reps and mutual funds salesmen, health food companies often give large discounts to stores and then simply load their product on the retailer, who must then sell the product (whether or not it's the right one, or the best one on the market to solve various health challenges). Sadly, most health food salespeople spend their time pushing paticular products rather than matching the best products with the people who need them the most.

At this point in our partnership, we confronted the problem which every manufacturer of any product must confront; how would we get these health food supplements to market — and what would be the signature product?

THE BIRTH OF O.C.T.A.

The signature product we needed to develop for Destiny Health Solutions, came to D'Souza in a flash. He awoke at 2:30 a.m thinking about the chemistry of atoms, and how they are stable if they satisfy the "octet rule" (when an atom has eight electrons in its valence). He wanted to create a vital, healing product which would be truly stable in every sense of the word — one that would remain stable — and popular — in the marketplace, unlike so many products, which peak and then collapse.

Stable, unique, not a fad — the "O.C.T.A. rule." He thought of the word "octa," which means eight in dozens of languages. (We soon realized that the letters could also stand for "Overall Care, Total Awareness.")

Albert had become an expert in Chinese and Ayurvedic herbs. He wanted to combine the best knowledge of those two ancient, populous lands, creating a product which would give its user more energy, normalize his or her body functions, and benefit one's blood sugar levels. I wanted to create *a product which would be formulated in such a way that it increased overall health; overall care — and invoked total awareness* (the latter, because he would use herbs which had been employed for thousands of years to improve memory).

The way D'Souza explains O.C.T.A., our flagship product, is that it is an all-natural body tonic made up of eight specific herbs, designed to target all aspects of the human body: the immune system (supporting its natural ability to fight disease and infection), the circulatory system (by acting as a superior antioxidant, to rid the body of harmful, fatty acids, and increase energy levels), the digestive system (through aiding digestion, and assisting in the absorption of nutrients at the cellular level); and the skin and hair (through components that are crucial to the clarity, smoothness and softness of the skin — our body's largest organ, by far — as well as strengthening the follicles of the hair, to increase their growth).

By combining these eight, precious, carefully-chosen herbs, Destiny Health Solutions was creating in O.C.T.A. a formula for achieving optimum health. D'Souza soon found that there were key, potential benefits to drinking this product daily. He found that O.C.T.A. was helpful in:

* Preventing insomnia
* Modifying or preventing diabetes
* Lessening hypertension
* Promoting weight loss
* Improving sexual function
* Assisting digestion
* Strengthening liver function
* Increasing mental clarity
* Broadening one's attention span
* Maximizing energy
* Reducing blood sugar levels
* Controlling appetite
* Cutting down the length and severity of the common cold

The herbs Albert decided to include in O.C.T.A. were ones which are better known in India and China — but then, in two countries of over a billion inhabitants each, he sensed that their classic forms of traditional medicine could still teach our sparsely-populated and very young countries of Canada and the United States a thing or two!

The herbs that he chose were: ashwaganda, Jala Brahmi, banaba leaf, jujube, noni, pomegranate, schisandra, and wolfberry. He had struggled long and hard — even before we met — to find the exact proportions of each, for the best possible results. He soon found a quality pharmaceutical manufacturing company to make O.C.T.A. for DHS; thanks to his background at Shoppers and Noah's, he knew and trusted these people, and they've given him total access to excellent raw materials; he has complete control over where they come from, and can ensure they are the highest grade on the market today.

Whenever possible, we have ensured that these eight herbs are organic. For instance, the noni comes directly from the Amazon, extracted straight-from that extraordinary plant. Naturally, our products list all contrary indications on the label, for possible drug or herb interactions (for instance, some nutrients can hamper the absorption of certain prescription drugs). Each DHS product will be accompanied by a booklet, listing any dangers of toxicities, and which people might not want to use the product. But as far as

the in-depth information D'Souza has gathered on these particular herbs —
and hundreds of others I've studied and will use in other DHS products —
they are all extremely safe, and have been used for thousands of years in
China and India.

MORE PRODUCTS, AND MORE DREAMS
TO BE REALIZED

We have formulated other excellent products as well, for our launch in spring,
2003, and there are another dozen I am working as this book goes to press,
which I hope will be available before the end of 2003, or soon after. Another
health product we'll be offering is the MENOP.A.T.H. SYSTEM, a combination
of three dietary supplements targeting all aspects of menopause. The outrageous dangers of hormone replacement therapy are now widely known.
These pills have been eagerly consumed by countless millions of women
around the world for many years now.

Many women feel betrayed; others feel hurt, still more are just plain terrified by the damage they may have inflicted on their bodies over years of
ingestion. And these were prescription drugs that were "highly recommended" as "totally safe" by their gynecologists.

So, we've combined twelve natural herbs exclusively for menopausal
women, which naturally raise estrogen levels, and alleviate many of the (perfectly normal) symptoms associated with menopause, such as hot flashes,
irregular periods, breast tenderness, headaches, memory lapses, and more.
The MENOP.A.T.H. SYSTEM also offers a combination of essential vitamins,
and herbs, which jointly act as a calcium replacement to fortify weakening
bones, another symptom of menopause. The goal, of course, is to prevent or
delay osteoporosis, which is a cruel side effect of the four decade menstrual
cycle coming to an end.

Our MENOP.A.T.H. system will also include a natural antidepressant, to
help conquer the mood swings, irritability, insomnia, anxiety, disorientation,
confusion and depression which sometimes affect women going through
this uncomfortable transition.

Another creation is the METAP.H.A.S.E. System, which combines three
dietary products, targeting all aspects of both men's and women's weight
control problems. We have included essential nutrients which the body

needs to burn fat both while awake, and when at rest.

Our dream, then, is to turn Destiny Health Solutions into a company that offers a wide range of fine products. Part of that dream, of course, is to get these quality health products into as many homes — and bodies — as quickly as we are able.

Do we have more dreams? You bet. We would love to see DHS become so successful that we can create Destiny Agronomics, and grow our own herbs organically, possibly in the Philippines, or even in my native Guyana. What an amazing opportunity to create even better products, as well as much-needed, gainful employment in Second and Third World countries, which so rarely benefit from North American entrepreneural success. (I still recall the horrible stories about a certain billion-dollar athletic shoe company, which sold its products for $200 and upwards a pair, while paying impoverished — and often underage — overseas labourers only pennies an hour. We would never allow that happen with DHS. We have both seen poverty in our native countries and know we can help by not taking advantage of cheap labour.)

Our dreams go beyond even this; we have an eight to ten-year plan, which will see Destiny Health Solutions expand into other countries and create tree-planting projects in conjunction with governments around the world — trees planted not only for beauty's sake, but for their potential commercial value, as well.

For example, there are communities in South India where the major source of income is the harvest from coconut trees. We can see DHS planting 10,000 coconut trees, which might keep over a dozen families supported financially. In addition, we'd make the world a little greener and make sure that the coconut trees are organically grown.

I was also impressed by another dream of Albert's — to set up a National Naturopathic College, offering a four-year homeopathy program, with *another* four years spent on herbology and other modalities of natural health care to the most qualified men and women who want to study alternative or complementary medicine. This way, the future naturopaths of Canada would complete a full eight years of studies in natural medicine, just like medical colleges in major universities demand of their graduates.

We also dream of restaurants, across North America, offering healthy, organic meals, and menus that give people choices of dishes which relate to healing, or at least alleviating, any particular medical problem they may have, from insomnia to high cholesterol; from hypoglycemia to fibromyalgia.

But these dreams are truly for the future — maybe a decade or more along the way.

For now, I thank God that I met Albert E. D'Souza, who sees what we are creating together with Destiny Health Solutions as doing for the health improvement of millions, what I tried to accomplish, often successfully, in the world of money management.

So that takes care of health and wealth. As for happines, well, I think that should follow almost inevitably, once each of us achieve the first two!

SECTION
FIVE

HAPPINESS

YOUR PATHWAY TO SUCCESS

CHAPTER NINETEEN

IT'S A
JOURNEY

Life is a journey, complete with its inevitable ups and downs. It is your experiences along the way, both good and bad, and how you react to them, that make you who you are, and determine who you will become.

Never short-change yourself. All of us, in one way or another, are unique; each of us have extraordinary intelligence, talent, ability, and skills, attributes we can develop and direct toward accomplishing exceptional things, and making a real difference in this world.

Everyone wants to be successful. Everyone wants to be healthy, achieve financial independence, and achieve happiness. Luckily, for most people, success is *not* a matter of your birth or upbringing. It's not our family, friends, or contacts who enable us to do great things. Instead, success comes from striving to become the best that we can be, every day of our lives. It's about constant and never-ending improvements.

Have you ever wondered why some people are more successful than others? Why it is that some enjoy better health, relationships, and greater success in their careers, and achieve financial independence (if not great wealth) — while so many others do not?

Earlier in this book, I described my formative years. Based on the accepted norms of our society, *I was not supposed to be successful.* My father did not believe in the value of education, and we were so very poor. No one in my family — immediate or extended — went to high school, much less university. There were no entrepreneurs, or business owners, in my family, or among any of my acquaintances, to serve as role models.

Yet here I am, on the cusp of my 50th birthday, and I have earned four degrees, have written four books, and am a multi-millionaire. And I am in the best physical and emotional shape of my life, while continuing to push myself to become a better person.

What is it that differentiates me from any other person? It's obviously not my upbringing; not my education; not money. It is *a burning desire to become the best that I can be.* To make a difference in society, and try to leave the world a better place than the way I found it. I have a burning desire, as well, to help others to succeed. (There is an old Negro spiritual from slavery times in the United States which goes, "If I can help somebody, as I pass along, then my living shall not be in vain.")

I learned a long time ago that the key to success is to set one great, challenging goal, and then to pay any price, overcome any obstacle, and persist through any difficulty, to achieve it.

By reaching goals, you create a pattern, a template for success in your subconscious mind. Ever after, you will be automatically directed and driven toward repeating that success in *other* things that you attempt.

My entire life has been about challenging myself to become a better person, a better father, a better entrepreneur. To overcome adversities, and to move on. I wanted to excel at everything I did, and from the earliest age. Whether it was in primary school, in my favourite sports, at golf, in building Fortune Financial or in creating Infinity Mutual Funds, or my vision of 2003 and beyond — to build the world's leading health care business.

Although Fortune Financial and Infinity became number one in their respective fields in Canada, and subsequently caused me a tremendous amount of pain and grief, due to poor management decisions, I still learned one crucial lesson, and that is, *success can be repeated.*

I also learned that the only sure way to learn in life, is by making mistakes. And that the only way to give yourself a chance to *make* those mistakes, is to venture into the world of the unknown. Give yourself a chance to make mistakes; the more you make, the more you will learn, and the faster you will be on your way to success and greatness.

Here is something I'd like every reader of these words to think about, at this very moment: *You have within you, right now, everything you could ever need or want, to be a great success in any area of your life that you consider to be important.*

You also have within you everything it takes to be very happy — to achieve happiness. No one can make you happy, except you. You and I do not have control over the things that are happening around us (the weather, wars and diseases overseas, etc.) But we *do* have control over how we react to, or manage, the situations around us.

What is your personal mission in life? I feel strongly that we have been put on this earth for a reason — to do great and good things with our lives, in the time allotted to us. (One more reason for taking care of our health.) We have, within us, enormous, untapped resources of talent and ability, just waiting to be harnessed and ridden towards great, worthwhile acts.

Be honest with yourself: what do you *really* want in life? If you could be or do or have anything in life, what would it be? Allow yourself to dream, and then go to work — hard work it can be — to make those dreams become reality. First, however, you must learn the rules of the game. Everything in life has rules, of course. At a very young age, we quickly learned the rules about crossing the street, about having to be in school five days a week, and so on. Later in life, we learned the rules of driving, of obeying stop signs and traffic lights and speed limits.

However, no one has taught us how to live, how to be happy, and how to deal with life's daily challenges! No one has given us a set of rules, detailing how to manage our relationships, our careers, finances, or our health.

Learn how to play the game, and you might be surprised at the results. No one but you has total control of your life. (Interestingly, and directly related to the Health section and my goals with DHS, even we may have trouble controlling our own lives, if we are too under-nourished to think straight!) If you don't stand up and fight for yourself, no one else will. Most times, you will find that the person you most need to stand up to is yourself.

An ancient Jewish text, some 2,000 years old, puts it best: "If I am not for myself, then who will be for me? And if I am for myself only, what am I? And if not now, then when?"

239

Be prepared to pay a price for whatever you aspire to, in life. Nothing in this world comes without a price. If you want to be in better shape physically, then learn the rules, and be prepared to pay the price to achieve that goal. (The price in this case could be anything from the cost of a health club membership, to a treadmill, to making the attempt to eat properly.)

If your relationship is not bringing the happiness that you deserve, make a decision and be prepared to live with the consequences. The same is true when it comes to your career, your finances, and everything else that is important in your life.

The great majority of people, certainly in North America, want their success and happiness on the cheap — handed to them on a plate, without paying full price for it, in advance, as nature demands. (Think of the millions who would sooner eat junk food every day, and then pop pills to bring down their high cholesterol.) This continual expectation of achievement without cost leads to frustration and failure.

Always remember that there are no free lessons. The good news, however, is that your biggest problems of the day have been sent to you to teach you what you need to know to be happier and more successful in the future.

Sometimes in business, and in life, you have to try, try again, and then try something else. Remember: *"Difficulties come not to obstruct, but to instruct."* Always be prepared to adapt, adjust, and respond by doing something else. Think of the humourous, yet powerful joke about the man who dropped his keys into the snow next to his car, but kept searching for them by the front porch, "because the light is better over here." If we are not willing to face challenges, or shift directions, then we will never grow.

Nature sends us pain of all kinds —physical, emotional, and financial — to tell us to stop doing certain things.

Then, there are the opinions of others. *Don't let your dreams be destroyed or crushed by the opinions of other people,* including close relatives. (If I had listened to my father, I would never have continued my studies, taught school, left Guyana, or become an entrepreneur. I could well be slaving over the family farm, like some of my siblings continue to do, to this very day.) You alone know what that important goal means to you; other people will always have a different perspective on your life and dreams, and their viewpoint is occasionally tainted with envy, anger, or simply ill will.

240

One of the most meaningful lines I have ever read, is from a play by the gifted Irish writer, George Bernard Shaw — a line which Robert Kennedy paraphrased frequently: *"You see things, and you say, 'Why?' But I dream things that never were, and I say, 'Why not?'"*

CHAPTER TWENTY

CREATE A LIFE STRATEGY FOR HAPPINESS

Creating a life strategy that will bring you health, wealth, and happiness, is a learned skill. This book has given you the knowledge you need to create a winning strategy that can bring you all the happiness you need.

If your life is not what you would like it to be, then this is your opportunity to create positive, lasting change. In my personal life, I have always let these three words be my guiding principle: *I am responsible.*

A starting point should be to set clear and specific goals for yourself. At the beginning of each year, I write my goals in five areas:

1. Career
2. Financial
3. Family
4. Health
5. Emotional

Please understand that these are *not* "New Year's Resolutions" which most people make and don't keep. These are clearly thought out goals which are written and read on a regular basis.

For our goals to be achieved, they must be managed, and you must accept full responsibility to be the manager. If things are not going the way I would like them to go in any of these five areas listed above, then it is my responsibility to analyze the reasons why things are not working, and then put a plan in place to get me the results that I expect.

As your life manager, you can assess your progress, or lack thereof, by continually asking yourself the following questions:

a. Am I creating opportunities for myself to get what I really want in life?
b. Do I keep reaching for those things that will keep me healthy, wealthy and happy?
c. Am I doing whatever is necessary to keep me safe and secure from foolish risks?
d. Am I putting myself in situations where I can use all of my skills and abilities?
e. Am I pursuing relationships in which I can be healthy and flourish?
f. Do I design my day so that I can enjoy some peace and tranquility?
g. Do I plan my life in such a way that there is time for fun and recreation?
h. Do I ensure that there is a balance in the areas of career, financial, family, health, and emotional health?

If it's Going to Be, it's Up to Me

No matter what happens in our lives, we have within us what it takes to accomplish almost anything that we want in life. But we must accept the fact that "if it's going to be, it's up to me."

Success demands that we pay the price which excellence demands. The price always calls for sacrifice. Goals that are only self-serving never deliver satisfying successes. And it must be clear to you what success means to you. If you are going to define success only in terms of how much money you have in the bank, then you are defining it from a very self-serving perspective.

However, if you define success, as I have done in my own life, as "constant and never-ending improvement," and the desire to leave this world a slightly better place than how you found it, then success, and happiness, becomes more meaningful.

By now you are, I hope, convinced that to achieve success and happiness in life, you must set meaningful, measurable, and manageable goals. Let me define what I mean:

Meaningful goals: These are weighed carefully in your mission statement for life. They have come from your passion to find a need, and fill it. They have crystallized your values and exposed the real you. You must also be prepared to pay the price, because your goals, once they are achieved, could make a big difference in your life, and that of others.

Measurable Goals: Results and rewards must be recognizable and quantifiable, all along the way. For that reason, it's helpful to have immediate, short-term, and long-term goals.

Manageable Goals: What are your long-term goals? Maybe one is to be financially secure? Retire early? Become and/or remain healthy? Whatever your ultimate goal may be, you're in the position to manage your development to achieve ultimate success. Good management minimizes the waste of your assets — your heart, your time, your money, your skills.

Don't be Afraid to Fail — All Successful People are Experienced in Failure
With a newfound maturity, I accept full responsibility for how good I can become at what is most important to me. With personal growth comes a fear of the unknown, and other new problems. Those problems are nothing more than the increasing shadow of my personal growth. And my personal growth has been as a result of lessons learned from my failures and successes in life to date.

My whole life has been about venturing into the world of the unknown. Leaving my childhood home at the age of 17 to teach in the jungles of Guyana; coming to Canada at the age of 20 with almost no money and nothing to fall back on; working full-time while studying full-time; starting a career in sales (and with commission income only!); supporting a wife and a growing family, while carrying a heavy mortgage; I could go on and on. Yet somehow, I managed to create, together with so many others, two wildly successful, multi-million-dollar companies. As you have read in this book, I did sell those firms in 1999, and endured tremendous heartache. When I think back to that agonizing time, I recall receiving a card from two friends, Dr. Raj Singh, a dentist, and his brother, Dr. Rudy Singh, a chiropractor. I wish to share that card, in the hope that, as you set new goals for yourself, you will be prepared to pay the price for the inevitable set-backs and disappointments.

> I'm sorry things haven't worked out
> the way you'd hoped. It's only natural
> to feel disappointed when you've worked
> so hard and come so far. But this is only
> a temporary setback, and I know it won't
> discourage you for long. You have the
> ability to accomplish anything you set
> your mind to and the determination to
> keep trying until you reach your goal.
>
> So don't let this get you down . . .
> you have what it takes to bounce back
> stronger than ever. And remember,
> I'm always in your corner cheering you on.

The words were written by someone named Linda Barnes. But just as meaningful were the handwritten notes from my two dear friends, at the bottom of the card: *"Somebody's testing you. I'm just curious to see how you'll turn these adversities into advantages."*

CHAPTER TWENTY-ONE

DON'T QUIT

S o here I am, in my 50th year of life, finishing my fourth book, and starting all over again in a brand new business. Will my health products
company enjoy the runaway success of both Fortune Financial and Infinity
Mutual Funds? Only God knows.

But like most of you, I occasionally come across quotations or poems
which I find speak to me deeply, and capture my philosophy of life — and of
happiness — in a more concise way than I could do in a hundred pages of
print.

One such poem is called "Don't Quit," and although it is usually
described as "Author Unknown" or "Anonymous," a trustworthy-sounding
letter on the Internet insists that it was written by a 15-year-old named Alice
Rowland, from Penticton, British Columbia. She had written it in response
to a newspaper advertisement calling for poetry submissions. She is 70 years
old this year, and was shocked to first see "Don't Quit" printed in the local
newspaper of her then-Albertan home in 1974, a quarter-century after she
had written it.

Ms. Rowland later told a reporter, "My poem is found on posters, cups,
bookmarkers, plaques, and 'do not disturb' motel tags, to name a few. The

poem always says 'author unknown,' which makes me a bit sad, but I really don't know how to change that after all these years. I don't receive any royalties from any of my work."

What a good metaphor for all of our lives! Here was a girl who wrote a poem which has inspired millions, yet she never earned a cent — and is even denied recognition for her accomplishment. But *she* didn't quit, or become bitter from the lack of acknowledgement for what she created.

I haven't quit, either. You can see that — in the creation of Destiny Health Solutions — and the good health that I am determined to bring to millions of men and women around the world, thanks to the knowledge and wisdom of Albert E. D'Souza.

Alice Rowland's poem, written a mere five years before I was born halfway around the world from her native British Columbia, seems the perfect way to conclude this book. Oh yes — my final message to all who read this volume: *do not quit.*

Don't Quit

When things go wrong as they sometimes will,
When the road you're trudging seems all uphill,
When the funds are low and the debts are high
And you want to smile, but you have to sigh,
When care is pressing you down a bit,
Rest, if you must, but don't quit.

Life is queer with its twists and turns,
As every one of us sometimes learns,
And many a failure turns about
When he might have won had he stuck it out;
don't give up though the pace seems slow
You may succeed with another blow.

Success is failure turned inside out —
The silver tint of the clouds of doubt,
And you never can tell just how close you are,
It may be near when it seems so far;
So stick to the fight when you're hardest hit —
It's when things seem worst that you must not quit.

Alice Rowland